Kaplan Publi[...] finding new way[...] ir studies and our exciting online resources really do offer something different to students looking for exam success.

This book comes with free MyKaplan online resources so that you can study anytime, anywhere. **This free online resource is not sold separately and is included in the price of the book.**

Having purchased this book, you have access to the following online study materials:

CONTENT	AAT	
	Text	Kit
Electronic version of the book	✓	✓
Progress tests with instant answers	✓	
Mock assessments online	✓	✓
Material updates	✓	✓

How to access your online resources

Kaplan Financial students will already have a MyKaplan account and these extra resources will be available to you online. You do not need to register again, as this process was completed when you enrolled. If you are having problems accessing online materials, please ask your course administrator.

If you are not studying with Kaplan and did not purchase your book via a Kaplan website, to unlock your extra online resources please go to www.mykaplan.co.uk/addabook (even if you have set up an account and registered books previously). You will then need to enter the ISBN number (on the title page and back cover) and the unique pass key number contained in the scratch panel below to gain access. You will also be required to enter additional information during this process to set up or confirm your account details.

If you purchased through Kaplan Flexible Learning or via the Kaplan Publishing website you will automatically receive an e-mail invitation to MyKaplan. Please register your details using this email to gain access to your content. If you do not receive the e-mail or book content, please contact Kaplan Publishing.

Your Code and Information

This code can only be used once for the registration of one book online. This registration and your online content will expire when the final sittings for the examinations covered by this book have taken place. Please allow one hour from the time you submit your book details for us to process your request.

Please scratch the film to access your MyKaplan code.

Please be aware that this code is case-sensitive and you will need to include the dashes within the passcode, but not when entering the ISBN. For further technical support, please visit www.MyKaplan.co.uk

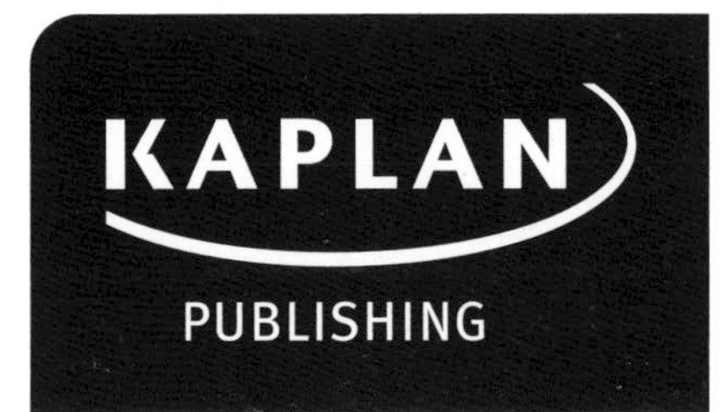

BUSINESS TAX

STUDY TEXT

Qualifications and Credit Framework

AQ2016

Finance Act 2016

For assessments from 1 January to 31 December 2017

This Study Text supports study for the following AAT qualifications:

AAT Professional Diploma in Accounting – Level 4

AAT Level 4 Diploma in Business Skills

AAT Professional Diploma in Accounting at SCQF Level 8

British Library Cataloguing-in-Publication Data

A catalogue record for this book is available from the British Library.

Published by
Kaplan Publishing UK
Unit 2, The Business Centre
Molly Millars Lane
Wokingham
Berkshire
RG41 2QZ

ISBN 978-1-78415-637-4

The text in this material and any others made available by any Kaplan Group company does not amount to advice on a particular matter and should not be taken as such. No reliance should be placed on the content as the basis for any investment or other decision or in connection with any advice given to third parties. Please consult your appropriate professional adviser as necessary. Kaplan Publishing Limited and all other Kaplan group companies expressly disclaim all liability to any person in respect of any losses or other claims, whether direct, indirect, incidental, consequential or otherwise arising in relation to the use of such materials.

Printed and bound in Great Britain.

We are grateful to HM Revenue and Customs for the provision of tax forms, which are Crown Copyright and are reproduced here with kind permission from the Office of Public Sector Information.

CONTENTS

INTRODUCTION

HOW TO USE THESE MATERIALS

These Kaplan Publishing learning materials have been carefully designed to make your learning experience as easy as possible and to give you the best chance of success in your AAT assessments.

They contain a number of features to help you in the study process.

The sections on the Unit Guide, the Assessment and Study Skills should be read before you commence your studies.

They are designed to familiarise you with the nature and content of the assessment and to give you tips on how best to approach your studies.

STUDY TEXT

This study text has been specially prepared for the revised AAT qualification introduced in September 2016.

It is written in a practical and interactive style:

- key terms and concepts are clearly defined
- all topics are illustrated with practical examples with clearly worked solutions based on sample tasks provided by AAT in the new examining style
- frequent activities throughout the chapters ensure that what you have learnt is regularly reinforced
- 'pitfalls' and 'assessment tips' help you avoid commonly made mistakes and help you focus on what is required to perform well in your assessment
- 'Test your understanding' activities are included within each chapter to apply your learning and develop your understanding.

ICONS

The study chapters include the following icons throughout.

They are designed to assist you in your studies by identifying key definitions and the points at which you can test yourself on the knowledge gained.

Definition

These sections explain important areas of knowledge which must be understood and reproduced in an assessment.

Example

The illustrative examples can be used to help develop an understanding of topics before attempting the activity exercises.

Test your understanding

These are exercises which give the opportunity to assess your understanding of all the assessment areas.

Quality and accuracy are of the utmost importance to us so if you spot an error in any of our products, please send an email to mykaplanreporting@kaplan.com with full details, or follow the link to the feedback form in MyKaplan.

Our Quality Coordinator will work with our technical team to verify the error and take action to ensure it is corrected in future editions.

UNIT GUIDE

Introduction

This unit introduces the learners to UK taxation relevant to businesses. It is about the computing of business taxation, preparation of tax returns and how taxation has an impact on the running of a business for sole traders, partnerships and limited companies.

In learning how to prepare tax computations, learners will gain skills in the tax treatment of capital expenditure, and adjustment of accounting profits for tax purposes for sole traders, partnerships and limited companies. In addition, they will be able to allocate profits between partners in a partnership and be able to calculate National Insurance (NI) contributions for the self-employed.

The learner will become familiar with the completion of tax returns. They will know when these returns need to be filed with the UK's Revenue and Customs authority (HMRC), and the implications of errors in tax returns, the late filing of returns and the late payment of tax.

They will understand how to compute tax on the sale of capital assets and they will have an introduction to some of the tax reliefs available to businesses.

Tax advice is an important part of many accountancy roles. Learners will be able to discuss the ethical issues facing business owners and managers in reporting their business tax and the responsibilities that an agent has in giving advice on tax issues to business clients.

Learning outcomes

On completion of this unit the learner will be able to:

- Complete tax returns for sole traders and partnerships and prepare supporting tax computations.
- Complete tax returns for limited companies and prepare supporting tax computations.
- Provide advice on the UK tax regime and its impact on sole traders, partnerships and limited companies.
- Advise business clients on tax reliefs, and their responsibilities and their agent's responsibilities in reporting taxation to HM Revenue & Customs.
- Prepare tax computations for the sale of capital assets.

Scope of content

The unit consists of five learning outcomes, which are further broken down into assessment criteria. These are set out in the following table with reference to the relevant chapter within the text.

In any one assessment, students may not be assessed on all content, or on the full depth or breadth of a piece of content. The content assessed may change over time to ensure validity of assessment, but all assessment criteria will be tested over time.

		Chapter
1	**Complete tax returns for sole traders and partnerships and prepare supporting tax computations**	
1.1	**Analyse trading profits and losses for tax purposes**	
	Students need to be able to:	
	• apply rules relating to deductible and non-deductible expenditure	9
	• classify expenditure as either revenue or capital expenditure	9
	• adjust accounting profit and losses for tax purposes.	9
1.2	**Identify the correct basis period for each tax year**	
	Students need to be able to:	
	• identify the basis periods using the opening year and closing year rules	11
	• determine overlap periods and overlap profits	11
	• explain the effect on the basis period of a change in accounting date.	11
1.3	**Identify and calculate capital allowances**	
	Students need to be able to:	
	• identify the types of capital allowances	9
	• calculate capital allowances including adjustments for private usage.	9

		Chapter
1.4	**Analyse taxable profits and losses of a partnership between the partners**	
	Students need to be able to:	
	• apportion profits between a maximum of four partners	10
	• determine the basis periods for continuing, new or departing partners	11
	• allocate profits between the partners.	10
1.5	**Calculate the NI contributions payable by self-employed taxpayers**	
	Students need to be able to:	
	• determine who is liable to pay NI contributions	14
	• calculate NI contributions.	14
1.6	**Complete the individual and partnership tax returns relevant to sole traders and partnerships**	
	Students need to be able to:	
	• accurately complete self-employed tax returns	9
	• accurately complete partnership tax returns.	10
2	**Complete tax returns for limited companies and prepare supporting tax computations**	
2.1	**Analyse trading profits and losses for tax purposes**	
	Students need to be able to:	
	• apply the rules relating to deductible and non-deductible expenditure	3
	• classify expenditure as either revenue or capital expenditure	3
	• adjust accounting profits and losses for tax purposes.	3

		Chapter
2.2	**Identify and calculate capital allowances**	
	Students need to be able to:	
	• identify types of capital allowances	4
	• calculate capital allowances.	4
2.3	**Calculate total taxable profits and corporation tax payable**	
	Students need to be able to:	
	• calculate the taxable total profits from trading income, property income, investment income and chargeable gains	2, 5
	• calculate the total profits and corporation tax payable for accounting periods longer than, shorter than or equal to 12 months.	2, 5
2.4	**Complete corporation tax returns**	
	Students need to be able to:	
	• accurately complete a corporation tax return.	5
3	**Provide advice on the UK's tax regime and its impact on sole traders, partnerships and limited companies**	
3.1	**Demonstrate an understanding of the tax return filing requirements and tax payments due**	
	Students need to know:	
	• tax return filing deadlines	7, 13
	• payment rules for sole traders and partnerships: amounts and dates	13
	• payment rules for limited companies: amounts and dates.	7

		Chapter
3.2	**Demonstrate an understanding of the penalties and finance costs for non-compliance**	
	Students need to know:	
	• penalties for late filing of tax returns and failing to notify chargeability	7, 13
	• late payment interest and surcharges	7, 13
	• the enquiry window and penalties for incorrect returns.	7, 13
4	**Advise business clients on tax reliefs, and their responsibilities and their agents responsibilities in reporting taxation to HMRC**	
4.1	**Appraise the effective use of trading losses**	
	Students need to be able to:	
	• assess and calculate available loss relief	6, 12
	• advise on the best use of a trading loss for sole traders, partnerships and limited companies.	6, 12
4.2	**Demonstrate an understanding of the current tax reliefs and other tax issues**	
	Students need to know:	
	• current tax reliefs available to businesses	6 and throughout
	• current tax issues and their implications for businesses.	6 and throughout
4.3	**Discuss the responsibilities relating to tax for the business and its agent**	
	Students need to know:	
	• what the badges of trade are and how they evolved	9
	• what records need to be maintained by a business, how long these records need to be maintained and the penalties for failing to keep these records	7, 13

		Chapter
	• the distinction between tax planning, tax avoidance and tax evasion	21
	• AAT's ethical standards relating to tax advice and professional conduct in relation to taxation.	21
5	**Prepare tax computations for the sale of capital assets**	
5.1	**Calculate capital gains tax payable by self-employed taxpayers**	
	Students need to be able to:	
	• apply the rules relating to chargeable persons, disposals and assets	15
	• calculate chargeable gains and allowable losses	18
	• apply the rules relating to the disposal of shares	19
	• apply the rules relating to the disposal of chattels and wasting assets	18
	• apply current reliefs and allowances	18, 20
	• apply capital gains tax rates.	18, 20
5.2	**Calculate chargeable gains and allowable losses for limited companies**	
	Students need to be able to:	
	• apply the rules relating to disposals and assets	16
	• calculate the computation of chargeable gains and allowable losses	16
	• apply the rules relating to the disposal of shares	17
	• apply current reliefs and allowances.	20

Delivering this unit

This unit has the following links across the AAT Professional Diploma in Accounting.

Unit name	Content links	Suggested order of delivery
Personal Tax	This unit is an optional unit at Professional level, so it does not need to be taken after another unit has been studied. The Professional level unit, Personal Tax, is associated with this unit, although these units can be taken separately. Knowledge developed in either of these units will be useful in the later study of the other unit.	N/A

THE ASSESSMENT

Test specification for this unit assessment

Assessment type	Marking type	Duration of exam
Computer based unit assessment	Partially computer/ partially human marked	2 hours

The assessment for this unit consists of 11 compulsory, independent, tasks.

The competency level for AAT assessment is 70%.

	Learning outcomes	Weighting
1	Complete tax returns for sole traders and partnerships and prepare supporting tax computations	29%
2	Complete tax returns for limited companies and prepare supporting tax computations	19%
3	Provide advice on the UK's tax regime and its impact on sole traders, partnerships and limited companies	15%
4	Advise business clients on tax reliefs, and their responsibilities and their agent's responsibilities in reporting taxation to HMRC	19%
5	Prepare tax computations for the sale of capital assets	18%
Total		100%

Reference material

Reference material is provided in this assessment. During your assessment you will be able to access reference material through a series of clickable links on the right of every task. These will produce pop-up windows which can be moved or closed.

The relevant section of the reference material has been included in the appropriate chapter of this study text. This is based on the version of the reference material that was available at the time of going to print.

STUDY SKILLS

Preparing to study

Devise a study plan

Determine which times of the week you will study.

Split these times into sessions of at least one hour for study of new material. Any shorter periods could be used for revision or practice.

Put the times you plan to study onto a study plan for the weeks from now until the assessment and set yourself targets for each period of study – in your sessions make sure you cover the whole course, activities and the associated test your understanding activities.

If you are studying more than one unit at a time, try to vary your subjects as this can help to keep you interested and see subjects as part of wider knowledge.

When working through your course, compare your progress with your plan and, if necessary, re-plan your work (perhaps including extra sessions) or, if you are ahead, do some extra revision/practice questions.

Effective studying

Active reading

You are not expected to learn the text by rote, rather, you must understand what you are reading and be able to use it to pass the assessment and develop good practice.

A good technique is to use SQ3Rs – Survey, Question, Read, Recall, Review:

1 **Survey the chapter**

   Look at the headings and read the introduction, knowledge, skills and content, so as to get an overview of what the chapter deals with.

2 **Question**

   Whilst undertaking the survey ask yourself the questions you hope the chapter will answer for you.

3 Read

Read through the chapter thoroughly working through the activities and, at the end, making sure that you can meet the learning objectives highlighted on the first page.

4 Recall

At the end of each section and at the end of the chapter, try to recall the main ideas of the section/chapter without referring to the text. This is best done after a short break of a couple of minutes after the reading stage.

5 Review

Check that your recall notes are correct.

You may also find it helpful to re-read the chapter to try and see the topic(s) it deals with as a whole.

Note taking

Taking notes is a useful way of learning, but do not simply copy out the text.

The notes must:

- be in your own words
- be concise
- cover the key points
- be well organised
- be modified as you study further chapters in this text or in related ones.

Trying to summarise a chapter without referring to the text can be a useful way of determining which areas you know and which you don't.

Three ways of taking notes

1 Summarise the key points of a chapter

2 Make linear notes

A list of headings, subdivided with sub-headings listing the key points.

If you use linear notes, you can use different colours to highlight key points and keep topic areas together.

Use plenty of space to make your notes easy to use.

3 Try a diagrammatic form

The most common of which is a mind map.

To make a mind map, put the main heading in the centre of the paper and put a circle around it.

Draw lines radiating from this to the main sub-headings which again have circles around them.

Continue the process from the sub-headings to sub-sub-headings.

Annotating the text

You may find it useful to underline or highlight key points in your study text – but do be selective.

You may also wish to make notes in the margins.

Revision phase

Kaplan has produced material specifically designed for your final assessment preparation for this unit.

These include pocket revision notes and an exam kit that includes a bank of revision questions specifically in the style of the new syllabus.

Further guidance on how to approach the final stage of your studies is given in these materials.

Further reading

In addition to this text, you should also read the 'Accounting Technician' magazine every month to keep abreast of any guidance from the assessors.

TAX RATES AND ALLOWANCES

These tables are provided in the reference material that you can access during your assessment. They will be available by clicking on the appropriate link to produce a pop-up window.

Taxation tables for business tax – 2016/17

Capital allowances

Annual investment allowance	
From 1/6 April 2014	£500,000
From 1 January 2016	£200,000
Plant and machinery writing down allowance	
Long life assets and integral features	8%
Other assets	18%
Motor cars	
CO_2 emissions up to 75 g/km	100%
CO_2 emissions between 76 and 130 g/km	18%
CO_2 emissions over 130 g/km	8%
Energy efficient and water saving plant	
First year allowance	100%

Capital gains

Annual exempt amount	£11,100
Standard rate (residential property/other disposals)	18/10%
Higher rate (residential property/other disposals)	28/20%
Entrepreneur's relief rate	10%
Entrepreneurs' relief limit	£10,000,000

National Insurance rates

Class 2 contributions:	£2.80 per week
Small earnings exemption	£5,965 p.a.
Class 4 contributions:	
Main rate	9%
Additional rate	2%
Lower earnings limit	£8,060
Upper earnings limit	£43,000

Corporation tax

Financial year	**2016**	**2015**
All profits and gains	20%	20%

1 Introduction to business tax

Introduction

This chapter presents an overview of business tax.

CONTENTS

1 Contents of the study text

1.1 Four categories

The study text can be split into four specific categories:

	Chapters
• Companies	2 – 7
• Unincorporated traders (sole traders and partnerships)	8 – 14
• Chargeable gains	15 – 20
• Duties and responsibilities of a tax adviser	21

The aim is to gradually consider each of the ways of taxing a business and then to consider the ethical implications for a tax adviser when giving advice.

Business taxation depends on whether an individual has decided to set up his business as a:

- company
- sole trader; or
- partnership.

2 Types of business entity

2.1 Company

A company is a legal entity, separate from its owners and managers.

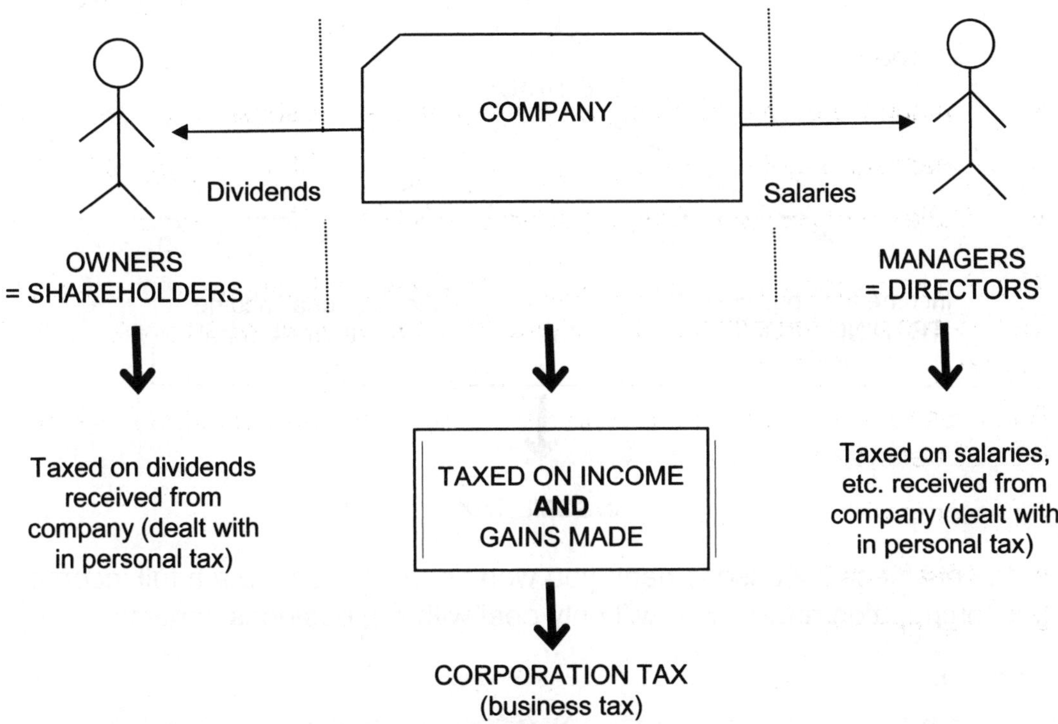

Note: In a lot of cases the shareholders and directors are the same people. However, this will have no effect on the business tax assessment.

2.2 Sole trader

An individual setting up an unincorporated business (i.e. not a company) on his/her own is known as a sole trader.

A sole trader is not a separate legal entity.

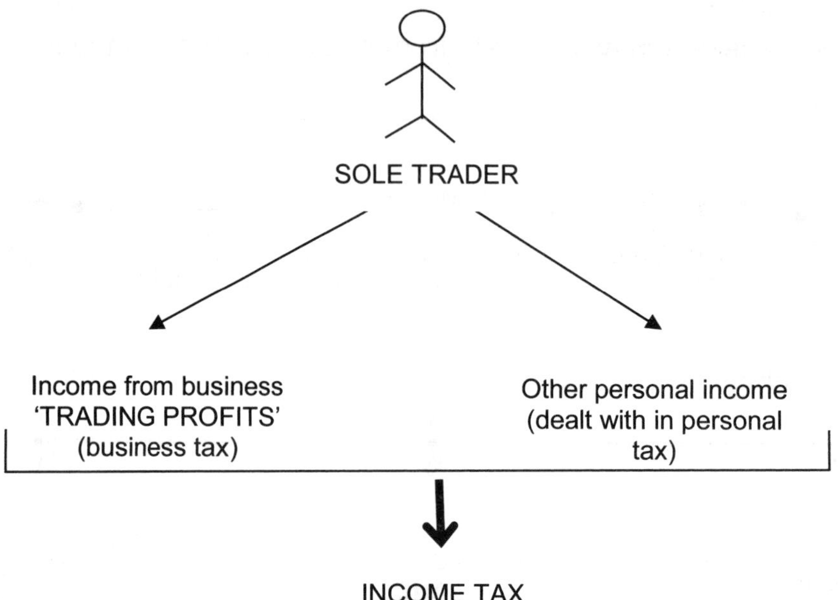

In the business tax assessment, you won't need to complete a full income tax computation/return. You will only deal with the business aspects.

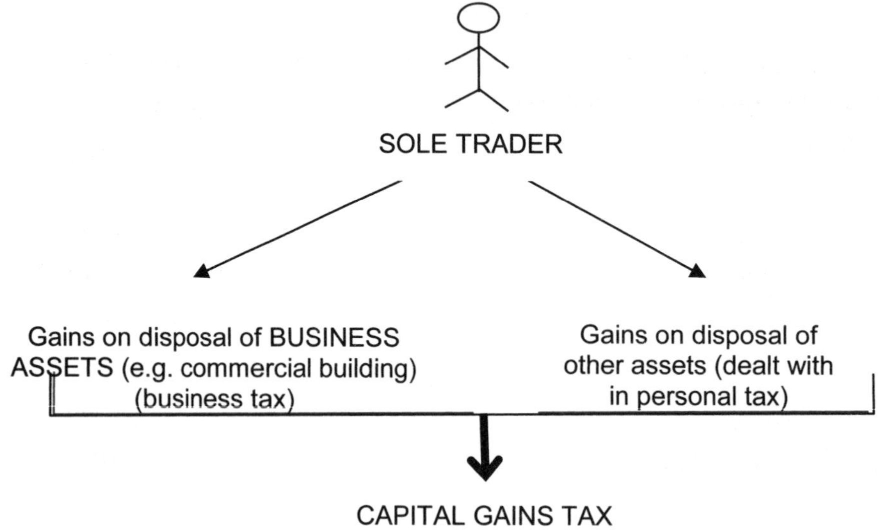

In the business tax assessment, you may be required to complete a capital gains tax computation. However, the sole trader will only have disposed of business assets.

2.3 Partnership

A partnership is another form of unincorporated business, but it is not a separate legal entity.

A partnership is formed when a number of individuals carry on a business together with a view to profit, i.e. a partnership is effectively a collection of sole traders working together.

Each partner pays his own income tax and capital gains tax on his share of the partnership's profits and gains.

3 Introduction to the UK tax system

3.1 Overall structure

Taxation is the raising of money by the State from the general public.

The UK Parliament passes tax legislation.

HMRC (Her Majesty's Revenue and Customs) is the body that controls and administers all areas of UK tax law.

3.2 Tax legislation

The basic rules of the UK tax system are contained in various statutes. These are amended and added to by annual Finance Acts.

Legislation can be given effect, or interpreted, in the following ways:

Statutory Instruments

Acts of Parliament confer powers on Ministers to make more detailed orders, rules or regulations by means of statutory instruments. An Act will often contain a broad framework and statutory instruments are used to provide the necessary detail that would be too complex to include in the Act itself.

Case law

Judges cannot make law relating to taxation, but they can be required to interpret the law which applies to the circumstances of the particular case. These rulings are binding and therefore provide guidance on the interpretation of tax legislation.

Extra-Statutory Concessions

In cases where there is doubt as to the meaning of the law, or where a strict application of the law produces an unacceptable result, HMRC does not always seek to apply the law strictly but instead makes an Extra-Statutory Concession.

HMRC Statements of Practice

These are public announcements of HMRC's interpretation of the legislation. They have no legal force and do not remove the taxpayer's right of appeal.

3.3 Tax avoidance and tax evasion

Tax avoidance

This means arranging your tax affairs, using legal methods, so that you pay less tax.

For example, individuals and businesses can reduce their tax bills by claiming all the reliefs and allowances to which they are entitled. Sometimes a transaction can be timed to give maximum tax advantage.

Tax avoidance is legal.

Tax evasion

Tax evasion, however, is a criminal offence.

Tax evasion means using illegal methods to reduce tax due.

Typically this might be through concealing a source of income, deliberately understating income or over-claiming expenses and reliefs.

AAT reference material

These topics are covered in the reference material set out in section 5.

4 Summary

There are three types of business entity to consider:

- company
- sole trader
- partnership.

Each has its own special rules for calculating profits, gains and tax.

HMRC administers tax law which is passed by Parliament.

Tax avoidance is the legal use of reliefs and allowances whilst tax evasion is illegal such as concealment of income or over-claiming of reliefs.

5 AAT Reference material

Introduction to business tax

Administration

- Taxation administered by HM Revenue & Customs (HMRC).
- Rules covering tax are contained in statute (law) which is passed every year (Finance Act).
- Decisions reached by the courts interpreting the law are known as case law.
- HMRC also issue guidance – Extra Statutory Concessions and Statements of Practice.

Taxes

- Corporation Tax – paid by companies on both income and capital gains.
- Income Tax – paid by individuals on their income.
- Capital Gains Tax – paid by individuals on their capital gains.

Tax avoidance and tax evasion

- Tax evasion

  Any action taken to evade tax by illegal means; this carries a risk of criminal prosecution.

  Examples of tax evasion include failing to declare income and claiming false expenses.

- Tax avoidance

  Use of legitimate means to minimise taxpayer's tax liability, for example by investing in a tax-free ISA (Individual Savings Account).

Principles of corporation tax

Introduction

It is very likely that one of the tasks in the assessment will include the preparation of a corporation tax computation. This chapter sets the scene.

ASSESSMENT CRITERIA

Calculate the taxable total profits from trading income, property income, investment income and chargeable gains (2.3)

Calculate the total profits and corporation tax payable for accounting periods longer than, shorter than or equal to 12 months (2.3)

CONTENTS

1 Introduction to corporation tax

1.1 Corporation tax

Corporation tax is paid by companies. A company can be recognised in the assessment because its name will end with:

- Ltd (which means limited company); or
- plc (which means public limited company).

Sole traders and partnerships do not pay corporation tax.

Example

Which of the following businesses pay corporation tax?

(a) Amy's Motor Dealers Ltd

(b) Bert & Sons

(c) Christopher Diamond plc

(d) Eric & Co

Solution

Corporation tax is paid by companies:

(a) Amy's Motor Dealers Ltd (name ends in Ltd); and

(c) Christopher Diamond plc (name ends in plc).

1.2 Corporation tax computation

Companies pay corporation tax on the total of their income and gains. Firstly, the period covered by the computation must be identified and then the income and gains to be included in the computation are calculated.

2 The principle of chargeable accounting periods

2.1 Chargeable accounting period

A 'period of account' is the period for which a company prepares a set of financial accounts.

However, a company must prepare a corporation tax computation for a 'chargeable accounting period' (CAP).

In a normal situation, a company prepares a 12 month set of financial accounts and has a matching CAP for corporation tax purposes.

Example

Fred Ltd has prepared accounts for the year ended 31 December 2016. Gordon plc has prepared accounts for the year ended 31 March 2017.

For what period will the companies prepare their corporation tax computations?

Solution

Fred Ltd – computation for year ended 31 December 2016.

Gordon plc – computation for year ended 31 March 2017.

2.2 Accounts of less than 12 months

A CAP can be any length up to 12 months.

Where a company prepares a set of financial accounts of less than 12 months, there is a short CAP for corporation tax purposes.

Example

Harry Ltd has previously prepared accounts to 31 December, until 31 December 2015. The company has now changed to preparing accounts to 30 September.

What is its first chargeable accounting period using the new date?

Solution

Harry Ltd has a CAP of 9 months ended 30 September 2016.

2.3 Accounts of more than 12 months

A CAP can never exceed 12 months.

Therefore, when a company prepares financial accounts for a period of more than 12 months, there must be two CAPs for corporation tax purposes.

The two CAPs are:

- CAP for the first 12 months; and
- a separate CAP for the balance period.

No other combination is acceptable.

A corporation tax computation is prepared for each CAP.

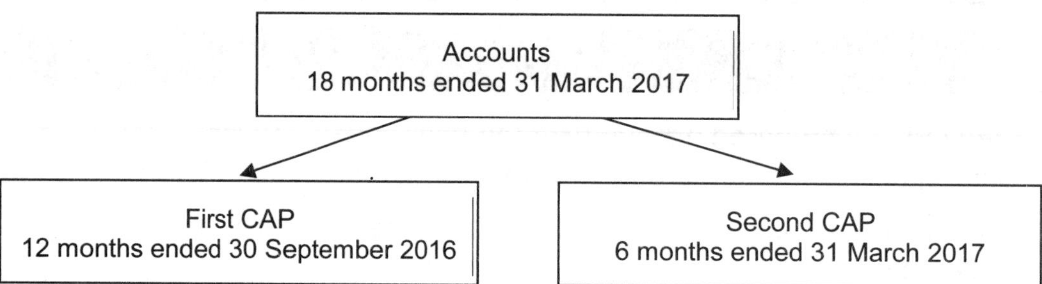

The method of allocating profits from the accounts between the two periods is covered in Chapter 5.

Test your understanding 1

Imogen Ltd has prepared accounts for the 15 months ended 31 July 2017.

What is/are the chargeable accounting period(s)?

A 15 months ended 31 July 2017

B 3 months ended 31 July 2016 and 12 months ended 31 July 2017

C 12 months ended 30 April 2017 and 3 months ended 31 July 2017

D 11 months ended 31 March 2017 and 4 months ended 31 July 2017

3 Pro forma corporation tax computation

In the assessment you may be expected to prepare a corporation tax computation using a similar layout to the pro forma set out below.

The pro forma will become more familiar as you work through the chapters.

The pro forma includes references to the chapters in the textbook where each entry is considered in detail.

Company name

Corporation tax computation for XX months ended.......(the CAP)

	£	**Chapter(s)**
Trading profit	X	3, 4
Non-trade interest	X	5
Property income	X	5
Chargeable gains	X	5, 16
	——	
Total profits	X	
Less: Qualifying charitable donations	(X)	5
	——	
Taxable total profits (TTP)	X	
	——	
Corporation tax liability (at relevant rate)	X	6
	——	

Test your understanding

Test your understanding 2

Period of assessment

Read the following statements and state whether they are true or false.

1 Any business carrying on trading activities will pay corporation tax.

2 Corporation tax computations are prepared for a period of account.

3 The chargeable accounting period will always be the same as the period of account.

4 When a period of account exceeds 12 months there will be two chargeable accounting periods; the first 12 months and then the balance of the period.

Test your understanding 3

Harris Ltd

Harris Ltd started trading on 1 March 2016 and prepares its first set of accounts to 30 April 2017.

What is Harris Ltd's first chargeable accounting period?

A 2 months ended 30 April 2016

B 12 months ended 28 February 2017

C 13 months ended 31 March 2017

D 14 months ended 30 April 2017

5 Summary

A corporation tax computation must be prepared for each chargeable accounting period.

Identifying the correct chargeable accounting period(s) is an essential first step in correctly calculating corporation tax.

Test your understanding answers

Test your understanding 1

The correct answer is C.

Explanation

The financial accounting period must be split into the first 12 months and then the remaining period.

Imogen Ltd therefore has the following chargeable accounting periods:

12 months ended 30 April 2017; and

3 months ended 31 July 2017.

Two corporation tax computations must be prepared.

Test your understanding 2

1	False	Corporation tax is only paid by companies (Ltd or plc).
2	False	Corporation tax computations are prepared for a chargeable accounting period.
3	False	A period of account can exceed 12 months but a chargeable accounting period cannot.
4	True	

Test your understanding 3

The correct answer is B.

Explanation

B is the correct answer because the long period of account is divided into two chargeable accounting periods as follows:

1 the first for the 12 months ended 28 February 2017

2 the second for the remaining 2 months to 30 April 2017.

Adjusted trading profits

Introduction

It is likely that in the assessment there will be a task that involves the computation of adjusted profits for sole traders, partnerships and limited companies.

This chapter deals with adjustments for companies.

See Chapter 9 for further information on the taxation of trading profits for a sole trader or partnership.

ASSESSMENT CRITERIA

Apply the rules relating to deductible and non-deductible expenditure (2.1)

Classify expenditure as either revenue or capital expenditure (2.1)

Adjust accounting profits and losses for tax purposes (2.1)

CONTENTS

1 Introduction to adjusted trading profits

The first entry shown on the pro forma corporation tax computation is the adjusted trading profits of the company.

The starting point in determining the amount of adjusted trading profits is the net profit as shown in the accounts (i.e. the statement of profit or loss, formerly known as the income statement). However, the accounts may, for example, contain expenditure items which are not allowable for tax purposes.

The net profit shown in the accounts of the company must be adjusted for tax purposes to give the adjusted trading profit.

2 Adjustment of profits calculation

2.1 Pro forma adjustment of profits calculation

	£	Detail in:
Net profit as per accounts	X	
Add: Disallowable expenditure	X	Section 3
	X	
Less: Income included in the accounts but not taxable as trading profit	(X)	Section 4
Adjusted trading profit before capital allowances	X	
Less: Plant and machinery capital allowances	(X)	Chapter 4
Adjusted trading profit	X	

The three categories of adjustment are considered in turn, in the sections and chapter indicated above. In this chapter you will calculate the 'adjusted trading profit before capital allowances'.

An adjustment of may be required in the assessment. It is essential that you understand the entries made.

Information about adjustment of profits is contained in the AAT reference material in section 8. Note that this reference material includes some out of date terminology – 'Gift Aid' – this terminology is explained in Chapter 5.

3 Disallowable expenditure

3.1 The principle of disallowable expenditure

Expenditure included in the accounts has the effect of reducing the profits of the company.

However, some items of expenditure are acceptable deductions for financial accounting purposes but are not acceptable for corporation tax purposes.

As a result, the reduction that was made in the accounts must be reversed for corporation tax purposes (i.e. the expenditure must be added back).

This is known as 'disallowable expenditure'.

The general principle to be applied in relation to any particular item of expenditure is that it will only be allowable in arriving at the taxable trading profits if it has been incurred 'wholly and exclusively' for the purposes of the trade.

If the expense is too remote from the trade it fails the remoteness test and will not be allowable. Expenditure is regarded as being too remote from the trade when it is incurred in some capacity other than that of trading.

Example

Jack Limited has the following statement of profit or loss for its year ended 31 March 2017:

	£
Sales	100,000
Less: Cost of sales	(40,000)
Gross profit	60,000
Less: Expenditure (Note)	(35,000)
Net profit per accounts	25,000

Note: The expenditure can be analysed as follows:

	£
Wholly and exclusively for the purposes of the trade	33,000
Not wholly and exclusively for the purposes of the trade (i.e. disallowable expenditure)	2,000
	35,000

Calculate the adjusted trading profits of Jack Limited for the year ended 31 March 2017.

Solution

Jack Limited – Adjusted trading profit – year ended 31 March 2017

	£
Net profit per accounts	25,000
Add: Disallowable expenditure	2,000
Adjusted trading profits	27,000

3.2 Examples of disallowable expenditure

The general principle of expenditure being incurred 'wholly and exclusively' for the purposes of the trade can be used in the assessment if you are in doubt.

However, there are many common examples of disallowable expenditure that tend to appear regularly in assessments. The common examples are set out in the remainder of section 3.

3.3 Fines

Fines on the business should be disallowed as the business is expected to operate within the law. Typical examples are penalties for late payment of VAT or for breaking health and safety regulations.

In practice, however, HM Revenue and Customs usually allow a deduction for parking fines incurred by employees while on company business. This does not, however, apply to directors' parking fines.

Example

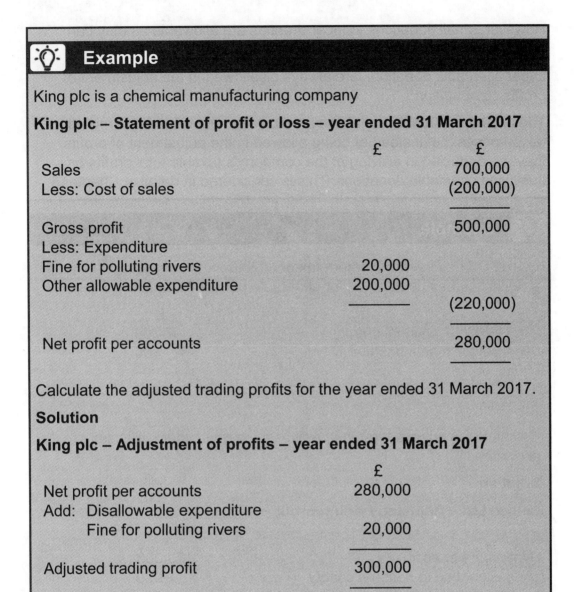

King plc is a chemical manufacturing company

King plc – Statement of profit or loss – year ended 31 March 2017

	£	£
Sales		700,000
Less: Cost of sales		(200,000)
Gross profit		500,000
Less: Expenditure		
Fine for polluting rivers	20,000	
Other allowable expenditure	200,000	
		(220,000)
Net profit per accounts		280,000

Calculate the adjusted trading profits for the year ended 31 March 2017.

Solution

King plc – Adjustment of profits – year ended 31 March 2017

	£
Net profit per accounts	280,000
Add: Disallowable expenditure	
Fine for polluting rivers	20,000
Adjusted trading profit	300,000

3.4 Fraud

Fraud undertaken by directors is disallowed. This is because the loss does not relate to the company's trading activities.

However, petty theft by non-senior employees which is not covered by insurance is generally allowable.

3.5 Donations

Donations to charity usually fail the wholly and exclusively test.

In practice, this means that there is no deduction for donations to national charities or political parties, unless there is some clear benefit to the trade.

However, small donations to local charities are allowable as they can effectively be classed as advertising.

Other charitable donations are always disallowed in the adjustment of profits computation.

These other charitable donations are however allowable for corporation tax purposes, but instead of being allowed in the adjustment of profits, they are deducted in arriving at the company's taxable total profits as qualifying charitable donations. This is considered in detail at Chapter 5.

Example

Louise Ltd has net profit before tax of £123,000. In calculating this profit a deduction has been made for charitable donations as follows:

	£
To NSPCC – national charity	7,000
To local children's hospital	300
	7,300

Calculate the adjusted trading profit assuming all other expenses are allowable.

Solution

Louise Ltd – Adjusted trading profit

	£
Net profit per accounts	123,000
Add: Donation to national charity	7,000
Adjusted trading profit	130,000

3.6 Capital expenditure

As a rule, capital expenditure charged to the statement of profit or loss (e.g. depreciation, purchase of small capital items) is not an allowable expense for tax purposes.

For this reason, 'repairs' expenditure requires careful review, as it often contains items of a capital nature.

In general, repairs and redecoration are considered to be revenue expenditure and are therefore allowable. Improvements, however, are disallowable.

In practice, the distinction between a repair and an improvement is not clear-cut. Repairs usually involve restoring an asset to its original condition or replacing part of an asset with a modern equivalent. Improvements usually involve enhancing the asset in some way.

For example, the replacement of a single glazed window with a double glazed window would be a repair, whilst installing a new window in a brick wall would be an improvement.

Second-hand non-current assets

If a non-current asset (i.e. fixed asset) is purchased in a dilapidated state, and the purchase price reflects this, then initial 'repairs' expenditure to bring the asset to a fit state for use in the business will not be allowable.

Two cases illustrate the difficulty of applying this rule in practice.

In *Law Shipping Co Ltd v CIR (1923)* the company purchased a ship which was not in a seaworthy condition. Expenditure on making the ship seaworthy was held to be capital and therefore disallowed.

In *Odeon Associated Theatres Ltd v Jones (1971)* the company purchased some cinemas which were in a run-down condition. Expenditure incurred in renovating the cinemas was held to be revenue and therefore allowable.

These two cases can be distinguished. In the *Law Shipping* case, the ship was not usable until the repairs were undertaken and the purchase price reflected the condition it was in. By contrast, in the Odeon case, the cinemas were capable of being used for the purpose of the trade prior to their renovation. In addition, the repairs were to remedy normal wear and tear.

You do not need to remember the names of the legal cases mentioned but the principle of the decision made is important.

Legal expenses of a capital nature

The general rule to determine whether legal expenses are allowable is to look at the nature of the expense.

If they relate to a capital item, such as the purchase of a building, then the expenses will be disallowed.

Note that for tax purposes, leases are always treated as capital in this context, therefore legal expenses relating to leases will normally be disallowed (but see exception below).

If they relate to a revenue item, such as the collection of trade receivables or employee issues such as drawing up contracts of employment, then they will be allowable.

There are some exceptions to the capital rule.

The following expenses are allowable:

- the legal costs of renewing a short lease (i.e. 50 years or less)
- the legal costs of defending title to a non-current asset (e.g. disputes over land boundaries).

Depreciation

Depreciation, together with any loss on the sale of non-current assets, is disallowed and must be added back.

Relief for capital expenditure may be given through capital allowances instead of depreciation (see Chapter 4).

Test your understanding 1

For each of the following items of expenditure, state if they would be treated as capital or revenue items for tax purposes.

1	Purchase of new office furniture	Revenue / Capital
2	Rates	Revenue / Capital
3	Repair to make asset usable after purchase	Revenue / Capital
4	Legal costs re purchase of new offices	Revenue / Capital
5	Legal costs re renewal of 20 year lease	Revenue / Capital

3.7 Irrecoverable debts (receivables)

The write off of a trade debt in the accounts as an irrecoverable debt is an allowable deduction from trading profits. Consequently the recovery of a trade debt previously written off is taxable.

The write off of a non-trade debt (e.g. a loan to a former employee or a supplier), is not an allowable deduction from trading profits.

Note that 'irrecoverable debts' are also sometimes referred to as 'impaired debts' or 'bad debts'.

A provision for bad debts, which is calculated in accordance with IFRS® Standards is allowable when computing adjusted trading profits.

As a company's accounts are required to be drawn up using IFRS Standards and these standards require objective evidence of impairment in a debt, a bad debt provision in a company's accounts will be specific in nature and allowable for tax purposes.

It is possible that a company's accounts could include a provision relating to matters other than receivables (e.g. inventory provision). Any movement in a provision described as general should be disallowed for tax purposes.

Example

The impaired debts account of Greenidge Ltd for the year ended 30 April 2017 appears as follows:

	£		£
Written off:		Provision for irrecoverable debts b/f	445
– Trade debts	274		
– Former employee	80	Recoveries – trade debts	23
Provision for irrecoverable debts c/f	419	Statement of profit or loss	305
	773		773

Show any adjustments required for tax purposes.

Solution

In this example, the information is presented in the form of a 'T' account.

The first stage is to establish a breakdown of the statement of profit or loss charge of £305.

Remember that this figure comprises amounts written off and recovered, and movements in provisions.

Statement of profit or loss charge:

	£	Allowable?
Decrease in provision for irrecoverable debts (£445 – £419)	(26)	✓
Amounts written off:		
Trade debt	274	✓
Former employee	80	✗
Recoveries – trade debts	(23)	✓
	305	

The write off of the debt owed by the former employee is disallowed.

The recovery of the trade debts is taxable.

The *decrease* in the provision for irrecoverable debts will be specific in nature and is therefore not adjusted for.

The adjustment to the trading profits for tax purposes is therefore:

Add: Former employee debt written off	£80
	——

Write-offs of non-trading loans (such as here to the former employee) are not allowable deductions from trading profits, however they are allowed as a deduction from non-trade related interest income – take care, as it is easy to miss this point (see Chapter 5).

3.8 Interest payable

For the purpose of computing a company's adjusted trading profits you need to distinguish between trading and non-trading payments.

Interest payable on trading loans is an allowable expense in calculating trading profits. For example, interest payable on bank overdrafts or loan notes (also referred to as debentures) used for trading purposes.

Interest payable on non-trading loans is not an allowable expense in calculating trading profits. A loan to purchase an investment would be an example of a non-trading loan. Interest on such a loan should be added back in the adjustment to profits computation.

However, interest in respect of non-trading loans is allowable as a deduction from non-trade related interest income (see Chapter 5).

3.9 Other miscellaneous adjustments

Pre-trading expenditure

Expenditure incurred up to seven years before a trade commences is allowed as an expense of the first CAP of trading, provided it would have been allowable had the trade existed at the time the expenditure was incurred.

Entertaining

The cost of entertaining customers and suppliers is disallowed. However, the cost of entertaining staff is allowable.

Gifts

Gifts to employees are allowable.

Other gifts, for example gifts to customers, are only allowable if they fulfil the following three conditions.

- They incorporate a conspicuous advertisement for the business.

- The total cost per donee is not more than £50 per annum.
- The gift is not food, drink (alcoholic or otherwise) or tobacco or a voucher.

Note that if the cost exceeds the £50 limit, the whole amount is disallowed. Therefore desk diaries or pens embossed with the company name usually qualify but a bottle of whisky carrying an advert for the company would not.

Trade samples

Trade samples which are not for resale are allowable.

Hire or lease charges

The rules for disallowing part of the leasing charges for cars are based on the level of CO_2 emissions.

Leasing charges for cars with CO_2 emissions of 130 g/km or less are allowed in full.

There is a standard disallowance of 15% of the leasing charges for a lease on a car with CO_2 emissions over 130 g/km.

Example

BSG Ltd starts to lease two cars on 1 May 2016. The details of the leased cars are as follows:

(1) The first car has a retail price of £21,000 and CO_2 emissions of 145 g/km. The leasing charges up to 31 December 2016 are £6,400.

(2) The other car has a retail price of £15,000 and CO_2 emissions of 120 g/km. The leasing charges up to 31 December 2016 are £4,700.

Show the amount disallowed for the purposes of calculating the adjusted trading profits in the year ended 31 December 2016.

Solution

The only disallowance is for the first car as the CO_2 emissions exceed 130 g/km.

The disallowed amount is (15% of £6,400) = £960

3.10 Dividends

Dividends are paid out of profits after they have been subjected to tax. They are not expenses incurred in earning those profits. They are therefore not allowable expenditure.

However, there is normally no adjustment required as the computation starts with the 'net profit' which for a company is before the deduction of dividends paid. In a correctly drawn up statement of profit or loss dividends have not been deducted from net profit and so do not need to be added back.

An adjustment is only required if a question specifically tells you that the net profit given is after dividends have been deducted.

3.11 Summary

Common items of allowable and disallowable expenditure are summarised below.

Expenditure	**Allowable**	**Disallowable**
Fines	Employee parking fines	Other fines and penalties
Fraud	Petty theft by non-senior employees	By directors
Donations	Small donations to local charities	Other donations
In relation to non-current assets	Capital allowances on plant and machinery	Depreciation Profit or loss on sale
Repairs	Revenue expenditure Repairs and redecoration	Capital expenditure Improvements Work required on a newly-purchased asset to make it fit for use
Legal expenses	Relate to revenue matters – debt collection, employee contracts	Relate to capital matters – but note exceptions Relate to breaking the law
Irrecoverable debts	Trade debts	Non-trade debts
Interest payable	On trading loans	On non-trading loans
Entertaining	Staff	Customers and suppliers
Gifts	To employees Other gifts provided conditions satisfied	All other gifts
Car leasing	CO_2 emissions of 130 g/km or less	Other cars – disallow 15% of leasing costs

Test your understanding 2

1 Jamelia Ltd operates a business selling high quality second hand clothes.

Which of the following costs is NOT deductible in arriving at the tax adjusted trading profits?

A Repairs to shop premises, carried out two weeks after the shop opened.

B Advertising in the local paper.

C Parking fine incurred by the Managing Director for parking outside the shop.

D Cost of writing off stock that wouldn't sell.

2 Bakers R Us Ltd incurred the following expenses for the year ended 31 March 2017, but is unsure of their treatment for tax purposes.

Which of the following is NOT deductible in arriving at Bakers R Us Ltd's tax adjusted trading profit?

A The cost of new plant and machinery that is used in the bread making process.

B The write off of a trade debt owed by a customer.

C Legal fees in chasing the debt owed by a customer.

D A provision against the debt owed by a customer.

Income included in the accounts but not taxable as trading profits

4.1 Types of income

The following are examples of income which may be included in the statement of profit or loss, but which is not taxable as trading profits.

- Income taxed in another way, for example rental income (property income), interest receivable.
- Dividends received.
- Profits on sales of non-current (i.e. capital) assets.

4.2 Effect

As these types of income are not taxable as trading profits, they must be deducted to arrive at the correct adjusted trading profits.

5 Detailed pro forma adjustment of profits

5.1 Pro forma for a company

	+	–
	£	£
Net profit per accounts	X	
Add: Disallowable expenditure:		
Depreciation	X	
Loss on sale of non-current assets	X	
Capital expenditure	X	
Legal expenses of capital nature	X	
Fines and penalties	X	
Donations (unless small and to local charity)	X	
Entertaining (other than staff)	X	
Gifts to customers	X	
Proportion of car leasing costs	X	
Less: Income in accounts but not trading profits:		
Rental income		X
Profit on sale of non-current assets		X
Interest receivable		X
Dividend income		X
	X	X
	(X) ←	
Adjusted trading profit before capital allowances	X	

Example

The statement of profit or loss of STD Ltd for the year ended 31 March 2017 showed a net profit of £42,000 after accounting for the following items:

Expenditure:		Income:	
	£		£
Depreciation	9,500	Insurance recovery re flood damage to trading inventory	6,500
Loan note interest (Note 1)	8,000	Profit on sale of machine	3,200
Irrecoverable debts:			
– Trade debts written off	4,000		
– Increase in provision	1,000		
Entertainment expenses (Note 2)	2,700		
Legal fees re new lease	3,200		
General expenses (Note 3)	1,800		

Notes:

(1) The loan note was issued to raise finance to purchase plant and machinery for the purpose of the trade.

(2) Entertainment consists of expenditure on:

	£
Entertaining customers	1,200
Staff dance (30 people)	900
Gifts to customers of food hampers	600

(3) General expenses comprise:

	£
Parking fines (relating to employees on company business)	300
Fees for employees attending training courses	1,500

Compute the adjusted trading profit for the above period.

Solution

Step 1: Start your solution with the company's net profit:

	+	–
	£	£
Net profit		42,000

Step 2: Add back any disallowable items of expenditure

Go through each expense in turn and decide whether or not it needs to be added back. If it does require adding back, add the figure to the plus column of your pro forma.

If you do not know how to treat a particular item, guess. You have a good chance of getting the right answer.

Step 3: Deduct income in the accounts which is not taxable as trading profits

Deal with any income in the order in which it appears in the accounts. For each item, ask yourself whether it relates to the company's trade.

If it does, no action is required. If it does not, include the figure in the minus column.

Step 4: Finish by totalling the pro forma

Note that it is not essential for you to put headings such as 'disallowable expenditure' on your pro forma. You could simply state 'add' and 'less'.

You do, however, need to list each adjusted item in words as well as figures.

Approach in computer based assessment (CBA)

You might be given a pro forma and will not have to type in expense headings and numbers. Instead you may have to select correct headings and numbers from drop down menus.

Alternatively, an assessment task may require you to drag and drop each item which needs adjustment into the appropriate part of the computation.

STD Ltd – Adjustment of profit for the year ended 31 March 2017

	+	–
	£	£
Net profit	42,000	
Depreciation	9,500	
Entertainment expenses	1,800	
Legal fees	3,200	
General expenses	–	
Profit on sale of machine		3,200
	56,500	(3,200)
	(3,200)	
Adjusted trading profit	53,300	

Explanation

1 Depreciation (capital expenditure) is not an allowable deduction.

2 Loan note interest is allowable (assuming the loan note proceeds were used for trading purposes).

3 Write-offs of trade debts and provisions in a company's accounts are allowable.

4 Expenditure on entertaining customers is not allowable. Expenditure on entertaining staff is allowable. The cost of the hampers is not allowable as they contain food.

5 The legal fees in respect of the new lease are a capital item, and are therefore not allowable.

6 Parking fines incurred by employees will generally be allowed. Training course fees are also allowable, assuming the course relates to the company's trade.

7 The insurance recovery is in respect of trading inventory. It is therefore taxable as trading profits, and no adjustment needs to be made.

8 Profits on the sale of non-current assets (such as plant and machinery) are effectively negative depreciation and are therefore not taxable.

In an assessment task you should try to work methodically through the statement of profit or loss and ensure you deal with all relevant items.

 **Example**

The statement of profit or loss of DTS Ltd for the year ended 31 March 2017 showed a net profit of £53,000 after accounting for the following items:

Expenditure:		Income:	
	£		£
Depreciation	8,300	Rents received	8,400
Loss on sale of lorry	6,000	Profit on sale of machine	7,400
Legal fees re employees' service contracts	600		
Penalty for late VAT return	2,200		
Repairs (Note)	6,400		

Note:

Included in the figure for repairs is an amount of £5,000 incurred in installing new windows in a recently acquired second-hand warehouse.

This building had suffered fire damage resulting in all of its windows being blown out shortly before being acquired by DTS Ltd. Other repairs were of a routine nature.

Compute the adjusted trading profit for the above period.

Solution

DTS Ltd – Adjustment of profit for the year ended 31 March 2017

	+	–
	£	£
Net profit	53,000	
Depreciation	8,300	
Loss on sale of lorry	6,000	
Legal fees re employees' service contracts	–	
Penalty for late VAT return	2,200	
Repairs	5,000	
Rents received		(8,400)
Profit on sale of machine		(7,400)
	74,500	(15,800)
	(15,800) ←	
Adjusted trading profit	58,700	

Explanation

1 Depreciation (capital expenditure) is not an allowable deduction.

2 Losses on the sale of non-current assets are treated in the same way as depreciation – they are added back. Conversely, profits on the sale of non-current assets are deducted.

3 Legal fees in connection with the service contracts are wholly and exclusively for the trade and are therefore allowable.

4 VAT penalties are not allowable.

5 The cost of new windows is not allowable. It is capital expenditure required to put a new asset into a usable state (*Law Shipping* case).

6 Rents received are taxable as property income and not trading profits, therefore deduct.

In an assessment you should try to work methodically through the information given and ensure you deal with all relevant items.

Test your understanding 3

Brazil Ltd

The following is the statement of profit or loss of Brazil Ltd for the year ended 30 April 2017:

	£	£
Sales		240,458
Less: Cost of sales		(183,942)
Gross profit		56,516
Other income		5,000
Salaries and wages	24,174	
Rent and rates	8,560	
Legal and professional charges	3,436	
General expenses	1,211	
Depreciation	3,047	
		(40,428)
Net profit		21,088

The following further information is given:

(1) **Other income**

This comprises bank deposit interest for the year received on 30 April 2017.

(2) **Legal and professional charges**

This item includes the following:

	£
Legal fees in connection with new lease	325
Legal fees in connection with action by employee for unfair dismissal	830
Payment to employee for unfair dismissal	1,200
Accountancy charges	1,081

(3) **General expenses**

These include a payment of £200 to the Friends of the Local Hospital, and a donation of £25 to Save the Children.

Required:

Calculate the adjusted trading profit for the year for tax purposes.

Test your understanding 4

Cashew Ltd

The following is the statement of profit or loss of Cashew Ltd for the year ended 31 March 2017:

	£	£
Gross profit		47,214
Other income		4,000
Salaries and wages	20,509	
Repairs to premises	3,263	
Travelling and entertaining expenses	1,964	
Irrecoverable debts	(630)	
Depreciation	2,120	
		(27,226)
Net profit		23,988

The following further information is given:

(1) **Other income**

This comprises bank deposit interest for the year which was received on 31 March 2017.

(2) **Repairs to premises**

Included in this item is £1,450 incurred in fitting a new shop-front to a former office and £250 for the initial repainting of a new shop.

(3) **Travelling and entertaining expenses**

These include expenses of entertaining UK customers of £326 and gifts to customers of Christmas hampers costing £528 (cost £48 each).

(4) **Irrecoverable debts**

The figure in the accounts is made up as follows:

	£
Trade debt recoveries	(232)
Decrease in provision for irrecoverable trade debts	(398)
	(630)

Required:

Calculate the adjusted trading profit for the year for tax purposes.

6 Test your understanding

Test your understanding 5

Katrina Ltd

Katrina Ltd incurred the following costs for the year ended 31 March 2017. For each item of expenditure state the tax treatment in arriving at Katrina Ltd's trading profits.

Choice of treatment is 'Deductible' or 'Not deductible'.

1 Fees incurred in chasing a debt which was over 6 months old.

2 Legal fees incurred in acquiring a 5 year lease over new shop premises.

3 Qualifying charitable donation to a national charity.

4 Small donation to a local charity.

5 Costs of purchasing computer equipment.

Test your understanding 6

Adjustment of profits

What adjustment, if any, should you make for the following items included in a company's statement of profit or loss when calculating adjusted trading profits?

State 'add back' or 'no adjustment'.

1 Managing director's salary (he owns 99% of the shares)

2 Overdraft interest

3 Interest on a loan to purchase an investment property

4 Gifts of diaries to customers, costing £5 each and embossed with the company's name

5 Gifts of bottles of wine to customers, costing £5 each and embossed with the company's name

Test your understanding 7

Tricks Ltd

Tricks Ltd's statement of profit or loss for the year ended 31 March 2017 was as follows:

	£	£
Sales		370,150
Loan note interest receivable		4,100
UK dividends received		12,000
Profit on the sale of an investment		2,750
		389,000
Allowable trading expenses	125,750	
Disallowable trading expenses	5,900	
Loan note interest payable (Note)	8,100	
		(139,750)
Net profit		249,250

Note: The funds raised by the issue of the loan note were used to purchase machinery for use in the business.

Required:

Calculate Tricks Ltd's adjusted trading profits for the year ended 31 March 2017.

Test your understanding 8

Cricket Limited

Cricket Limited has the following results for the year ended 31 December 2016:

	£		£
Salaries, wages	20,041	Gross trading profit	802,350
Legal charges (Note 1)	2,436		
Impaired debts (Note 2)	480		
Depreciation – Factory	20,000		
– Machine	10,000		
Repairs (Note 3)	7,800		
Sundry expenses (allowable)	3,492		
Net profit	738,101		
	802,350		802,350

Notes:

(1) **Legal charges**

	£
Debt collection	1,136
Staff service agreements	300
In connection with lease of new office premises	1,000
	2,436

(2) **Impaired debts**

	£
Loan to former employee written off	200
Increase in provision for impaired debts	280
	480

(3) **Repairs**

	£
Repainting	200
New office furniture	7,600
	7,800

Required:

Show Cricket Limited's adjusted trading profits for the year ended 31 December 2016.

Test your understanding 9

Uranus Ltd

The following items are charged against profit in the accounts of Uranus Ltd for the year ended 31 March 2017:

1 Running expenses of the managing director's BMW totalling £10,000 (including depreciation of £6,000). His total mileage in the year was 12,000 of which 6,000 was private. The car was owned by Uranus Ltd.

2 Entertainment expenditure totalling £25,000 of which £10,000 was incurred on overseas customers, £11,000 on UK customers and £4,000 on the annual company dinner for 200 employees.

3 Lease rental of £6,000 on sales director's car costing £20,000. The lease commenced on 1 April 2016. The car has CO_2 emissions of 145 g/km.

Required:

State how you would deal with each of the above items when preparing the company's computation of adjusted trading profits for the year ended 31 March 2017.

Test your understanding 10

Saturn Ltd

The following items are charged against profit in the accounts of Saturn Ltd for the year ended 31 March 2017:

1 A payment of £616 to the Royal National Lifeboat Institution (a registered national charity).

2 The write off of £8,000 against a trade debt of the company, being 80% of the debt. The liquidator of the debtor company had advised Saturn Ltd of this figure but in the event £5,000 of the debt was paid in May 2017.

3 Trade samples costing £7,000 in total which are put through the letter boxes of 2,000 homes in the East Midlands.

Required:

State how you would deal with each of the above items when preparing the company's computation of adjusted trading profits for the year ended 31 March 2017.

7 Summary

You should now be able to successfully attempt questions requiring you to calculate the adjusted trading profit for corporation tax purposes.

The starting point for computing adjusted trading profits is the net profit shown in the company's accounts. This must be adjusted in respect of the following items:

- Disallowable expenditure.

  The main types of disallowable expenditure are:

  – expenditure not wholly and exclusively for the purpose of the trade

  – expenditure disallowed under the detailed rules.

- Income included in the accounts but not taxable as trading profits. For example:

  – rents and interest

  – profits on the sale of capital assets.

When writing out answers on paper, it is advisable to use a '+' and '–' column and deal with each adjustment as you work methodically through the question. There is no need to arrange your answer into the two types of adjustment shown above. Either presentation may be seen in the assessment.

8 AAT Reference material

Adjustment of profits – sole traders, partnerships and companies

Pro forma for adjustment of profits

	£	£
Net profit as per accounts		X
Add: Expenses charged in the accounts that are not allowable as trading expenses	X	
		X
		X
Less: Income included in the accounts which is not assessable as trading income	X	
		(X)
Adjusted profit/(loss)		X

Disallowed expenses

- Expenses that fail the remoteness test so not "wholly and exclusively" for trading purposes.
- Fines on the business or fraud by directors/owners.
- Qualifying charitable donations (such as Gift Aid donations) will be allowed for companies. Political donations are never allowable.
- Capital expenditure, e.g. purchase of equipment included in profit and loss account.
- Depreciation. Capital allowances granted instead.
- Costs of bringing newly acquired second-hand assets to useable condition.
- Legal and professional expenses relating to capital items or breaking the law.
- Customer entertaining. Staff entertaining can be allowable.
- Customer gifts, unless gift incorporates business advertising, cost is less than £50 per annum per customer, and gift is not food, drink, tobacco or cash vouchers.

Non-assessable income

- Income taxed in any other way, e.g. interest or property income for individuals.
- Profits on sale of fixed assets.

Test your understanding answers

Test your understanding 1

1	Capital	The purchase of a new non-current asset is capital expenditure
2	Revenue	Rates are payable every year and are revenue expenditure
3	Capital	As the asset was purchased in a damaged condition and needed to be repaired before use, it is capital expenditure
4	Capital	Legal fees in relation to a capital purchase are treated as capital expenditure
5	Revenue	Legal fees in relation to the renewal of a short lease are specifically allowed as revenue expenditure

Test your understanding 2

Jamelia Ltd

1 The correct answer is C.

Bakers R Us Ltd

2 The correct answer is A.

Explanation

1 Fines incurred by directors are not deductible.

Parking fines incurred by employees whilst on business activity are generally deductible, but not those incurred by directors.

The other costs are deductible.

2 A is a capital cost, whereas the others are revenue costs, all of which are allowable as trading expenses, given the context.

The cost of plant and machinery will qualify for capital allowances (see Chapter 4).

Test your understanding 3

Brazil Ltd

Adjusted trading profit for tax purposes for year ended 30 April 2017.

	£	£
Net profit as per accounts	21,088	
Add: Legal fees re new lease	325	
National charity donation	25	
Depreciation	3,047	
Less: Bank deposit interest		(5,000)
	24,485	(5,000)
	(5,000)	
Adjusted trading profit	19,485	

Explanation

- Legal fees and payment in connection with unfair dismissal are allowable, as part of the cost of employing staff.
- The donation of £200 to the local charity is allowable as a business expense (small and local). Any donation to a national charity is not allowable.

Test your understanding 4

Cashew Ltd

Adjusted trading profit for tax purposes for year ended 31 March 2017.

	£	£
Net profit as per accounts	23,988	
Add: New shop-front	1,450	
Entertaining customers	326	
Gifts	528	
Depreciation	2,120	
Less: Bank deposit interest		(4,000)
	28,412	(4,000)
	(4,000)	
Adjusted trading profit	24,412	

Explanation

- The £250 initial repainting costs in respect of the new shop are considered to be allowable, following the decision in *Odeon Theatres case.*
- Although the hampers cost less than £50 each, the cost is disallowed as the gift is of food.
- Recoveries of trade debts and movements in provisions for irrecoverable trade debts both relate to the trade and are therefore taxable and no adjustment is required.

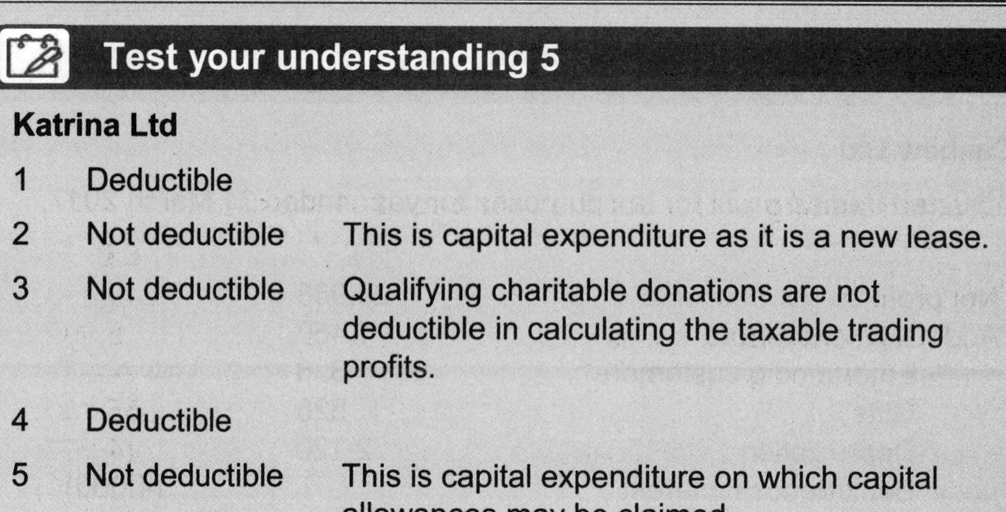

Test your understanding 5

Katrina Ltd

1	Deductible	
2	Not deductible	This is capital expenditure as it is a new lease.
3	Not deductible	Qualifying charitable donations are not deductible in calculating the taxable trading profits.
4	Deductible	
5	Not deductible	This is capital expenditure on which capital allowances may be claimed.

Test your understanding 6

Adjustment of profits

1. No adjustment required – allowable expense.
2. No adjustment required – allowable expense.
3. Add back – not allowable deduction from trading profits but is deductible from non-trade related interest income.
4. No adjustment required – allowable expense.
5. Add back – gift of drink.

   Note that the gift of any type of drink is not allowable (not just alcohol).

Test your understanding 7

Tricks Ltd

Adjusted trading profits for the year ended 31 March 2017

	£
Net profit	249,250
Add: Disallowable expenses	5,900
	255,150
Less: Loan note interest receivable	(4,100)
UK dividends	(12,000)
Profit on sale of investment	(2,750)
Adjusted trading profits	236,300

The funds raised by the issue of the loan note were used for the purposes of the trade and the interest paid is therefore an allowable deduction in computing the adjusted trading profits.

Note that this alternative presentation to the two columns shown previously is also acceptable.

Test your understanding 8

Cricket Limited

Adjusted trading profits for the year ended 31 December 2016

		£
Net profit per accounts		738,101
Add:	Legal charges re new office premises	1,000
	Loan to former employee written off	200
	New furniture	7,600
	Depreciation	30,000
Adjusted trading profit		776,901

Test your understanding 9

Uranus Ltd

1 Running expenses, except for depreciation, are an allowable deduction. The depreciation must be disallowed but relief for the cost of the car will be available through capital allowances.

The private use of the car by an employee of a company is irrelevant for profit adjustment purposes.

Therefore, add back £6,000.

2 Disallow all entertaining except staff entertaining.

Therefore, add back £21,000.

3 Part of this lease cost will be disallowed as the car has CO_2 emissions exceeding 130 g/km.

The disallowable portion added back is as follows:
(15% × £6,000) = £900

Test your understanding 10

Saturn Ltd

1 Donations to national charities are disallowed and treated as qualifying charitable donations. Therefore, add back £616.

2 No adjustment is required.

The write-off of a trade debt is allowable. There will be a credit in the following year's accounts, when the £5,000 is recovered, which will be taxable as part of the trading profit.

3 Trade samples, which are not for resale, are allowable. So no adjustment required.

Capital allowances – plant and machinery

Introduction

In the assessment it is likely that there will be tasks testing adjusting of profits (as per Chapter 3) and calculation of plant and machinery capital allowances.

Capital allowances are a very important topic.

ASSESSMENT CRITERIA

Identify types of capital allowances (2.2)

Calculate capital allowances (2.2)

CONTENTS

1 Introduction to capital allowances

1.1 Capital allowances

Capital allowances are a form of depreciation that is allowable for tax purposes. The allowances are only given on certain items of capital expenditure.

This syllabus includes plant and machinery capital allowances only.

1.2 Capital allowances v depreciation

Each business can decide its own rate of depreciation for accounting purposes. In theory, identical businesses with the same assets could have different amounts of depreciation.

In order for everyone to be treated the same, HMRC use a standard calculation of capital allowances for tax purposes.

The capital allowances are deducted instead of depreciation, to arrive at the adjusted trading profit.

Example

Marcus Ltd and Nigel Ltd are two companies making the same products.

In the year ended 31 December 2016, both companies made profits before depreciation/capital allowances of £200,000. Both have only one piece of machinery that they bought in the year for £150,000.

The companies have different methods of calculating depreciation, giving the following amounts:

Marcus Ltd	£25,000
Nigel Ltd	£35,000

For tax purposes, both companies would have capital allowances of £150,000.

Compare the accounting profits and adjusted trading profits of both companies.

Solution

	Marcus Ltd	Nigel Ltd
	£	£
Profit before depreciation	200,000	200,000
Less: Depreciation	(25,000)	(35,000)
Accounting profits	175,000	165,000
Adjustment of profits computation		
Accounting profits	175,000	165,000
Add: Depreciation	25,000	35,000
Adjusted profit before capital allowances	200,000	200,000
Less: Capital allowances	(150,000)	(150,000)
Adjusted trading profit	50,000	50,000

In reality there are likely to be many more adjustments that could give rise to different adjusted trading profits for tax purposes (as per Chapter 3).

However, this example illustrates that identical businesses could have different accounting profits, but have the same adjusted trading profits on which their tax is calculated.

2 Qualifying expenditure

2.1 What qualifies as plant and machinery?

There is no automatic right to tax relief for capital expenditure.

In order to qualify for capital allowances, expenditure must usually be in respect of plant or machinery.

There is no statutory definition of plant, however the courts have established a **function test**:

Does the asset perform:	**This means that the asset is:**	**Plant and machinery?**
An active function	Apparatus **with which** the business is carried on	Yes
A passive function	The setting **in which** the business is carried on	No

The dividing line between an asset that is functional and one that is merely setting is not always clear. Examples below show how the Courts have reacted to claims for capital allowances in these circumstances.

- A canopy covering petrol filling pumps was held to be part of the setting and not plant and machinery. (It did not assist in serving petrol to customers.)
- False ceilings in a restaurant were not plant. (All they did was hide pipes.)
- Swimming pools at a caravan park were held to be plant and machinery – the caravan park as a whole was the setting.

The most common types of capital expenditure found in a set of financial accounts that are treated as 'plant and machinery' for tax purposes are:

- plant and machinery including moveable partitioning
- fixtures and fittings
- motor vehicles including cars, vans and lorries
- computer equipment and software.

In addition, the cost of alterations to buildings needed for the installation of plant qualifies as plant and machinery.

3 The allowances

3.1 Main types of capital allowances

The following are the main types of capital allowances that may be available to a company in respect of plant and machinery.

(a) Writing-down allowance (WDA)

- given at 18% on a reducing balance basis on most assets
- given at 8% on a reducing balance basis for cars with CO_2 emissions exceeding 130 g/km (see section 5 below).

(b) Annual investment allowance (AIA)

- a 100% allowance for the first £200,000 of expenditure incurred by a company on plant and machinery in a 12-month period
- where a company spends more than the maximum AIA the excess expenditure may qualify for a WDA.

(c) First year allowance (FYA)

- a 100% allowance is available on:
  - new low emission cars with CO_2 emissions of 75 g/km or less (see section 5 below)
  - energy efficient and water saving technologies that are environmentally friendly (see section 4.8 below)
- additions qualifying for the FYA are added into the capital allowances computation after the deduction of WDAs.

Example

Olivia Ltd purchased a machine costing £210,000 on 1 May 2016 in its year ended 31 December 2016. This is its only capital item.

Calculate the capital allowances for the first three years of ownership.

Assume the rates of allowances for the year ended 31 March 2016 continue into the future.

Solution

Olivia Ltd – Capital allowances

	£	Allowances £
Year ended 31 December 2016		
Cost	210,000	
AIA (max)	(200,000)	200,000
	10,000	
WDA (18% × £10,000)	(1,800)	1,800
	8,200	201,800
Year ended 31 December 2017		
WDA (18% × £8,200)	(1,476)	1,476
	6,724	
Year ended 31 December 2018		
WDA (18% × £6,724)	(1,210)	1,210
	5,514	

4 Calculating the allowances

4.1 Expenditure not pooled

As companies may have many assets, it would be extremely time-consuming to calculate allowances separately for each asset. Therefore, all qualifying expenditure is added to the main pool, apart from:

- cars with CO_2 emissions exceeding 130 g/km; and
- assets for which a short life asset election has been made.

4.2 General pool (or main pool)

Most items of plant and machinery go into the general pool (also known as the main pool). Once an asset enters the pool, it loses its identity. This means that the writing down allowance (WDA) is calculated on the balance of the whole pool of assets, rather than on the individual assets.

When a new asset is acquired, the purchase price increases the value of the pool. When an asset is disposed of, the pool value is reduced by the lower of the sale proceeds or the original cost of the asset (see section 4.6 below).

Allowances are given for chargeable accounting periods. Allowances commence in the year in which the expenditure is incurred. A full WDA is given in the year of purchase irrespective of the date of purchase within that year.

4.3 Annual investment allowance (AIA)

The AIA is a 100% allowance for the first £200,000 of expenditure incurred by a company on plant and machinery in a 12-month period.

The AIA:

- is not available for expenditure on cars
- applies for a 12-month accounting period. The allowance is pro-rated for short accounting periods.

Where expenditure on plant and machinery in a 12-month period exceeds the maximum the excess is added to the pool balance on which a WDA can be claimed.

Example

Marble Ltd commenced trading on 1 February 2016. In its first year of trading the company made the following purchases:

- plant and machinery (purchased 1 September 2016) £337,500
- a car for the office manager (CO_2 emissions 120 g/km) £11,000

Required:

(a) Calculate how much of Marble Ltd's capital expenditure is eligible for writing down allowances after deduction of the AIA.

(b) What would your answer to part (a) be if the plant and machinery had cost £180,000?

Solution

(a) **Year ended 31 January 2017**

		General pool
	£	£
Additions:		
Not qualifying for AIA:		
Car		11,000
Qualifying for AIA:		
Plant and machinery	337,500	
Less: AIA	(200,000)	
Balance eligible for 18% WDA	137,500	137,500
Eligible for WDA		148,500

(b) If the plant and machinery had cost £180,000

		General pool
	£	£
Additions:		
Not qualifying for AIA:		
Car		11,000
Qualifying for AIA:		
Plant and machinery	180,000	
Less: AIA (Note)	(180,000)	
		Nil
Eligible for WDA		11,000

Note: The unused AIA of £20,000 (£200,000 – £180,000) is lost.

4.4 First year allowance (FYA)

A first year allowance is given in the year that a qualifying asset is purchased.

A 100% FYA is given for expenditure on low emission cars (see section 5) and energy efficient and water saving technologies (see section 4.8).

4.5 Writing down allowances (WDA)

An annual WDA of 18% is given on a reducing balance basis.

It is given on:

- the unrelieved expenditure in the pool brought forward at the beginning of the accounting period (known as the tax written down value (TWDV))
- plus any additions eligible for WDAs
- less disposals of plant and machinery.

The TWDV brought forward includes all prior period expenditure, less capital allowances already claimed.

Example

Plaster Ltd commenced trading on 1 April 2016 preparing accounts to 31 March each year.

On 1 May 2016 the company purchased £315,000 of machinery and a car costing £22,000 with CO_2 emissions of 125 g/km.

Calculate the capital allowances available to Plaster Ltd for the year ended 31 March 2017.

Plaster Ltd – Capital allowances computation

		General pool	**Allowances**
	£	£	£
Addition not qualifying for AIA			
Car		22,000	
Addition qualifying for AIA	315,000		
Less: AIA (Note)	(200,000)		200,000
Balance expenditure	115,000	115,000	
		137,000	
WDA (18% × £137,000)		(24,660)	24,660
TWDV c/f		112,340	
Total allowances			224,660

4.6 Disposal in the general pool

When a pool item is sold, the sale proceeds are deducted from the pool. However, this deduction cannot exceed the asset's original cost.

The following example illustrates the working of the general pool, including disposals.

Example

Apple Ltd prepares accounts to 31 March each year.

On 1 May 2016 Apple Ltd incurred expenditure of £10,000 on the purchase of shop fittings and machinery. On 1 June 2016 the company sold some machinery for £6,000 (cost £4,000).

On 5 May 2017 the company sold equipment for £2,395 which had cost £11,200 in May 2012.

The tax written down value of the pool at 1 April 2016 was £8,260.

Compute the capital allowances for the years ended 31 March 2017 and 31 March 2018.

Assume the rates of allowances for the year ended 31 March 2017 continue into the future.

Solution

Step 1: Identify the balance brought forward at the beginning of the accounting period

This is the *tax written down value* (Tax WDV or TWDV).

	Pool
	£
Year ended 31 March 2017	
TWDV brought forward	8,260

Step 2: Identify the accounting periods in which the additions and disposals occur

In the year ended 31 March 2017, Apple Ltd acquired plant costing £10,000 and sold plant for £6,000 (cost £4,000).

The second disposal occurs in the second accounting period.

Step 3: Identify any additions on which the AIA can be claimed

The plant acquired on 1 May 2016 qualifies for the AIA.

Deal with this addition *before* calculating the WDA for that year on the other items in the general pool.

Step 4: Prepare the capital allowances computation

Deal with one accounting period at a time.

		General pool	Allowances
	£	£	£
Year ended 31 March 2017			
TWDV b/f		8,260	
Additions qualifying for AIA	10,000		
Less: AIA	(10,000)		10,000
		Nil	
Disposals			
1 June 2016 (proceeds restricted to cost)		(4,000)	
		4,260	
WDA at 18%		(767)	767
TWDV c/f		3,493	
Total allowances			10,767

		General pool	Allowances
	£	£	£
Year ended 31 March 2018			
TWDV b/f		3,493	
Disposals			
5 May 2017		(2,395)	
		1,098	
WDA at 18%		(198)	198
TWDV c/f		900	
Total allowances			198

4.7 Balancing charges

If on the disposal of an asset in the main pool, the disposal proceeds exceed the pool balance (after additions to the pool in the year have been added) a negative balance will be left on the pool.

This gives rise to a 'balancing charge'.

A balancing charge is added to the pool to bring the pool balance back to £Nil.

A balancing charge is treated as a negative capital allowance (i.e. added to the adjusted trading profit).

4.8 Small pools writing down allowance

The WDA is claimed each accounting period and if there are no additions in an accounting period to be added to the pool, the WDA will be claimed on an ever decreasing amount for many years. It will be quite common in many small businesses and companies for there to be no additions to the pool, since any purchases in the period are usually covered by the AIA.

To prevent the inconvenience of keeping records of small balances of expenditure, a 'small pool WDA' can be claimed.

The annual WDA available:

- applies to the main pool and special rate pool (see section 5.2 below)
- does not apply to short life assets (see section 6.1 below)
- is any amount up to £1,000, and
- is time apportioned for long or short accounting periods. (Watch out for this in questions.)

Therefore, an allowance of up to £1,000 can be claimed on the main or special rate pool where the unrelieved expenditure on the pool (after dealing with additions qualifying for WDAs and disposals in the period) is £1,000 or less. This allows the balance on a 'small pool' to be written off at once.

The claim is optional. However, it is likely that the taxpayer will want to claim as much as possible and reduce the remaining balance on the pool to nil.

Example

Annabelle is in business as a sole trader and preparing accounts to 31 March. During the year ending 31 March 2017 she incurred the following expenditure:

15 May 2016 Purchased new office furniture for £23,000.

In addition on 1 July 2016 she sold office equipment for £10,000 (original cost £18,000).

As at 1 April 2016 the tax written down value on her main pool was £10,800.

Calculate Annabelle's capital allowances for the year ended 31 March 2017.

Solution

		General pool	Allowances
	£	£	£
Year ended 31 March 2017			
TWDV b/f		10,800	
Additions qualifying for AIA	23,000		
Less: AIA	(23,000)		23,000
		Nil	
Disposals			
1 July 2016		(10,000)	
		800	
Small pool WDA		(800)	800
TWDV c/f		Nil	
Total allowances			23,800

4.9 Energy efficient and water saving technologies

A first year allowance (FYA) of 100% is available on purchases of plant and machinery which is energy efficient, reduces water use or improves water quality.

100% FYA also applies to new (not second hand) electric vans.

The additions qualifying for FYA are included in the capital allowances computation after the deduction of the WDAs.

First year allowances are given in full in the period of purchase, **regardless** of the length of the accounting period (i.e. the FYA is never time apportioned).

5 Capital allowances treatment of cars

5.1 Motor vehicles v motor cars

In financial accounts we tend to group all motor vehicles together. For example, we include cars, vans, lorries, motor bikes, etc. together as motor vehicles.

For tax purposes, vans, lorries and motorbikes are treated like all other plant and machinery. They are included in the general pool and qualify for:

- AIA in the accounting period of purchase
- WDA.

However, motor cars have a different treatment.

5.2 Capital allowances treatment of motor cars

The capital allowances available in respect of motor cars depend on the level of the car's CO_2 emissions.

- Motor cars with CO_2 emissions between 76 and 130 g/km are added to the general pool and attract a WDA of 18%.
- If the car has emissions exceeding 130 g/km then it must be put into the special rate pool where the WDA is only 8%.
- New low emission motor cars are however eligible for a first year allowance (FYA) in the year of purchase.

  The rate of the FYA is 100% and it is only for new cars with low CO_2 emissions (75 g/km or less).

  Second hand low emission cars are treated as cars with CO_2 emissions between 76 – 130 g/km, however, if the question does not specify, you should assume that the car is new.

  Very few cars are low emission cars.

You will be told the level of CO_2 emissions for each car in the assessment.

Remember also that motor cars **never** qualify for the 100% AIA.

5.3 Disposals of cars

(a) *Main pool cars*

Deduct lower of disposal proceeds and original cost from main pool balance before WDA is calculated (i.e. like normal pool disposals).

(b) *Low emission cars*

As for (a)

(c) *Special rate pool cars*

Deduct lower of disposal proceeds and original cost from special rate pool balance.

If a positive balance remains – give WDA at 18% (main pool cars) or 8% (special rate pool cars) (Note this applies **even if there are no cars left** in the special rate pool).

If a negative balance remains – a balancing charge applies (see 4.7 above).

Example

Patrick Ltd has a year ended 31 March 2017. Its general pool had a TWDV brought forward of £31,000 at 1 April 2016.

In the year ended 31 March 2017, it has purchased two assets:

(a) a new car (CO_2 emissions 120 g/km) costing £9,000; and

(b) a van (not zero emission) costing £4,000 (on 1 February 2017).

There were no disposals in the year.

Required:

(a) Calculate the capital allowances for the year.

(b) What would your answer be to (a) if the car was low emission.

Solution

(a) Patrick Ltd – Capital allowances – year ended 31 March 2017

		General pool	Allowances
	£	£	£
TWDV b/f		31,000	
Additions not qualifying for AIA		9,000	
Additions qualifying for AIA			
Van	4,000		
AIA	(4,000)		4,000
		Nil	
Disposals		Nil	
		40,000	
WDA (£40,000 × 18%)		(7,200)	7,200
TWDV c/f		32,800	
Total capital allowances			11,200

(b) Patrick Ltd – Capital allowances – year ended 31 March 2017

		General pool	Allowances
	£	£	£
TWDV b/f		31,000	
Addition qualifying for AIA			
Van	4,000		
Less: AIA	(4,000)		4,000
		Nil	
Disposals		Nil	
		31,000	
WDA (£31,000 × 18%)		(5,580)	5,580
Addition qualifying for FYA			
Car	9,000		
Less: FYA (100%)	(9,000)		9,000
		Nil	
TWDV c/f		25,420	
Total capital allowances			18,580

Example

Joist Ltd prepares accounts to 31 March each year.

In the year ended 31 March 2017 it purchased the following cars:

(1) Car costing £16,000 with CO_2 emissions of 118 g/km

(2) Car costing £20,000 with CO_2 emissions of 180 g/km

The tax WDV brought forward on the general pool was £21,480.

Calculate Joist Ltd's capital allowances for the year ended 31 March 2017.

Solution

Joist Ltd – Capital allowances – year ended 31 March 2017

	General pool	**Special rate pool**	**Allowances**
	£	£	£
TWDV b/f	21,480		
Additions not qualifying for AIA			
Car – CO_2 76–130 g/km	16,000		
Car – CO_2 >130 g/km		20,000	
	37,480		
WDA at 18%	(6,746)		6,746
WDA at 8%		(1,600)	1,600
TWDV c/f	30,734	18,400	
Total capital allowances			8,346

Example

Grin Ltd prepares accounts to 31 March each year.

At 1 April 2016 the tax written down values brought forward were:

General pool £15,400
Special rate pool £17,000

During the year ended 31 March 2017 the company purchased plant for £20,000 and two cars with CO_2 emissions of 170 g/km costing £20,000 each.

There were no additions in the year ended 31 March 2018.

There were no disposals in the year ended 31 March 2017 but in the year ended 31 March 2018, one of the cars purchased in the previous year was sold for £13,500.

Required:

Calculate Grin Ltd's capital allowances for the years ended 31 March 2017 and 2018.

Assume the rates of allowances for the year ended 31 March 2017 continue into the future.

Solution

The first task is to decide how many columns are needed to answer this question. There are two balances brought forward which require their own columns and a column is required on the left to deduct the AIA.

A pro forma can then be set up as below

		General pool	**Special rate pool**	**Allowances**
	£	£	£	£
Year ended 31 March 2017				
TWDV b/f		15,400	17,000	

Now the additions can be put into the appropriate column and the allowances calculated.

Grin Ltd – Capital allowances

		General pool	Special rate pool	Allowances
	£	£	£	£
Year ended 31 March 2017				
TWDV b/f		15,400	17,000	
Additions:				
Not qualifying for AIA or FYA				
Cars over 130 g/km			40,000	
Qualifying for AIA			57,000	
Plant	20,000			
AIA	(20,000)			20,000
WDA at 18%		(2,772)		2,772
WDA at 8%			(4,560)	4,560
Tax WDV c/f		12,628	52,440	
Total allowances				27,332
Year ended 31 March 2018				
Disposals			(13,500)	
			38,940	
WDA at 18%		(2,273)		2,273
WDA at 8%			(3,115)	3,115
Tax WDV c/f		10,355	35,825	
Total allowances				5,388

The example below demonstrates the full capital allowances working.

Example

JNN Ltd started trading on 1 April 2016, preparing accounts to 31 March each year.

The following assets have been purchased since the company began trading.

Date of purchase	Asset	Cost
		£
9 November 2016	Used car	1,472
10 December 2016	Used car	928
15 December 2016	Plant and machinery	202,800
8 June 2017	New car	19,500
20 October 2018	New car	18,071

The cars acquired on 9 November 2016 and 10 December 2016 have CO_2 emissions between 76 – 130 g/km.

The new car acquired on 8 June 2017 has CO_2 emissions of 180 g/km and the one acquired on 20 October 2018 has CO_2 emissions of 70 g/km.

All the cars are used by employees 60% for business and 40% privately.

Calculate the capital allowances due for the three years ending 31 March 2019.

Assume the rates of allowances for the year ended 31 March 2017 continue into the future.

Solution

The approach is as follows:

- Allocate additions and disposals to the relevant accounting periods. Any acquisitions made prior to the commencement of trading are treated as if made on the first day of trading.
- Identify which additions qualify for AIA and FYA.
- Ignore information about private use as this is not relevant to companies.

JNN Ltd – Capital allowances computation

		General pool	Special rate pool	Total allowances
	£	£	£	£
Y/e 31 March 2017				
TWDV b/f				
Additions: No AIA:				
Cars (£1,472 + £928)		2,400		
Qualifying for AIA				
Plant and machinery	202,800			
Less: AIA (max)	(200,000)			200,000
		2,800		
		5,200		
WDA (18% × £5,200)		(936)		936
TWDV c/f		4,264		
Total allowances				200,936
Y/e 31 March 2018				
Additions: No AIA:				
Car – CO_2 > 130 g/km			19,500	
WDA @ 18%/8%		(768)	(1,560)	2,328
TWDV c/f		3,496	17,940	
Total allowances				2,328
Y/e 31 March 2019				
WDA @ 18%/8%		(629)	(1,435)	2,064
Additions qualifying for FYA				
Low emission car	18,071			
Less: FYA @ 100%	(18,071)			18,071
		Nil		
TWDV c/f		2,867	16,505	
Total allowances				20,135

Test your understanding 1

ENT Ltd prepares accounts to 31 December annually.

On 1 January 2016 the tax written down value of plant and machinery brought forward on the general pool was £24,000.

The following transactions took place in the year to 31 December 2016.

15 April 2016	Purchased car for £12,600 (emissions 180 g/km)
30 April 2016	Sold plant for £3,200 (original cost £4,800)
16 July 2016	Purchased car for £9,200 (emissions 120 g/km)
17 August 2016	Purchased car for £9,400 (emissions 125 g/km)
12 December 2016	Purchased energy saving plant for £2,615

In the following year to 31 December 2017, ENT Ltd sold for £7,900 the car originally purchased on 17 August 2016. The car originally purchased on 15 April 2016 was sold for £9,400 on 9 November 2017. There were no other transactions.

Required:

Compute the capital allowances and balancing adjustments for the years ended 31 December 2016 and 31 December 2017.

Assume the rates of allowances for the year ended 31 March 2017 continue into the future.

6 Short life assets

6.1 Short life asset treatment

Where an asset is expected to have a useful life of less than eight years from the end of the period of account in which it was acquired, it may be beneficial to remove it from the general pool and treat it as a short life asset.

Capital allowances are calculated separately for each short life asset. When the asset is sold there will be a balancing adjustment.

- Where it is sold for less than its TWDV there will be a tax deductible balancing allowance equal to the excess of the TWDV over the sales proceeds.
- Where it is sold for more than its TWDV there will be a taxable balancing charge equal to the excess of the sales proceeds over the TWDV.

A short life asset election will be advantageous if it is anticipated that the asset will be sold for less than its TWDV, such that a balancing allowance will arise, within the following eight accounting periods.

The following conditions apply:

- short life asset treatment is not available for cars
- if a short life asset is not sold within eight years of the end of the accounting period in which it was purchased, its TWDV will be transferred back into the general pool
- a short life asset election must be made within two years of the end of the accounting period in which the expenditure was incurred.

However, note that the AIA is available against short life assets and the business can choose the expenditure against which the AIA is matched.

If eligible for the AIA, there may be no expenditure left to 'de-pool' and the short life asset election will not be made.

If there is expenditure in excess of the maximum AIA on assets eligible for the AIA, it may be advantageous for the AIA to be allocated against the general pool expenditure rather than a short life asset and for the short life asset election to be made.

Example

View Ltd prepares accounts to 31 March each year.

On 1 May 2015 the company purchased a lathe for £20,000. The lathe was required for an 18-month contract and was sold on 30 November 2016 for £7,000. View Ltd claimed to treat the lathe as a short life asset.

The company purchased other machinery in the year ended 31 March 2016 such that the AIA limit was exceeded. The AIA was not claimed in respect of the lathe.

Required:

Calculate the capital allowances available in respect of the lathe for the years ended 31 March 2016 and 2017.

Solution

Capital allowances are calculated separately for the lathe and it is not included in the general pool.

View Ltd – Capital allowances

	Short life asset	Allowances
	£	£
Year ended 31 March 2016		
Additions:		
Not qualifying for AIA or FYA		
Lathe	20,000	
WDA at 18%	(3,600)	3,600
Tax WDV c/f	16,400	
Year ended 31 March 2017		
Disposals	(7,000)	
	9,400	
Balancing allowance	(9,400)	9,400
Tax WDV c/f	–	

View Ltd has accelerated the capital allowances in respect of the lathe by treating it as a short life asset. If no short life asset claim had been made, the tax written down value would have remained in the general pool and View Ltd would have continued to claim WDAs in respect of it.

Note that if the lathe had been sold for more than £16,400, the claim would not have been beneficial as it would have resulted in a balancing charge.

7 Pro forma computation for capital allowances on plant and machinery

7.1 Plant and machinery allowances

Capital allowances are an important element of the syllabus. To answer capital allowances questions successfully, it is vital to use a methodical approach to work through the information in the question.

The following approach to computational questions together with the following pro forma will help you to deal with the information in the correct order.

Note that a pro forma is supplied in the AAT reference material set out in section 12 below. This uses two separate columns for the AIA and FYA instead of one. Either approach is fine.

7.2 Approach to computational questions

For plant and machinery capital allowances, adopt the following step-by-step approach:

1. Read the information in the question and decide how many columns you will require.
2. Draft the layout and insert the TWDV b/f (does not apply in a new trade).
3. Insert additions not eligible for the AIA or FYA into the appropriate column.
4. Insert additions eligible for the AIA in the first column, and then allocate the AIA to the additions. If additions exceed the maximum AIA available then the remaining expenditure is added to the general pool and eligible for the WDA.
5. Deal with any disposal by deducting the lower of cost and sale proceeds.
6. Calculate the WDA at the appropriate rate on each of the pools.
7. Insert additions qualifying for 100% FYA in the first column and give the FYA.
8. Calculate the TWDV to carry forward to the next accounting period and add the 'total allowances' column.
9. Deduct the total allowances from the tax adjusted trading profits.

Pro forma capital allowances computation

		General pool	Special rate pool	Short life asset	Allowances
	£	£	£	£	£
TWDV b/f		X	X	X	
Additions:					
Not qualifying for AIA or FYA:					
Cars (76 – 130 g/km)		X			
Cars (over 130 g/km)			X		
Qualifying for AIA:					
Plant and machinery purchased	X				
Less: AIA (do not exceed maximum)	(X)				X
Balance of AIA qualifying expenditure to general pool		X			
Disposals (lower of original cost and sale proceeds)		(X)	(X)	(X)	
		X	X	X	
Balancing allowance/(Balancing charge)				X/(X)	X/(X)
				Nil	
WDAs at appropriate rates		(X)	(X)		X
Qualifying for FYA:					
Low emission cars (up to 75 g/km) and other qualifying assets	X				
Less: FYA at 100%	(X)				X
		Nil			
TWDV c/f		X	X		
Total allowances					X

7.3 Approach to assessment questions

In the CBA you will be given a blank grid to enter capital allowance figures.

It will not be necessary to enter lines dividing totals and subtotals, but otherwise you should be able to produce a computation that is the same as that which you would draw up on paper. It is recommended that you prepare the computation on the paper provided before entering it on screen.

This activity will be manually marked.

8 Impact of the length of the accounting period

8.1 Short chargeable accounting periods

Capital allowances are computed for chargeable accounting periods and deducted in calculating trading profits.

The allowances calculated so far were all for 12-month accounting periods.

Where the accounting period is less than 12 months long, the AIA and WDA must be scaled down accordingly. You must perform this calculation to the nearest month.

If the period for which accounts are drawn up exceeds 12 months, the capital allowances are computed in two stages – the first 12 months, then the balance (see Chapter 2, section 2.3).

Note that first year allowances are never time apportioned.

Therefore expenditure on low emission cars, energy efficient and water saving plant and machinery are always given the FYA in full, even if the length of the accounting period is less than 12 months.

Example

KNN Ltd started to trade on 1 January 2016 and, on that day, purchased a machine costing £205,000.

Calculate the capital allowances due for the first period of account on the assumption that accounts are prepared to

(i) 31 December 2016

(ii) 31 October 2016

(iii) 31 May 2017

Solution

	(i) 31 Dec 2016 (12 months)	(ii) 31 Oct 2016 (10 months)	(iii) 31 May 2017 (17 months)
	£	£	£
First period of account:			
First CAP (max 12 months)			
Addition:			
Qualifying for AIA:			
Plant and machinery	205,000	205,000	205,000
Less: AIA	(200,000)		(200,000)
(max 10/12 × £200,000)		(166,667)	
	5,000	38,333	5,000
WDA (18%)	(900)		(900)
WDA (18%) × 10/12		(5,750)	
TWDV c/f	4,100	75,083	4,100
Second CAP			
(balance of period of account)			
WDA (18% × 5/12)	n/a	n/a	(308)
TWDV c/f	4,100	32,583	3,792

Note that in example (iii) corporation tax is charged separately on an accounting period of 12 months ending on 31 December 2016 and on an accounting period of 5 months ending on 31 May 2017 (see Chapter 2).

Test your understanding 2

ABC Ltd buys a car costing £16,000 in its accounting period of nine months to 31 December 2016. The car has CO_2 emissions of 120 g/km.

What capital allowances are available?

A £2,880

B £1,280

C £960

D £2,160

9 Business cessation

9.1 Final accounting period

In the accounting period of cessation no allowances are given other than balancing adjustments.

Any additions and disposals in the final period are allocated to the appropriate columns in the capital allowances working.

At the end of the period there will be no tax WDV carried forward, so there must be a balancing adjustment on all columns in the capital allowances working.

- If there is a positive balance remaining, a balancing allowance is given.
- If there is a negative balance remaining, a balancing charge arises.

Example

DRN Ltd, a company that had been trading for many years preparing accounts to 31 March, ceased trading on 30 September 2017.

The tax written down value of the pool at 1 April 2016 was £12,600. On 1 October 2016, DRN Ltd purchased some plant for £4,600.

All items of plant were sold on 30 September 2017 for £8,000 (no item was sold for more than cost).

Calculate the capital allowances due for the year ended 31 March 2017 and the six months ended 30 September 2017.

Solution

DRN Ltd – Capital allowances computation

		General pool	Allowances
	£	£	£
Year ended 31 March 2017			
TWDV b/f		12,600	
Addition qualifying for AIA			
1 October 2016	4,600		
Less: AIA	(4,600)		4,600
		Nil	
Less: WDA (18%)		(2,268)	2,268
TWDV c/f		10,332	
Total allowances			6,868
6 months ended 30 September 2017			
Disposal		(8,000)	
		2,332	
Balancing allowance		(2,332)	2,332

Note: If plant is not sold until after the date of cessation, the proceeds eventually realised are used as the market value on cessation.

In effect it is treated as if sold on cessation for market value.

Test your understanding 3

JKL Ltd ceased trading on 31 March 2017 and sold all of its plant and machinery on that date. The tax written down value of the pool at 1 April 2016 was £2,000.

What capital allowances are due based on the disposal proceeds below?

Please tick whether it is a balancing allowance or balancing charge and complete the amount.

Disposal proceeds	Balancing allowance	Balancing charge	Amount £
Scrapped for no proceeds			
Sold for £500			
Sold for £2,200			

10 Test your understanding

Test your understanding 4

Plant and machinery allowances

Which one of the following statements is false?

A The cost of alterations to buildings needed for the installation of plant is specifically eligible for plant and machinery capital allowances

B The AIA is not available on cars, unless it is a low emission car

C If the period of account of a business is less than 12 months, the AIA and WDA are scaled down proportionately

D A short life asset election cannot be made in respect of a car

Test your understanding 5

Annual Investment Allowance

Which of the following acquisitions will qualify for the annual investment allowance?

A A warehouse

B Display equipment in a shop

C A car used partly for business purposes by an employee

D A pool car used exclusively for business use

Test your understanding 6

Banks Ltd

Banks Ltd prepared accounts for the three month period ended 31 March 2017.

On 1 February 2017 a car with CO_2 emissions of 162 g/km was purchased for the sales director at a cost of £16,000. It is used by him 60% for business purposes.

What are the capital allowances available on this car for the three months ended 31 March 2017?

Test your understanding 7

Faraday Ltd

Faraday Ltd has the following non-current asset information for the year ended 31 December 2016.

Balances brought forward at 1 January 2016:	£
General pool	398,100
Special rate pool	28,060
Additions:	
Machinery	193,345
Energy saving plant	20,850
Office furniture	33,610
Managing Director's car (CO_2 emissions 178 g/km)	48,150
Disposals:	
Machinery (Cost £25,000)	16,875
Director's car (CO_2 emissions 198 g/km, cost £31,000))	23,100

Required:

Calculate Faraday Ltd's total capital allowances and show the balances to carry forward to the next accounting period.

Test your understanding 8

Deni Ltd

Deni Ltd is a manufacturing business preparing accounts to 31 January each year.

At 1 February 2016, the written-down value of plant and machinery in the general pool was £25,000 and £7,100 for a short life asset which had been purchased in October 2012.

During the year ended 31 January 2017, the following transactions were undertaken:

Purchases		£
1 March 2016	Machinery	211,250
15 March 2016	Second-hand machinery	10,000
20 May 2016	MD's car with CO_2 emissions of 120 g/km (used 80% for business)	19,600
Sales		
25 February 2016	Machinery (cost £6,000)	1,750
31 March 2016	Short life asset	500

Required:

Compute Deni Ltd's capital allowances for the accounting period ended 31 January 2017.

Test your understanding 9

TEN Ltd

TEN Ltd prepares accounts to 31 December annually. On 1 January 2016, the balance of plant and machinery brought forward was £16,000.

The following transactions took place in the year to 31 December 2016.

15 April 2016	Purchased car for £15,000 (CO_2 emissions 125 g/km)
30 April 2016	Sold plant for £2,000 (original cost £1,600)
26 July 2016	Purchased two new cars for £9,300 each. Both of these cars qualify as low-emission cars.

In the following year to 31 December 2017, TEN Ltd sold for £7,600 one of the cars originally purchased on 26 July 2016.

The car originally purchased on 15 April 2016 was sold for £8,000 on 9 May 2017. There were no other transactions.

Required:

Compute the capital allowances for the years ended 31 December 2016 and 31 December 2017.

Assume the rates of allowances for the year ended 31 March 2017 continue into the future.

Test your understanding 10

Booker Ltd

Booker Ltd trades as a manufacturer in York and prepares accounts to 31 March each year. In 2016 it decided to change its year end and prepared accounts for the 9 month period to 31 December 2016.

The balance on the general pool was £18,150 at 1 April 2016. In July 2016, the company sold for £4,900 a car bought in 2012 for £7,800 (the car had CO_2 emissions of 117 g/km). The company also purchased a second-hand car with CO_2 emissions of 125 g/km for £5,750 in July 2016. There was 10% private use of both cars by employees.

In December 2016 it also purchased plant for £153,750.

Required:

Calculate Booker Ltd's capital allowances for the 9 m/e 31 December 2016 and show the tax written-down values carried forward.

11 Summary

Capital allowances are available, instead of depreciation, to give tax relief for the cost of capital assets over the life of the assets.

A tabular layout is essential for computing capital allowances on plant and machinery.

The table should have separate columns for each of the following:

- general pool
- special rate pool.

When an asset is expected to have a short life and to be sold for less than its tax written down value, it may be beneficial to exclude it from the general pool and treat it as a short life asset.

When an accounting period is less than 12 months long, the maximum annual investment allowance and writing down allowances must be scaled down accordingly.

First year allowances are never scaled down.

12 AAT reference material

Capital allowances on plant and machinery

Layout of capital allowances on plant and machinery computation

(see taxation tables for rates)

	First Year Allowance (FYA)	Annual Investment Allowance(AIA)	General pool	Special rate pool	Short Life Asset	Total allowances
	£	£	£	£	£	£
WDV b/f			X	X	X	
Additions	X	X	X			
Disposals			(X)		(X)	
	X	X	X	X	X	
Balancing allowance/balancing charge(BA/BC)					X/(X)	X/(X)
					Nil	
AIA/FYA	(X)	(X)				X
Writing down allowance @ 18% pa			(X)			X
Writing down allowance @ 8% pa				(X)		X
WDV c/f	Nil	Nil	X	X		
Total allowances						X

- Plant – defined by 'function/setting' distinction and case law.
- AIA – 100% allowance for expenditure (other than cars) in 12 month period (pro rata). Expenditure in excess of AIA qualifies for writing down allowance (WDA).
- Full WDA for the period is given regardless of date of purchase of item. WDA is scaled for periods other than 12 months.
- FYA – 100% allowance given on purchase of environmentally friendly cars and energy saving/water efficient plant. FYA is not scaled for short accounting periods.
- If the written down value (WDV) on the general pool (= WDV b/f + additions – disposals) is £1,000 or less then pool is written off as small pools annual writing down allowance.
- Short life assets (SLA) – de-pool asset if life expected to be less than 8 years. Not available for cars.

Test your understanding answers

Test your understanding 1

ENT Ltd – Capital allowances computation

		General pool	Special rate pool	Total allowances
	£	£	£	£
Y/e 31 Dec 2016				
TWDV b/f		24,000		
Additions: No AIA:				
Cars:				
15 April 2016			12,600	
16 July 2016		9,200		
17 August 2016		9,400		
Disposals		(3,200)		
		39,400		
WDA @ 18%/8%		(7,092)	(1,008)	8,100
Energy saving plant	2,615			
Less: FYA (100%)	(2,615)			2,615
		Nil		
TWDV c/f		32,308	11,592	
Total allowances				10,715
Y/e 31 Dec 2017				
Disposals		(7,900)	(9,400)	
		24,408	2,192	
WDA @ 18%/8%		(4,393)	(175)	4,568
TWDV c/f		20,015	2,017	
Total allowances				4,568

Test your understanding 2

The correct answer is D.

Explanation

A WDA of (£16,000 × 18% × 9/12) = £2,160 is due.

Test your understanding 3

Capital allowances computation

Disposal proceeds	Balancing allowance	Balancing charge	Amount £
Scrapped for no proceeds	✓		2,000
Sold for £500	✓		1,500
Sold for £2,200		✓	200

Test your understanding 4

Plant and machinery allowances

The correct answer is B.

Explanation

The AIA is not available on any cars.

If the car is a low emission car it is entitled to a 100% first year allowance, but this is a FYA, not the AIA.

The other statements are all true.

Test your understanding 5

Annual Investment Allowance

The correct answer is B.

Explanation

The other acquisitions will not qualify for AIA because:

A Buildings are not plant and machinery.

C/D Cars do not attract the AIA regardless of whether they are for business or private use.

Test your understanding 6

Banks Ltd

The correct answer is £320.

Explanation

There is no adjustment to capital allowances as a result of private use of assets by employees. The WDA is time apportioned as the period is only three months.

3 months ended 31 March 2017		**Allowances**
	£	£
Additions – no AIAs		
Car with emissions >130 g/km	16,000	
Less: WDA (8% × 3/12)	(320)	320
TWDV c/f	15,680	

Test your understanding 7

Faraday Ltd – Capital allowances

	£	General pool £	Special rate pool £	Allowances £
Year ended 31 Dec 2016				
TWDV b/f		398,100	28,060	
Additions – no AIA				
Car			48,150	
Additions – AIA				
Machinery	193,345			
Office furniture	33,610			
	226,955			
Less: AIA	(200,000)			200,000
Balance of AIA exp.		26,955		
Disposal		(16,875)	(23,100)	
		408,180	53,110	
WDA (18%)/(8%)		(73,472)	(4,249)	77,721
Additions – FYA				
Energy saving plant	20,850			
FYA (100%)	(20,850)			20,850
		Nil		
TWDV c/f		334,708	48,861	
Total allowances				298,571

Test your understanding 8

Deni Ltd

Capital allowances

		General pool	Short life asset	Allowances
Year ended 31 January 2017	£	£	£	£
TWDV b/f		25,000	7,100	
Addition not qualifying for AIA				
Car		19,600		
Additions qualifying for AIA				
Machinery				
(£211,250 + £10,000)	221,250			
Less: AIA (note)	(200,000)			200,000
		21,250		
Disposal		(1,750)	(500)	
		64,100	6,600	
Balancing allowance			(6,600)	6,600
WDA (18% × £64,100)		(11,538)		11,538
TWDV c/f		52,562		
Total allowances				218,138

Note: The short life asset is sold which must give rise to a balancing charge or allowance. In this case it is an allowance as the asset is sold for less than the TWDV brought forward.

Test your understanding 9

TEN Ltd

Capital allowances

		General pool	Allowances
Year ending 31 December 2016		£	£
TWDV b/f		16,000	
Additions not qualifying for AIA			
15 April 2016		15,000	
Disposals			
30 April 2016 (restrict to cost)		(1,600)	
		29,400	
WDA (£29,400 × 18%)		(5,292)	5,292
Additions qualifying for FYA			
Cars (2 × £9,300)	18,600		
FYA at 100%	(18,600)		18,600
		Nil	
TWDV c/f		24,108	
Total allowances			23,892
Year ending 31 December 2017			
Disposals (£7,600 + £8,000)		(15,600)	
		8,508	
WDA (18% × £8,508)		(1,531)	1,531
TWDV c/f		6,977	
Total allowances			1,531

Test your understanding 10

Booker Ltd

Capital allowances computation

		General pool	**Allowances**
	£	£	£
9 months to 31 Dec 2016			
TWDV b/f		18,150	
Additions			
Not qualifying for AIA or FYA			
Car		5,750	
Qualifying for AIA			
Plant and machinery	153,750		
Less: AIA (max 9/12 × £200,000)	(150,000)		150,000
Balance of AIA qualifying expenditure		3,750	
Disposal		(4,900)	
		22,750	
WDA (18% × 9/12)		(3,071)	3,071
TWDV c/f		19,679	
Total allowances			153,071

Corporation tax computation

5

Introduction

In the previous chapters we have been working towards calculating the adjusted trading profit of a company, the major source of income found on most corporation tax computations.

In this chapter we add to that knowledge to enable a full computation of a company's corporation tax liability.

Finally, we cover the completion of the corporation tax return.

ASSESSMENT CRITERIA

Calculate the taxable total profits from trading income, property income, investment income and chargeable gains (2.3)

Calculate the total profits and corporation tax payable for accounting periods longer than, shorter than or equal to 12 months (2.3)

Accurately complete a corporation tax return (2.4)

CONTENTS

1 Pro forma corporation tax computation

1.1 Pro forma

The first stage of a single company computation is to ascertain the company's taxable total profits. This comprises income and gains, less qualifying charitable donations.

The pro forma that was set out in Chapter 2 is set out again below. It will be referred to throughout this chapter.

Company name

Corporation tax computation for XX months ended…(the CAP)

	£
Trading profit	X
Non-trade interest	X
Property income	X
Chargeable gains	X
Total profits	X
Less: Qualifying charitable donations	(X)
Taxable total profits	X
Corporation tax liability at relevant rate	X

The AAT reference material set out in section 7 below contains a pro forma corporation tax computation.

2 Taxable total profits

2.1 Adjusted trading profit

The adjusted trading profit and capital allowances have been covered in the previous chapters, so you can now compute the trading profit that is entered in the computation of taxable total profits.

	Chapter	£
Adjusted trading profit	3	X
Less: Capital allowances		
Plant and machinery	4	(X)
Trading profit		X

2.2 Interest income (the loan relationship rules)

We consider the loan relationship rules at this point because of their relevance to the computation of trading profit and non-trade interest.

The loan relationship rules apply when a company pays or receives interest, or incurs any cost relating to a loan.

The legislation distinguishes between trading purposes and non-trading purposes, in relation to the interest.

For assessment purposes:

If a company **receives** interest you can normally assume that it is for non-trading purposes.

For example:

- interest received on a building society account
- interest received on a bank deposit account.

If a company **pays** interest you can normally assume that it is for trading purposes.

For example:

- interest paid on a bank overdraft
- interest paid on a loan to purchase new machinery.

You will, however, need to read the question carefully to make sure that these assumptions are not contradicted.

Net or gross?

Most interest paid by or received by a company is paid or received gross (with the exception of interest paid to individuals).

All amounts shown on corporation tax computations must be shown gross.

If interest is paid to an individual by a company it is paid net of 20% tax. Hence, the interest must be grossed up.

The gross interest is calculated as follows:

Interest paid to individual × 100/80

Example

Rye Ltd pays and receives the following amounts of interest.

		£
(a)	Interest received on deposit account with Bat East Bank plc	5,000
(b)	Interest paid on overdrawn business bank account	(2,000)
(c)	Interest paid on loan made to the company by Mr Smith	(2,000)

Compute the gross figures to be used in the corporation tax computation.

Solution

Gross amounts to be included in calculation of taxable total profits:

		£
(a)	Interest received	5,000
(b)	Interest paid on overdraft	(2,000)
(c)	Interest paid on loan by Mr Smith (£2,000 × 100/80)	(2,500)

Trading loans

Interest paid

All interest on trading loans deducted in the statement of profit or loss is an allowable deduction from trading profits.

This means you will not need to make any adjustments in converting the accounting profit into the adjusted trading profit.

Interest received

You are unlikely to see any interest received for trading purposes.

However, if you do, such interest is included in the trading profit and therefore needs no adjustment.

Non-trading loans

Interest paid

Interest deducted in the statement of profit or loss in relation to non-trading loans is disallowed in computing adjusted trading profits (i.e. add it back in the adjustment of profit computation).

Instead, the interest is an allowable deduction from non-trade interest income.

The main example of this type of interest will be interest paid on a loan to buy an investment property or shares.

Interest received

Interest income shown in the statement of profit or loss (e.g. interest on a deposit account) will be from a non-trade loan and therefore must be deducted from net profit in the adjustment of trading profit computation and instead treated as non-trade interest income.

Other costs incurred in respect of loan relationships

All other costs in relation to non-trading loan relationships are disallowed in computing adjusted trading profits, but are allowed as a deduction from non-trade interest income instead.

The main example of this will be loans to former employees, customers or suppliers which have been written off.

The AAT reference material included in section 7 refers to the treatment of interest.

Accruals basis

All interest in corporation tax computations must be dealt with on an accruals basis (not received and paid basis).

The accruals basis means the amount due within the accounting period.

Example

Sam Limited has received the following interest on its bank deposit account that was opened on 1 April 2016:

Date received	£
30 June 2016	1,000
31 December 2016	3,000
30 June 2017	4,000

Assuming interest accrues evenly between each date; calculate the non-trade interest income to be shown in the corporation tax computation for the year ended 31 March 2017.

Solution

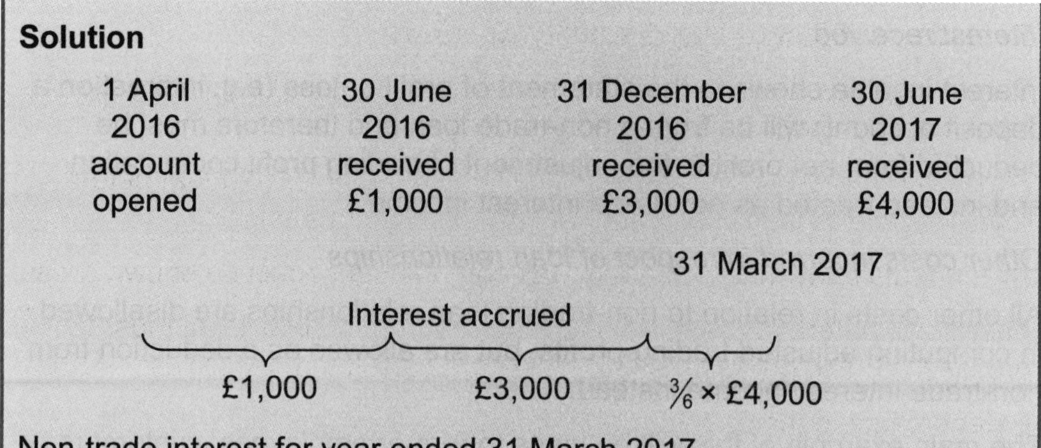

Non-trade interest for year ended 31 March 2017
= (£1,000 + £3,000 + £2,000) = £6,000

The figure shown in the accounts will normally be the accrued amount. You are therefore unlikely to have to calculate this.

Test your understanding 1

The statement of profit or loss of ABC Ltd includes interest received on an investment in Government securities.

How should this be dealt with in the computation of the taxable total profits?

A Deducted from net profit only

B Included as non-trading income only

C Deducted from net profit and included as non-trading income

D No adjustment

2.3 Patent royalties

Patent royalties paid or received by companies are dealt with for tax purposes on an accruals basis.

Royalties payable

Royalties are relieved as a trading expense against trading profits on a normal accruals basis. So if they have been correctly charged through the accounts no adjustment should be needed.

Royalties receivable

Royalties receivable on patents are taxed as trading profits. Again, if the income has been correctly shown on an accruals basis no adjustment should be needed.

Royalties subject to income tax deductions

Patent royalties are usually received gross, except that patent royalties received from individuals are received net of 20% tax.

Similarly, all patent royalties are usually paid gross, except that patent royalties paid to individuals are paid net of basic rate tax.

All amounts shown in corporation tax computations must be shown gross.

Therefore, patent royalties paid to/received from an individual must be grossed up. The gross patent royalties are calculated as follows:

Patent royalties (cash amount) × 100/80

Example

Tom Ltd receives the following patent royalties.

What are the gross figures to be used in the corporation tax computation?

(a)	Received from Rye Ltd	£3,000
(b)	Received from Eric	£3,900

Solution

Gross amounts to be used:

(a)	From Rye Ltd	£3,000
(b)	From Eric (£3,900 × 100/80)	£4,875

2.4 Dividend income

Dividend income received by companies is not chargeable to corporation tax. In a correctly prepared set of financial statements, dividends are not included in arriving at net income. If dividend income is included in the net income, it must be deducted when computing the adjusted trading profits.

This is because dividend income is paid out of after-tax profits of another company (i.e. the profits generating the dividend have already been subject to UK corporation tax in that other company).

2.5 Property income

The calculation of property income is not in the business tax syllabus.

If a company has property income you will be given the figure to use in calculating the taxable total profits.

2.6 Chargeable gains

A company's taxable total profits include chargeable gains as well as income.

The calculation of the chargeable gain or loss on the disposal of capital assets is covered in a later chapter.

For the purpose of this chapter, all gains and losses on asset disposals are already computed. You will, however, need to be able to produce a summary of the position for the purpose of calculating taxable total profits.

This is shown as follows:

	£
Gain (transaction 1)	X
Gain (transaction 2)	X
Loss (transaction 3)	(X)
	X
Less: Capital losses brought forward	(X)
Net chargeable gains	X

Current period gains and losses are netted off automatically.

Excess capital losses are covered in Chapter 16.

Test your understanding 2

1 GHI Ltd made a chargeable gain on the disposal of shares during 2016 of £60,000. It had capital losses brought forward of £25,000.

How much should be included in taxable total profits?

2 How would your answer differ if capital losses brought forward had amounted to £75,000?

2.7 Qualifying charitable donations

The final component in calculating taxable total profits is to deduct from the total profits (income and gains) any qualifying charitable donations. These are paid gross by companies.

The gross amount deductible for a CAP is the amount *paid* in that CAP. This may be a different figure from the amount accrued in the accounts.

A qualifying charitable donation is basically any donation made by a company to a charity unless it already qualifies as a trading expense. Only donations that are 'small' and 'local in effect' will normally be allowed as a trading expense. It is therefore usually donations made to national charities which are treated as qualifying charitable donations.

Note that in the past it was necessary for a donation to be made under gift aid to be allowable. However this requirement no longer applies to company donations (but is still required for donations by individuals).

However, you may still come across references to gift aid donations. In particular they are included in the AAT reference material, which is included in section 7.

Test your understanding 3

Laserjet Ltd (1)

Laserjet Ltd provided you with the following information for its year to 31 January 2017.

	£
Adjusted trading profit before capital allowances	500,600
Capital allowances	16,000
Rental income (net of expenses)	32,000
Bank loan interest payable on a loan to purchase rental property (accrued)	4,000
Building society interest receivable (accrued)	20,000
10% loan note interest receivable (accrued)	6,000
Donation paid to national charity	14,000

Required:

Calculate the taxable total profits for the year ended 31 January 2017.

Approach to the question

You need a methodical approach to calculate taxable total profits.

Step 1: Set up a skeleton CT computation pro forma (this may be given in the assessment).

	£
Trading profit (W1)	
Non-trade interest (W2)	
Property income	
	–––––
Total profits	
Less: Qualifying charitable donations	
	–––––
Taxable total profits	
	–––––

Note that the labels in the computation are not required to be in any particular order, but it is accepted best practice to put the trading profit first.

Step 2: Prepare any necessary workings separately from the pro forma

Work through the information methodically. The figure for trading profit often (though not in this example) requires more than one working for the component parts of:

- adjusted trading profit
- capital allowances on plant and machinery.

As you complete each working, slot the result into the pro forma.

2.8 Long periods of account

As you know, although a company can draw up financial accounts for a period of more than 12 months, a company's 'chargeable accounting period' (CAP) for corporation tax purposes can never exceed 12 months.

Therefore, if the financial accounts cover more than 12 months, two chargeable accounting periods are required; one for the first 12 months and one for the balance.

This section tackles the allocation of income, chargeable gains and qualifying charitable donations between the two periods in finding taxable total profits.

Item	Method of allocation
Trading profit before deducting capital allowances	Time apportioned
Capital allowances (see Chapter 4)	Separate computation for each CAP
Property income	Time apportioned
Non-trade interest	Period in which accrued (Note)
Chargeable gains	Period of disposal
Qualifying charitable donation	Period in which paid

Note: If information to apply the strict accruals basis is not available, then time apportion.

Be very careful when calculating the number of months in the second period – double check it – as it is crucial for time apportioning calculations and easy to get wrong.

Note that the rules for long periods of account are covered in the AAT reference material set out in section 7 below.

Example

Printer Ltd has prepared accounts for the 16 months to 31 August 2016, with the following information.

	£
Adjusted trading profit before capital allowances	381,000
Building society interest	
Received 30 June 2015 (of which £1,950 related to year ended 30 April 2015)	2,450
Received 30 June 2016	2,675
Accrued on 31 August 2016	200
Rents from property	26,010
Chargeable gains	
Disposal on 31 March 2016	25,700
Disposal on 1 May 2016	49,760
Qualifying charitable donations:	
Paid 31 July 2015	6,000
Paid 31 January 2016	6,000

Capital allowances for the two CAPs derived from the 16 month period of account are £20,000 and £6,250 respectively.

Show how the company's period of account will be divided into CAPs and compute the taxable total profits for each CAP assuming, where relevant, that all income is deemed to accrue evenly.

Solution

The procedure to be followed is exactly the same as for a 12 month period, but incorporating the allocation rules.

	12 months to 30 April 2016	**4 months to 31 August 2016**
	£	£
Trading profit (W1)	265,750	89,000
Non-trade interest (W2)	2,531	844
Property income (W3)	19,507	6,503
Chargeable gains	25,700	49,760
Total profits	313,488	146,107
Less: Qualifying charitable donations (W4)	(12,000)	Nil
Taxable total profits	301,488	146,107

Note: The chargeable gains are allocated according to the date of the transaction.

Workings:

(W1) Trading profit

	Total	**12m**	**4m**
	£	£	£
Adjusted profit (see note)	381,000	285,750	95,250
Less: Capital allowances		(20,000)	(6,250)
Trading profit		265,750	89,000

Note: The adjusted trading profit before capital allowances is time **apportioned** (it is acceptable to apportion on a monthly basis in the assessment).

(W2) Non-trade interest – Building society interest

As the accrual at 30 April 2016 is not given, the total amount which would be included in the statement of profit or loss for the 16 month period on the accruals basis is calculated, then time apportioned:

		Total	12m	4m
		£	£	£
Received	30 June 2015	2,450		
	30 June 2016	2,675		
Add	Closing accrual	200		
Less	Opening accrual	(1,950)		
		3,375	2,531	844

(W3) Property income

Rental income is assessable as property income, which is assessed on an accruals basis for the 16 months and then time apportioned into the two CAPs:

	Total	12m	4m
	£	£	£
Property income	26,010	19,507	6,503

(W4) Qualifying charitable donations

	£	
31 July 2015	6,000	
31 January 2016	6,000	
	12,000	In y/e 30 April 2016

Nil in 4 months to 31 August 2016 as none paid.

Test your understanding 4

Chinny Ltd

Chinny Ltd has for many years prepared accounts to 30 September, but changed its accounting date to 31 December by preparing accounts for the 15 months ended 31 December 2016.

The accounts show a profit, as adjusted for tax purposes (but before deducting capital allowances), of £250,000.

Capital allowances for the two CAPs based on the 15 month period of account were £13,450 and £5,818 respectively.

The company also had income in the period as follows:

		£
Building society interest receivable	1 Oct 2015 – 30 Sept 2016	4,420
	1 Oct 2016 – 31 Dec 2016	780
Chargeable gains	Disposal 15 Dec 2016	55,000
Rents received	31 July 2016	8,000

The rents accrued at 30 September 2015 and 31 December 2016 were £3,000 and £5,000 respectively.

Required:

Calculate the amounts of taxable total profits for this 15 month period of account.

3 The corporation tax liability

3.1 Calculating the corporation tax liability

Once you have computed a company's taxable total profits, the next stage of the computation is to calculate the corporation tax liability.

Corporation tax is calculated using the rate (or rates) in force during the chargeable accounting period.

The rates of tax are fixed for a financial year (FY), which is the year that runs from 1 April to the following 31 March. For example, FY2016 is the period from 1 April 2016 to 31 March 2017 (note that it is labelled based on the year in which the period starts).

For FY2016 and FY 2015 the rate of corporation tax for all companies is 20%. This is also known as the main rate.

Example

Tilly Ltd has taxable total profits of £350,000 in its year ended 31 March 2017.

Calculate Tilly Ltd's corporation tax liability.

Solution

The year ended 31 March 2017 is the FY2016, therefore the tax is calculated at 20%.

Corporation tax liability (£350,000 × 20%) = £70,000.

Test your understanding 5

Osmond Ltd

Osmond Ltd had the following results for the year ended 31 March 2016:

	£
Trading profit	510,000
Loan note (debenture) interest receivable	8,000
UK dividends received	18,000
Chargeable gain on the sale of an investment	7,500

Required:

Calculate Osmond Ltd's corporation tax liability for the year ended 31 March 2016.

3.2 Non 31 March year ends

The CAP of a company with a year end of 31 December 2016 falls into two financial years as follows:

- three months of the year (1 January 2016 to 31 March 2016) is the last three months of FY2015
- nine months of the year (1 April 2016 to 31 December 2016) is the first nine months of FY2016.

However, because the main rate of corporation tax is 20% in both of these financial years, the corporation tax liability is simply 20% of the taxable total profits.

If the two financial years had different main rates of corporation tax, the corporation tax liability would be calculated by:

- time apportioning the taxable total profits between the two financial years by reference to the number of months in each financial year
- then multiplying the taxable total profits for each financial year by the appropriate main rate of corporation tax.

For example:

		£
FY2015	Taxable total profits × 3/12 × x%	X
FY2016	Taxable total profits × 9/12 × y%	X
		X

Example

Calculate the corporation tax liability for Printer Ltd in the example in section 2 for its two chargeable accounting periods.

Solution

The 12 months to 30 April 2016 falls partly into FY2015 (11 months) and partly into FY2016 (1 month). However, because the main rate of corporation tax is 20% for both financial years, the corporation tax liability is simply 20% of the taxable total profits.

12 months to 30 April 2016	£
(£301,488 × 20%)	60,297.60

4 months to 31 August 2016	£
(£146,107 × 20%)	29,221.40

Test your understanding 6

Unpredictably Uptown Limited

Unpredictably Uptown Limited (UUL) is a UK resident company which makes fashionable ladies clothing. The company has previously prepared accounts to 31 March but has now changed its accounting date to 30 September.

In the 18 months period to 30 September 2016 the company had the following results:

	£
Adjusted trading profits (Note 1)	990,000
Donation to charity (Note 2)	(20,000)
Bank interest receivable (Note 3)	12,500
Dividend received on 28 February 2016	17,500

Note 1: Adjusted trading profits

No capital allowances are due.

Note 2: Donation

On 31 December 2015 the company made a payment of £20,000 to a national charity.

Note 3: Bank interest

	£
30 September 2015 received	5,000
31 March 2016 received	4,000
30 September 2016 received	3,500
	12,500

The interest is non-trading interest. The amounts received were the amounts accrued to date.

Required:

Calculate the corporation tax liability of UUL for the period ended 30 September 2016.

4 Corporation tax return

4.1 Form CT600

The corporation tax return, Form CT600, must be completed for the chargeable accounting period.

Only the following boxes are relevant in the assessment.

145	Total turnover
155	Trading profit
160	Trading losses brought forward claimed against profits See Chapter 6
165	Net trading profit (Box 155 minus box 160
170	Non-trade interest income
185	Income from which income tax has been deducted The gross amount of patent royalties received from an individual
190	Property income
210	Gross chargeable gains
215	Allowable losses including losses brought forward
220	Net chargeable gains (Box 210 minus box 215
235	Profits before other deductions and reliefs Sum of boxes 165, 170, 185, 190 and 220

4.2 Taxable total profits on Form CT600

We have not dealt with entries to go in all boxes. However, the main ones considered are:

	Boxes
Total turnover	145
Trading profit	155
Less: trading losses b/f	160
Net trading profit	165
Non-trade interest income	170
Patent royalties from an individual	185
Property income	190
Gross chargeable gains	210
Current year and brought forward capital losses	215
Net chargeable gains	220
Total profits (income and gains)	235

In the assessment you will be given most of the information to enter into the form but you may have to calculate some of the figures such as totals and subtotals.

The following is important in connection with the completion of forms in the assessment.

- When completing the form in the assessment, figures must be entered in the correct boxes.
- You will only be asked to complete one page of the form.
- Commas need not be entered for numbers of four digits or more.
- You do not need to fill in every box, only the relevant ones.

The parts of the return which you may be required to complete in the assessment are reproduced below.

Tax calculation

Turnover

145 Total turnover from trade £ . 0 0

150 Banks, building societies, insurance companies and other financial concerns – *put an 'X' in this box if you do not have a recognised turnover and have not made an entry in box 145*

Income

155 Trading profits £ . 0 0

160 Trading losses brought forward claimed against profits £ . 0 0

165 Net trading profits – *box 155 minus box 160* £ . 0 0

170 Bank, building society or other interest, and profits from non-trading loan relationships £ . 0 0

172 Put an 'X' in box 172 if the figure in box 170 is net of carrying back a deficit from a later accounting period

175 Annual payments not otherwise charged to Corporation Tax and from which Income Tax has not been deducted £ . 0 0

Income *continued*

180 Non-exempt dividends or distributions from non-UK resident companies £ . 0 0

185 Income from which Income Tax has been deducted £ . 0 0

190 Income from a property business £ . 0 0

195 Non-trading gains on intangible fixed assets £ . 0 0

200 Tonnage Tax profits £ . 0 0

205 Income not falling under any other heading £ . 0 0

Chargeable gains

210 Gross chargeable gains £ . 0 0

215 Allowable losses including losses brought forward £ . 0 0

220 Net chargeable gains – *box 210 minus box 215* £ . 0 0

Profits before deductions and reliefs

225 Losses brought forward against certain investment income £ . 0 0

230 Non-trade deficits on loan relationships (including interest) and derivative contracts (financial instruments) brought forward £ . 0 0

235 Profits before other deductions and reliefs – *net sum of boxes 165 to 205 and 220 minus sum of boxes 225 and 230* £ . 0 0

Example

Victor Ltd has the following results for its year ended 31 January 2017.

Enter the figures on the Form CT600 as indicated.

	£	*CT 600 box*
Turnover	850,000	145
Trading profit	100,000	155
Non-trade interest income	20,000	170
Property income	5,000	190
Chargeable gains	8,000	210
Current year capital losses	(1,000)	215
Capital losses b/f	(2,000)	215
Total profits	130,000	235

Don't forget to include a sub-total in boxes a65 and 220.

Solution

Tax calculation

Turnover

Box	Description	£
145	Total turnover from trade	850000·00
150	Banks, building societies, insurance companies and other financial concerns – *put an 'X' in this box if you do not have a recognised turnover and have not made an entry in box 145*	

Income

Box	Description	£
155	Trading profits	100000·00
160	Trading losses brought forward claimed against profits	·00
165	Net trading profits – *box 155 minus box 160*	100000·00
170	Bank, building society or other interest, and profits from non-trading loan relationships	20000·00
172	Put an 'X' in box 172 if the figure in box 170 is net of carrying back a deficit from a later accounting period	
175	Annual payments not otherwise charged to Corporation Tax and from which Income Tax has not been deducted	·00

Income *continued*

Box	Description	£
180	Non-exempt dividends or distributions from non-UK resident companies	·00
185	Income from which Income Tax has been deducted	·00
190	Income from a property business	5000·00
195	Non-trading gains on intangible fixed assets	·00
200	Tonnage Tax profits	·00
205	Income not falling under any other heading	·00

Chargeable gains

Box	Description	£
210	Gross chargeable gains	8000·00
215	Allowable losses including losses brought forward	3000·00 (2,000 + 1,000)
220	Net chargeable gains – *box 210 minus box 215*	5000·00

Profits before deductions and reliefs

Box	Description	£
225	Losses brought forward against certain investment income	·00
230	Non-trade deficits on loan relationships (including interest) and derivative contracts (financial instruments) brought forward	·00
235	Profits before other deductions and reliefs – *net sum of boxes 165 to 205 and 220 minus sum of boxes 225 and 230*	130000·00

Test your understanding 7

Complete the extract of Form CT600 for Laserjet Ltd from TYU 3.

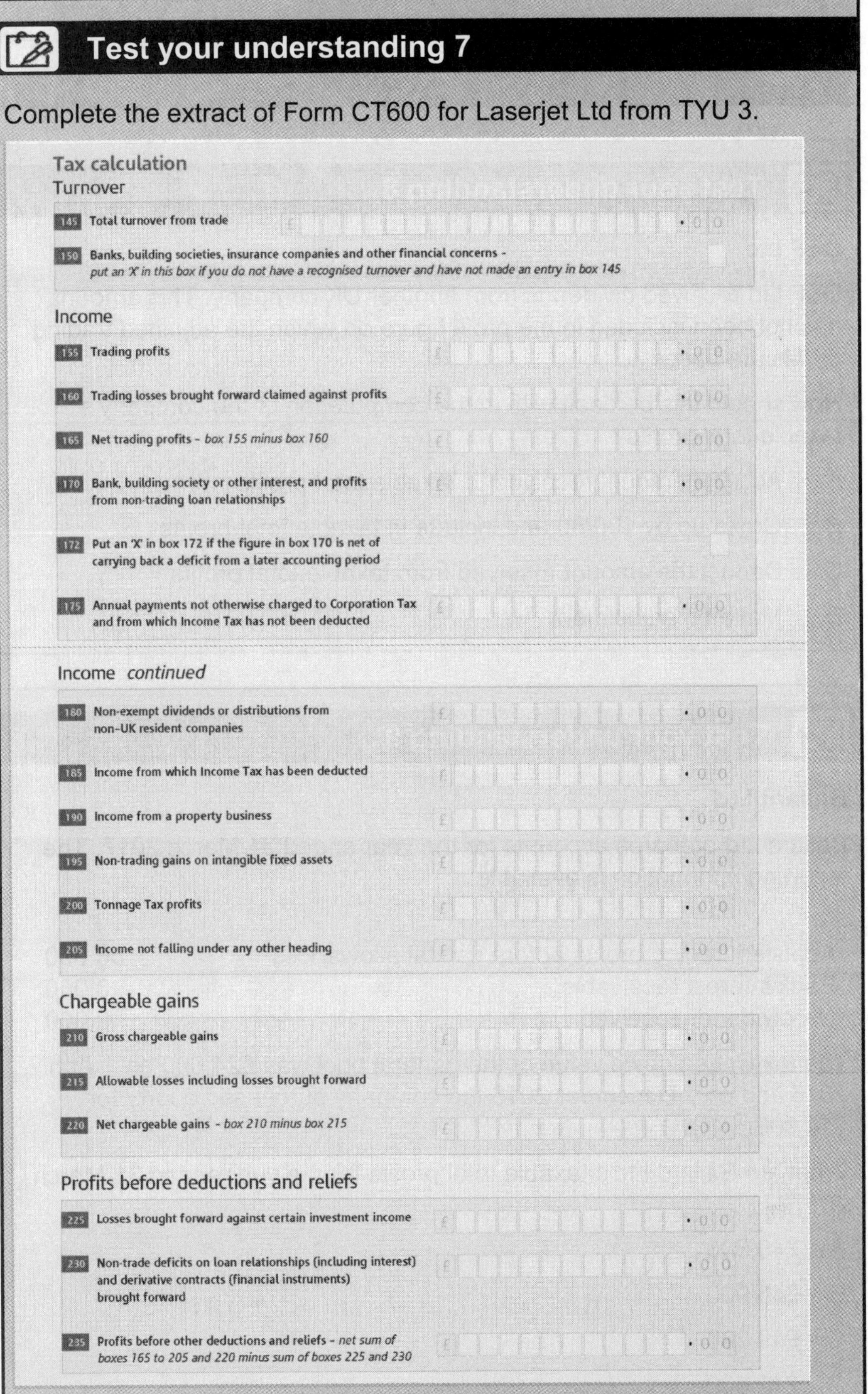

Tax calculation

Turnover

145 Total turnover from trade £ .00

150 Banks, building societies, insurance companies and other financial concerns – *put an 'X' in this box if you do not have a recognised turnover and have not made an entry in box 145*

Income

155 Trading profits £ .00

160 Trading losses brought forward claimed against profits £ .00

165 Net trading profits – *box 155 minus box 160* £ .00

170 Bank, building society or other interest, and profits from non-trading loan relationships £ .00

172 Put an 'X' in box 172 if the figure in box 170 is net of carrying back a deficit from a later accounting period

175 Annual payments not otherwise charged to Corporation Tax and from which Income Tax has not been deducted £ .00

Income *continued*

180 Non-exempt dividends or distributions from non-UK resident companies £ .00

185 Income from which Income Tax has been deducted £ .00

190 Income from a property business £ .00

195 Non-trading gains on intangible fixed assets £ .00

200 Tonnage Tax profits £ .00

205 Income not falling under any other heading £ .00

Chargeable gains

210 Gross chargeable gains £ .00

215 Allowable losses including losses brought forward £ .00

220 Net chargeable gains – *box 210 minus box 215* £ .00

Profits before deductions and reliefs

225 Losses brought forward against certain investment income £ .00

230 Non-trade deficits on loan relationships (including interest) and derivative contracts (financial instruments) brought forward £ .00

235 Profits before other deductions and reliefs – *net sum of boxes 165 to 205 and 220 minus sum of boxes 225 and 230* £ .00

5 Test your understanding

Test your understanding 8

DEF Ltd

DEF Ltd received dividends from another UK company. This amount has not been included in the profit figure on which the adjusted trading profits are based.

How should this be dealt with in the computation of the company's taxable total profits?

A Add the amount received to taxable total profits

B Gross up by 100/80 and include in taxable total profits

C Deduct the amount received from taxable total profits

D Make no adjustment

Test your understanding 9

Ballard Ltd

Ballard Ltd prepares accounts for the year ended 31 March 2017. The following information is available:

	£
Adjusted trading profits before capital allowances	56,000
Bank interest receivable	3,000
UK dividends received	9,000

The tax written down value of the general pool was £24,000 on 1 April 2016 and on 1 December 2016 the company purchased a lorry for £14,000.

What are Ballard Ltd's taxable total profits for the year ended 31 March 2017?

A £40,680

B £45,000

C £49,680

D £42,000

Test your understanding 10

Pitch Ltd (1)

Pitch Ltd has the following results for the year ended 31 December 2016:

	£
Adjusted trading profits (before capital allowances)	766,801
Capital allowances	24,688
Chargeable gains	136,400
Capital loss brought forward	63,200
Rents receivable	3,500
Patent royalties from an individual (£11,200 × 100/80)	14,000
Bank deposit interest receivable	2,400
Dividends received from UK companies	4,800
Qualifying charitable donation paid	(1,000)

Pitch Ltd has trading losses brought forward of £87,200, which will be deducted from its tax adjusted trading profits.

Required:

Show Pitch Ltd's taxable total profits for the year ended 31 December 2016.

Test your understanding 11

Pitch Ltd (2)

You are required to complete the following extract of Form CT600 for Pitch Ltd for the year to 31 December 2016 (see below).

Solution

Tax calculation

Turnover

Box	Description	£
145	Total turnover from trade	£ • 0 0
150	Banks, building societies, insurance companies and other financial concerns – *put an 'X' in this box if you do not have a recognised turnover and have not made an entry in box 145*	

Income

Box	Description	£
155	Trading profits	£ • 0 0
160	Trading losses brought forward claimed against profits	£ • 0 0
165	Net trading profits – *box 155 minus box 160*	£ • 0 0
170	Bank, building society or other interest, and profits from non-trading loan relationships	£ • 0 0
172	Put an 'X' in box 172 if the figure in box 170 is net of carrying back a deficit from a later accounting period	
175	Annual payments not otherwise charged to Corporation Tax and from which Income Tax has not been deducted	£ • 0 0

Income *continued*

Box	Description	£
180	Non-exempt dividends or distributions from non-UK resident companies	£ • 0 0
185	Income from which Income Tax has been deducted	£ • 0 0
190	Income from a property business	£ • 0 0
195	Non-trading gains on intangible fixed assets	£ • 0 0
200	Tonnage Tax profits	£ • 0 0
205	Income not falling under any other heading	£ • 0 0

Chargeable gains

Box	Description	£
210	Gross chargeable gains	£ • 0 0
215	Allowable losses including losses brought forward	£ • 0 0
220	Net chargeable gains – *box 210 minus box 215*	£ • 0 0

Profits before deductions and reliefs

Box	Description	£
225	Losses brought forward against certain investment income	£ • 0 0
230	Non-trade deficits on loan relationships (including interest) and derivative contracts (financial instruments) brought forward	£ • 0 0
235	Profits before other deductions and reliefs – *net sum of boxes 165 to 205 and 220 minus sum of boxes 225 and 230*	£ • 0 0

Test your understanding 12

Long period of account

When a company has a period of account that exceeds 12 months, how are the following apportioned:

	Time apportioned	Separate computation	Period in which arises
Adjusted trading profits			
Capital allowances			
Rental income			
Interest income			
Chargeable gains			
Qualifying charitable donation paid			

Tick the appropriate treatment.

Test your understanding 13

G Ltd

The following details relate to the corporation tax computation of G Ltd for the 12 month accounting period ended 31 March 2017:

	£
Tax adjusted trading profit (after disallowing the write off of a loan to a customer of £600 and a national charity donation of £1,800)	677,500
Bank interest receivable	2,800
Loan interest received	22,000
UK dividends received	36,000

Required:

Calculate G Ltd's corporation tax liability for the year ended 31 March 2017.

6 Summary

Make sure you are very familiar with the pro forma corporation tax computation.

Setting out your computations as shown in the pro forma will help to ensure that your computations and submissions to HM Revenue and Customs (HMRC) are always made in accordance with the current law and take account of current HMRC practice.

If you are given a period of account of more than 12 months, the first step is to split it into the two CAPs and compile the two separate taxable total profits/augmented profits figures using the apportioning rules.

Each CAP is then dealt with separately.

In FY2015 and FY2016 the rate of corporation tax is 20%.

Take care when filling in Form CT600 in the assessment, it is important to be as accurate as you can.

7 AAT reference material

An outline of corporation tax

- Companies pay corporation tax on their profits for each accounting period.
- There is one rate of corporation tax set each financial year.
- Profits = Income + Gains – Qualifying charitable donations.
- Accounting periods are usually 12 months long but can be shorter.
- If a company's accounts are longer than 12 months, the first 12 months will be one accounting period and the remainder a second accounting period.
- All UK property income is pooled as a single source of income and taxed on an accruals basis.
- Borrowing or lending money by a company is a loan relationship.
- Trading loan relationships are part of trading income.
- Non-trading loan relationships (NTL-R) are pooled to give NTL-R credits or deficits.
- Donations to national charities (such as Gift Aid donations) are qualifying charitable donations.
- Company A is a related 51% group company of company B if:
  - A is a 51% subsidiary of B, or
  - B is a 51% subsidiary of A, or
  - A and B are both 51% subsidiaries of the same company.

  'A' is a 51% subsidiary of 'B' if more than 50% of its ordinary share capital is beneficially owned (directly or indirectly) by 'B'.

The calculation of total profits and corporation tax payable

ABC Ltd

Corporation tax computation for the year/period ended DD/MM/20XX

	£
Trading income – accruals basis	X
Interest income – accrual basis	X
Property income – accruals basis	X
Chargeable gains	X
	X
Less Qualifying charitable donations	(X)
Total profits	X
Corporation tax payable – Total profits × Corporation tax rate	X

Key points

- Trading income is adjusted from net profit per company accounts less capital allowances.
- All income in computation to be gross.
- Some income may need to be grossed up. Companies receive interest gross.
- Virtually all interest receivable is taxed as interest income.
- Dividends payable by a company are not an allowable expense.
- UK dividends receivable by a company are not taxable.
- Net-off current year capital losses against current year capital gains. If there is a net capital loss carry it forward.
- See taxation tables for corporation tax rates.

Non 31 March year-ends

- For example – year ended 31 December 2016. 3 months of period falls in financial year 2015 (FY15) and 9 months in FY16.
- Apportion Total Profits to FY. Apply correct tax rate for FY.

Long periods of account

- Will consist of two accounting periods = first 12 months and remainder of period.
- Split profits as follows:
  - Adjusted trading profit and property income – time apportion.
  - Capital allowances – separate computations for each CAP.
  - Interest income – accruals basis.
  - Chargeable gains – according to date of disposal.
  - Qualifying charitable donations – according to date paid.

Test your understanding answers

Test your understanding 1

ABC Ltd

The correct answer is C.

Explanation

The interest received will be included in the net profit per the accounts. It therefore needs to be deducted in the adjusted trading profit computation. It is then included as non-trade interest income in the calculation of taxable total profits.

Test your understanding 2

GHI Ltd

1 £35,000

2 £Nil

Explanation

1 GHI Ltd would include chargeable gains of (£60,000 – £25,000) = £35,000 in taxable total profits.

2 No chargeable gains would be included in taxable total profits as the losses exceed gains by = £15,000 (£75,000 – £60,000). The excess loss will be carried forward and deducted from the next gains.

Test your understanding 3

Laserjet Ltd (1)

Corporation tax computation – year ended 31 January 2017

	£
Trading profit (W1)	484,600
Non-trade interest (W2)	22,000
Property income	32,000
Total profits	538,600
Less: Qualifying charitable donations	(14,000)
Taxable total profits	524,600

Workings:

(W1) Trading profit

	£
Adjusted trading profit	500,600
Less: Capital allowances	(16,000)
Trading profit	484,600

Take care not to adjust a profit which has already been adjusted.

(W2) Non-trade interest

	£
Building society interest receivable	20,000
Loan note interest receivable	6,000
	26,000
Less: Loan interest payable – rental property (note)	(4,000)
Non-trade interest	22,000

Note: This interest is not an allowable deduction from property income but has to be dealt with as a 'non-trading' loan and is deductible from non-trade interest income.

Test your understanding 4

Chinny Ltd

Corporation tax computations

	Year ended 30 September 2016	*3 months to 31 December 2016*
	£	£
Trading profit (W1)	186,550	44,182
Non-trade interest	4,420	780
Property income (W2)	8,000	2,000
Chargeable gains	–	55,000
Taxable total profits	198,970	101,962

Workings:

(W1) Trading profit

	Year ended 30 September 2016	*3 months to 31 December 2016*
	£	£
Adjusted trading profits (12/15:3/15)	200,000	50,000
Less: Capital allowances	(13,450)	(5,818)
Trading profit	186,550	44,182

(W2) Property income

Rent receivable for 15 months:

(£8,000 – £3,000 + £5,000) = £10,000

	Year ended 30 September 2016	*3 months to 31 December 2016*
	£	£
Time apportioned	8,000	2,000

Test your understanding 5

Osmond Ltd

Corporation tax computation – year ended 31 March 2016

	£
Trading profit	510,000
Non-trade interest	8,000
Chargeable gains	7,500
Taxable total profits	525,500
Corporation tax liability (£525,500 × 20%)	105,100.00

Test your understanding 6

Unpredictably Uptown Limited

Corporation tax payable – period 30 September 2016

	12 months to 31 Mar 2016	*6 months to 30 Sept 2016*
	£	£
Trading profit (W)	660,000	330,000
Non-trade interest	9,000	3,500
Total profits	669,000	333,500
Less Qualifying charitable donation	(20,000)	–
Taxable total profits	649,000	333,500
Corporation tax liability (£649,000/£333,500 × 20%)	129,800.00	66,700.00

Working:

(W) Trading profit

			£
Apportioned	12 months to 31 Mar 2016	$^{12}/_{18}$ × £990,000	660,000
	6 months to 30 Sep 2016	$^{6}/_{18}$ × £990,000	330,000
			990,000

Test your understanding 7

Laserjet Ltd (2)

Income

Box	Description	£
155	Trading profits	484600·00
160	Trading losses brought forward claimed against profits	·00
165	Net trading profits – *box 155 minus box 160*	484600·00
170	Bank, building society or other interest, and profits from non-trading loan relationships	22000·00 (20,000 + 6000 - 4000)
172	Put an 'X' in box 172 if the figure in box 170 is net of carrying back a deficit from a later accounting period	
175	Annual payments not otherwise charged to Corporation Tax and from which Income Tax has not been deducted	·00

Income *continued*

Box	Description	£
180	Non-exempt dividends or distributions from non-UK resident companies	·00
185	Income from which Income Tax has been deducted	·00
190	Income from a property business	32000·00
195	Non-trading gains on intangible fixed assets	·00
200	Tonnage Tax profits	·00
205	Income not falling under any other heading	·00

Chargeable gains

Box	Description	£
210	Gross chargeable gains	·00
215	Allowable losses including losses brought forward	·00
220	Net chargeable gains – *box 210 minus box 215*	·00

Profits before deductions and reliefs

Box	Description	£
225	Losses brought forward against certain investment income	·00
230	Non-trade deficits on loan relationships (including interest) and derivative contracts (financial instruments) brought forward	·00
235	Profits before other deductions and reliefs – *net sum of boxes 165 to 205 and 220 minus sum of boxes 225 and 230*	538600·00

Test your understanding 8

DEF Ltd

The correct answer is D.

Explanation

Dividends from another company are not subject to corporation tax and are therefore not included in taxable total profits.

Test your understanding 9

Ballard Ltd

The correct answer is A.

Explanation

	£
Adjusted trading profits	56,000
Less: Capital allowances (W)	(18,320)
Tax adjusted trading profits	37,680
Bank interest receivable	3,000
Taxable total profits	40,680

Note: UK dividends are not chargeable to corporation tax

Working: Capital allowances

	£	*Pool* £	*Allowances* £
TWDV b/f		24,000	
Addition with AIA	14,000		
Less: AIA	(14,000)		14,000
		Nil	
WDA (18% × £24,000)		(4,320)	4,320
TWDV c/f		19,680	
Total allowances			18,320

Test your understanding 10

Pitch Ltd (1)

Taxable total profits – year ended 31 December 2016

	£
Trading profit (W)	654,913
Property income	3,500
Non-trade interest	2,400
Chargeable gains (£136,400 – £63,200)	73,200
Patent royalties	14,000
Total profits	748,013
Less: Qualifying charitable donations	(1,000)
Taxable total profits	747,013

Working: Trading profit

	£
Adjusted trading profit	766,801
Less: Capital allowances	(24,688)
Trading losses brought forward	(87,200)
Trading profit	654,913

Test your understanding 11

Pitch Ltd (2)

Tax calculation

Turnover

Box	Description	£
145	Total turnover from trade	·00
150	Banks, building societies, insurance companies and other financial concerns – *put an 'X' in this box if you do not have a recognised turnover and have not made an entry in box 145*	

Income

Box	Description	£
155	Trading profits	742113·00
160	Trading losses brought forward claimed against profits	87200·00
165	Net trading profits – *box 155 minus box 160*	654913·00
170	Bank, building society or other interest, and profits from non-trading loan relationships	2400·00
172	Put an 'X' in box 172 if the figure in box 170 is net of carrying back a deficit from a later accounting period	
175	Annual payments not otherwise charged to Corporation Tax and from which Income Tax has not been deducted	·00

Income *continued*

Box	Description	£
180	Non-exempt dividends or distributions from non-UK resident companies	·00
185	Income from which Income Tax has been deducted	14000·00
190	Income from a property business	3500·00
195	Non-trading gains on intangible fixed assets	·00
200	Tonnage Tax profits	·00
205	Income not falling under any other heading	·00

Chargeable gains

Box	Description	£
210	Gross chargeable gains	136400·00
215	Allowable losses including losses brought forward	63200·00
220	Net chargeable gains – *box 210 minus box 215*	73200·00

Profits before deductions and reliefs

Box	Description	£
225	Losses brought forward against certain investment income	·00
230	Non-trade deficits on loan relationships (including interest) and derivative contracts (financial instruments) brought forward	·00
235	Profits before other deductions and reliefs – *net sum of boxes 165 to 205 and 220 minus sum of boxes 225 and 230*	748013·00

Test your understanding 12

Long period of account

	Time apportioned	**Separate computation**	**Period in which arises**
Trading income	✓		
Capital allowances		✓	
Rental income	✓		
Interest income			✓
Chargeable gains			✓
Qualifying charitable donation paid			✓

Note: Rental income usually accrues evenly and can therefore be time apportioned.

Test your understanding 13

G Ltd – Corporation tax computation – year ended 31 March 2017

	£
Trading profit	677,500
Interest income (W)	24,200
Total profits	701,700
Less: Qualifying charitable donation	(1,800)
Taxable total profits	699,900

	£
Corporation tax liability (£699,900 × 20%)	139,980.00

Working: Interest income	£
Bank interest	2,800
Loan interest	22,000
Less: Customer loan written off	(600)
Interest income	24,200

Note: Loans written off are not allowable against trading income and are added back in the adjustment of profits computation. However, they are allowable against interest income as an allowable deduction relating to a non-trading loan relationship.

Corporation tax reliefs and other tax issues

Introduction

This chapter covers two forms of relief available to companies and one other tax issue.

The relief for trading and capital losses is dealt with first.

Secondly the research and development tax credit scheme that applies to small and medium sized enterprises is discussed.

Individuals may seek to minimise tax by the use of a personal service company. Anti-avoidance rules often referred to as IR35 seek to reduce any advantages.

ASSESSMENT CRITERIA

Assess and calculate available loss relief (4.1)

Advise on the best use of a trading loss for sole traders, partnerships and companies (4.1)

Demonstrate an understanding of current tax reliefs available to businesses (4.2)

Demonstrate an understanding of current tax issues and their implications for business (4.2)

CONTENTS

1 Trading losses

1.1 Adjusted trading losses

In Chapter 3 we considered how to calculate an adjusted trading profit.

An adjusted trading loss is computed in the same way. However, when a company makes an adjusted trading loss, its trading profit assessment for the accounting period is nil.

Example

Carlos Ltd has had the following results for its year ended 31 March 2017:

		£	£
Gross profit			30,000
Less:	Depreciation	5,000	
	Allowable expenses	12,000	
			(17,000)
Net profit per accounts			13,000

The capital allowances for the year amount to £21,000.

Calculate the adjusted trading profit/(loss) for the year.

Solution

Step 1: Set up an adjustment of profits pro forma as in Chapter 3.

Step 2: Calculate the adjusted trading profit/(loss)

Work through the statement of profit or loss line by line as previously to calculate the adjusted trading profit/(loss).

Carlos Ltd

Adjustment of profit/(loss) – year ended 31 March 2017

		£
Net profit per accounts		13,000
Add:	Disallowable expenses	
	Depreciation	5,000
		18,000
Less:	Capital allowances	(21,000)
Adjusted trading loss		(3,000)
Trading profit assessment		Nil

The trading profit figure to be entered onto the pro forma corporation tax computation is nil.

The accounts may show a net **loss** to be adjusted. If this is the case, adding disallowable expenses will REDUCE the loss.

Example

Assume Carlos Ltd in the previous example had a net loss per accounts of (£10,000). Calculate the adjusted trading loss.

Solution

	£
Net loss per accounts	(10,000)
Add: Depreciation	5,000
	(5,000)
Less: Capital allowances	(21,000)
Adjusted trading loss	(26,000)

1.2 Summary of trading loss reliefs

There are three forms of relief available to a company which makes a trading loss:

- current year relief
- carry back relief
- carry forward relief.

Details of these reliefs are set out below and a summary is provided in the AAT reference material, which is included in section 7.

1.3 Current year relief

A trading loss can be relieved against total profits of the loss making accounting period. The set off is against profits before the deduction of qualifying charitable donations.

A claim for current year (or carry back) relief must be made within two years of the end of the loss making accounting period.

Example

Sage Ltd had the following results for the year ended 31 March 2017.

	£
Adjusted trading loss	(40,000)
Property income	10,000
Chargeable gain	50,000
Qualifying charitable donation	10,000

Show how relief would be obtained for the loss in the current period.

Approach to the example

It is *essential* once a loss has been identified to set up a loss memorandum as a working and allocate the loss to it, so that the relief for the loss does not exceed the actual amount of loss available.

Even where there is a trading loss, this does not alter the basic approach to a question.

- Present the CT computation in the standard pro forma.
- Support it with workings where necessary (one of which will be the loss memorandum).

Solution

Sage Ltd – Corporation tax computation – y/e 31 March 2017

	£
Trading profit	Nil
Property income	10,000
Chargeable gain	50,000
Total profits	60,000
Less: Loss relief – Current year	(40,000)
	20,000
Less: Qualifying charitable donation	(10,000)
Taxable total profits	10,000

Working:

(W1) Loss memorandum

	£
Year ended 31 March 2017	
Current period loss	(40,000)
Relieved in current period	40,000
Loss c/f	Nil

Setting off the loss before the deduction of qualifying charitable donations (QCDs) may result in the QCDs becoming unrelieved. Excess amounts of QCDs are lost.

Example

What if Sage Ltd in the previous example made a loss of £60,000?

Solution

	£
Total profits i.e. before QCDs (as before)	60,000
Less: Loss relief – Current year	(60,000)
	Nil
Less Qualifying charitable donation	Wasted
Taxable total profits	Nil

The QCD is unrelieved. It has not been used as there are insufficient profits to set it against.

It is an important principle in the use of most loss reliefs that, where there is an available loss, no restriction in set off is permitted.

This means that it would *not* have been possible here to restrict the loss relief to (£50,000) so as to then relieve a QCD of (£10,000), and find an alternative use for the remaining (£10,000) loss.

Unused qualifying charitable donations cannot be carried forward or back and are therefore wasted.

1.4 Carry back relief

A trading loss may be carried back for relief against total profits in the preceding 12 months, but only *after* the loss has first been relieved against any available current period total profits.

The loss is set off against total profits *before* deducting QCDs.

In other words, the order in which the loss is applied is as follows.

- First, against total profits of the current year (*before* QCDs).
- Second, against total profits of the previous 12 months (again, *before* the deduction of QCDs).

In questions this is often referred to as 'setting off the loss as soon as possible'.

When a company ceases to trade, it can carry back the loss for 36 months rather than 12.

Approach to losses questions

A longer style task in the assessment may involve utilising company losses over several years; a methodical approach is very important for these tasks.

- Lay out the years side by side in a table, leaving space to insert any loss reliefs.
- Keep a separate working for the trading loss – the memorandum.
- Firstly set the loss against the total profits (before QCDs) of the year of loss.
- Then carry the balance of the loss back against total profits (before QCDs) of the previous 12 months.
- State whether there is any unrelieved loss remaining.
- Keep a running tally in the loss memorandum working.

Here is a pro forma. The loss has been incurred in 2017.

Pro forma corporation tax loss computation

	2016	2017
	£	£
Trading profit	X	Nil
Non-trade interest	X	X
Property income	X	X
Chargeable gains	X	X
Total profits	X	X
Less: Loss relief		
– Current period		(X)
– Carry back	(X)	
	Nil	Nil
Less: Qualifying charitable donations	Wasted	Wasted
Taxable total profits	Nil	Nil

Loss memorandum:

	£
Current year loss (2017)	X
Less: Current year relief	(X)
Carry back relief	(X)
Loss still available	X

Example

Marjoram Ltd has the following results for the three accounting periods to 31 December 2017.

Year ended 31 December	**2015**	**2016**	**2017**
	£	£	£
Trading profits/(loss)	11,000	9,000	(45,000)
Building society interest	500	500	500
Chargeable gains	–	–	4,000
Qualifying charitable donations	250	250	250

Show the taxable total profits for all periods affected, assuming that loss relief is taken as soon as possible.

Solution

Marjoram Ltd

Corporation tax computations

Year ended 31 December	**2016**	**2017**
	£	£
Trading profit	9,000	Nil
Non-trade interest	500	500
Chargeable gains	Nil	4,000
Total profits	9,500	4,500
Less: Loss relief		
– Current loss relief		(4,500)
– Carry back relief	(9,500)	
	Nil	Nil
Less: Qualifying charitable donations	Wasted	Wasted
Taxable total profits	Nil	Nil

Note: The year ended 31 December 2015 is not affected; the loss cannot be carried back that far.

Loss working

	£
Loss for the year ended 31 December 2017	45,000
Less: Current year relief	(4,500)
	40,500
Less: Carry back 12 months	(9,500)
Loss still available at 1 January 2018	31,000

Test your understanding 1

Banks Ltd has the following results:

Year ended 31 March	2016	2017
	£	£
Adjusted trading profit/(loss)	50,000	(120,000)
Bank interest	2,000	3,000
Qualifying charitable donation	1,000	500

On the assumption that Banks Ltd uses its loss as early as possible, what is the trading loss carried forward to the year ended 31 March 2018?

A £117,000

B £68,000

C £66,500

D £65,000

Short previous accounting period

Losses can be carried back 12 months. This usually means the loss can be deducted from the profits of the previous accounting period. However, if the previous accounting period is less than 12 months long, it will be possible to carry the loss back to cover a proportion of the profits for the period preceding that.

Example

Amla Ltd has the following results for the three accounting periods to 31 December 2016.

	12m to 30 April 2015	8m to 31 Dec 2015	12m to 31 Dec 2016
	£	£	£
Trading profits/(loss)	40,000	18,000	(100,000)
Bank interest	2,000	1,500	1,700
Qualifying charitable donations	1,000	1,000	1,000

Show the taxable total profits for all periods affected, assuming that loss relief is taken as soon as possible.

Solution

Amla Ltd

Corporation tax computations

	12m to 30 April 2015	**8m to 31 Dec 2015**	**12m to 31 Dec 2016**
	£	£	£
Trading profits	40,000	18,000	Nil
Bank interest	2,000	1,500	1,700
Total profits	42,000	19,500	1,700
Less: Loss relief			
– Current loss relief			(1,700)
– c/b relief		(19,500)	
(max 4/12 × £42,000)	(14,000)		
	28,000	Nil	Nil
Qualifying charitable donations	(1,000)	Wasted	Wasted
Taxable total profits	27,000	Nil	Nil

Note: The loss can be carried back 12 months. This covers the whole of the 8 months to 31 December 2015 and 4 months of the year ended 30 April 2015. The maximum loss that can be deducted for the year ended 30 April 2015 is equal to 4/12 of the total profits i.e. £14,000.

Loss working

	£
Loss for the year ended 31 December 2016	100,000
Less: Current year relief	(1,700)
	98,300
Less: Carry back 8m to 31 Dec 2015	(19,500)
	78,800
Carry back to year ended 30 April 2015	(14,000)
Loss still available at 1 January 2017	64,800

Test your understanding 2

Uncut Undergrowth Ltd

Uncut Undergrowth Ltd is a UK resident company that began trading on 1 July 2014. The company's results are summarised as follows:

	Year ended 30 Jun 2015	6 months to 31 Dec 2015	Year ended 31 Dec 2016
	£	£	£
Trading profit/(loss)	35,000	25,000	(350,000)
Non-trade loan interest receivable	–	15,000	22,000
Property income	25,000	–	–
Chargeable gains/(loss)	(40,000)	–	30,000
Donation to national charity	1,000	1,000	1,000

Required:

Calculate the taxable total profits for all of the years in the question after giving maximum relief at the earliest time for the trading losses sustained and any other reliefs.

Also show any balance of losses carried forward.

1.5 Carry forward relief

Where any loss remains unrelieved after the current year and carry back claims have been made, the carry forward of the remaining loss is automatic. This also applies where no current year and carry back claims are made, as there is no compulsory requirement to use such reliefs.

The carry forward relief automatically allows trading losses to be set against future trading profits of the same trade as soon as they arise.

They cannot be relieved against any other profits. Such losses have to be used against the first available trading profits.

Example

Mint Ltd began trading on 1 April 2014 and has the following results:

Year ended 31 March	2015	2016	2017
	£	£	£
Adjusted trading profit/(loss)	15,000	(100,000)	40,000
Non-trade interest	5,000	10,000	10,000
Chargeable gain	–	40,000	–

Show how the loss relief would be claimed where relief is required as soon as possible.

Solution

Mint Ltd – Corporation tax computations

Year ended 31 March	2015	2016	2017
	£	£	£
Trading profit	15,000	Nil	40,000
Less: Loss relief b/f			(30,000)
			10,000
Non-trade interest	5,000	10,000	10,000
Chargeable gain	–	40,000	–
Total profits	20,000	50,000	20,000
Less: Loss relief			
– Current year		(50,000)	
– Carry back	(20,000)		
Taxable total profits	Nil	Nil	20,000

Working: Loss memorandum

	£
Loss for the year ended 31 March 2016	100,000
Less: Current year relief	(50,000)
Carry back relief	
– Year ended 31 March 2015	(20,000)
	30,000
Less: Used in year ended 31 March 2017	(30,000)
Loss left to c/f	Nil

Test your understanding 3

Potter Limited

The following is the income of Potter Limited which commenced to trade on 1 October 2015.

Year ended 30 September	**2016**	**2017**
	£	£
Adjusted trading profit (loss)	(35,000)	94,000
Bank interest receivable	11,400	8,400
Rents receivable (after deducting expenses)	21,300	21,400
Donation to national charity paid 30 Sept	500	500

Required:

Calculate the taxable total profits for the years ending 30 September 2016 and 2017, indicating how you would obtain relief as soon as possible for the loss.

1.6 Factors to be considered when choosing loss relief

Companies have the following choices when considering loss relief:

- current year claim then carry back claim then carry forward the remaining loss or
- current year claim then carry forward the remaining loss or
- carry forward all the loss.

When deciding which choice to make there are two main considerations:

(1) **Cash flow**

Where the company wants earliest relief a current and carry back claim would be preferred.

This enables the company to claim tax repayments for the previous year which is a useful cash flow for a company suffering losses.

(2) **Rate of relief**

Where the company wants to obtain the highest possible tax saving then the rate of tax saved is important.

A company would prefer to claim relief in the periods when it is paying tax at the highest rate of tax.

For example, it would prefer to carry back a loss if it paid tax at a higher rate in the previous year than it will pay in the current year.

You may have to make a choice of relief in the assessment and/or may be asked to select what factors a company should take into account when choosing the best relief.

2 Capital losses

Both trading and capital losses may be examined in the assessment.

Capital losses may occur in questions in isolation, but where a mixture of losses appear it is essential to distinguish the reliefs available.

The treatment of capital losses will be covered in detail in Chapter 16. However, in summary:

- A capital loss incurred in the current period is automatically relieved against current period gains. Any excess is then carried forward for relief against gains in future accounting periods.
- There is no carry back facility and a capital loss cannot be used against any other profit.

Test your understanding 4

Coriander Ltd

Coriander Ltd began trading on 1 January 2014 and has the following results:

	Trading profit or (loss)	Non-trade interest	Qualifying charitable donation	Capital gains or (losses)
	£	£	£	£
Year ended 31 Dec:				
2014	37,450	1,300	3,000	(5,000)
2015	(81,550)	1,400	3,000	
2016	20,000	1,600	3,000	12,000

Required:

Calculate taxable total profits for all years, assuming all reliefs are claimed at the earliest opportunity. State the amounts of losses carried forward.

Approach to the question

- Set up CT pro formas for all years leaving space to enter any loss reliefs.
- Set up a loss memorandum for the trading loss for the year ended 31 December 2015.
- There is also a capital loss to deal with which has more restrictive use than a trading loss.

Test your understanding 5

Read the following statements and state whether they are true or false.

1 Trading losses can be relieved by carry back before being offset in the year of loss.

2 Trading losses are deducted from other income after deducting qualifying charitable donations.

3 Trading losses carried forward can only be set against trading profits from the same trade.

4 Capital losses can be offset against other income in the year of the loss, but only against chargeable gains in future years.

3 Research and development tax credits

3.1 Introduction

In order to encourage more spending on research and development (R&D), additional tax reliefs are given for qualifying revenue expenditure incurred by companies.

There is a tax credit scheme for small or medium sized enterprises (SMEs).

An SME is a company with less than 500 employees with either:

- an annual turnover under 100 million euros, or
- a balance sheet under 86 million euros.

This definition is given in the AAT reference material, which is included in section 7, so you do not have to learn it.

3.2 Scheme details

The scheme works as follows.

- Enhanced relief is available if the company spends money on qualifying R&D.

- SMEs can deduct an additional 130% of qualifying expenditure for tax purposes, i.e. for every £100 spent on R&D the company can deduct the original £100 plus a further £130 as allowable expenses for tax purposes. This gives total tax relief of 230% of the £100.
- If the deduction creates a loss it may be surrendered in return for a cash payment from HMRC (see section 3.3 below).

Qualifying R&D expenditure must be revenue expenditure on a project that seeks to achieve an advance in science or technology that is relevant to the company's trade.

It can include expenditure on the following:

- staffing costs
- materials, water, fuel and power for R&D
- software directly used in R&D.

It cannot include:

- contributions to other bodies for independent research
- expenditure covered by a grant or subsidy.

Example

Dax plc is a profitable company manufacturing audio visual equipment. It is a small enterprise for the purposes of R&D.

The company has recently decided to investigate the market for a new type of classroom projection equipment and has spent the following amounts in the year ended 31 December 2016 on the project:

	£
Market research	8,000
Staff directly involved in researching the project	20,000
Heat and light in the R&D department	9,000
Administrative support for staff in the R&D department	5,000
New software	4,000
	46,000

Advise the company of any tax relief available in respect of its expenditure.

Solution

The cost of market research and administrative support is not covered by the SME scheme so only the normal 100% deduction is available.

The cost of staff directly involved in the project, heat and light in the R&D department and new software qualifies for the enhanced deduction.

	£
Allowable expense for tax purposes:	
Market research	8,000
Administrative support for staff in the R&D department	5,000
	13,000
Staff directly involved in researching the project	20,000
Heat and light in the R&D department	9,000
New software	4,000
	33,000
Total amount allowed in the calculation of adjusted profits	
100% of £13,000	13,000
230% of £33,000	75,900
	88,900

3.3 Losses

If the deduction of the R&D relief creates a loss then the company can choose:

- to use the loss in the normal way, or
- surrender the loss in return for a cash payment.

The cash payment will be 14.5% of the loss.

Note that the rate of the relief is not mentioned in the AAT reference material. However, the reference material states that the amount of tax credit is limited to the total of PAYE and National Insurance contribution liabilities of the company. The R&D credit was previously limited to this amount, but this has not been the case since 1 April 2012. This is the version of the reference material that was available at the time of going to print. The reference material may be amended in due course.

Example

Curzon plc is a small company. Their adjusted trading profit before any R&D expense is £40,000 for the year ended 31 March 2017. They have incurred £50,000 of qualifying R&D expenditure.

Advise the company of the amount of loss which arises in the year ended 31 March 2017 and the amount of tax credit which will be received if it is surrendered.

Solution

Loss:

	£
Adjusted trading profit before R&D expense	40,000
R&D (£50,000 × 230%)	(115,000)
Trading loss	(75,000)

The company can choose to use the loss as normal or claim a cash repayment of £10,875 (£75,000 × 14.5%).

Test your understanding 6

Read the following statements and state whether they are true or false.

1 A small company incurs £42,000 of qualifying R&D. It can deduct a total expense of £54,600 from its business profits.

2 An SME can have more than 500 employees provided its turnover is below 100 million euros and its balance sheet is under 43 million euros.

3 Ezri plc is a small company which has an adjusted trading profit of £21,000 before R&D expense and has spent £35,000 on qualifying R&D. It has an adjusted trading loss of £59,500.

4 Personal service companies (IR35)

4.1 Introduction

This section deals with tax avoidance by using personal service companies (PSCs). The legislation is often referred to as IR35, which was the name of the HMRC press release that first introduced the legislation.

4.2 What is a personal service company?

If an employee is employed and earning a salary then his employer has to deduct income tax and employee's national insurance contributions (NICs) from the salary paid to the employee, via the PAYE system. The employer also has to pay employer's NICs. These taxes are all covered in detail in the personal tax syllabus.

Alternatively, the employee could resign from his employment, set up his own company and then use that company to offer his services to his former employer. In that case, his company would invoice his former employer, who would pay the invoice without having to deduct income tax or NICs before making the payment, and would avoid having to pay employers' NICs at all.

The PSC pays corporation tax at only 20% on profits, net of any expenses wholly and exclusively incurred for the trade.

The former employee, now the company owner, could pay himself a small salary (which would avoid employee's NICs) and withdraw funds as dividends, which are not liable to NICs. This would result in a lower overall tax charge.

4.3 Relevant engagements

The PSC legislation is aimed at situations which are essentially disguised employments.

It is not limited to employees contracting with their former employer, but covers anything that is deemed to be a 'relevant engagement'.

A relevant engagement is a contract between the PSC and the client, which would have been a contract of employment if the client had contracted directly with the individual doing the work.

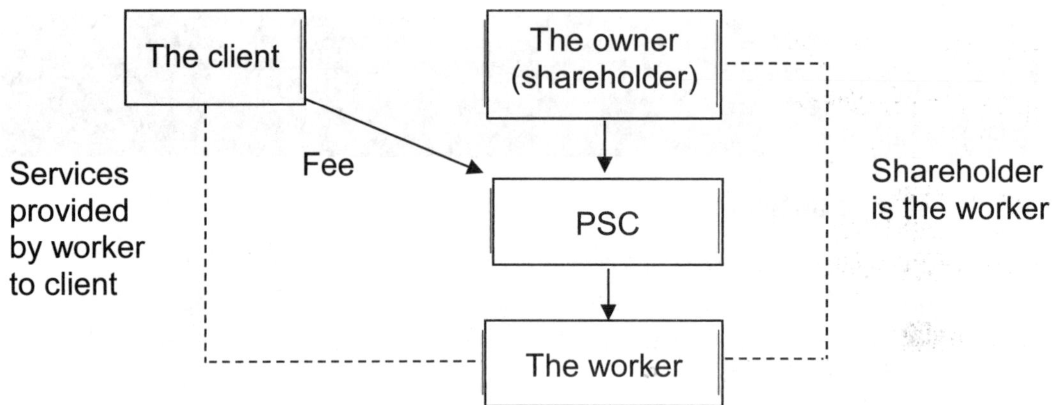

Factors to consider when deciding if a contract is a relevant engagement include:

- An obligation on the worker to accept work offered, and on the client to offer work would indicate a relevant engagement.
- If the manner and method of the work is controlled by the client, this indicates a relevant engagement.
- When the hours of work are fixed by the client, this would suggest a relevant engagement. If the worker can determine their own hours of work, this is a factor arguing against this being a relevant engagement.
- In a relevant engagement, it is likely that the worker is being paid an agreed, regular remuneration. If the worker is bearing the financial risk, it is less likely to be a relevant engagement.
- If the worker is provided with tools and equipment by the client, this is an indication of a relevant engagement.
- Having rights under employment legislation, such as holiday or sick pay, would indicate a relevant engagement.
- Having to perform the work themselves is a normal requirement for an employee and an indication that this is a relevant engagement. If the worker can send a substitute to do the work, this would indicate it is not a relevant engagement.

4.4 Deemed employment income tax charge

The client company is not affected by the PSC legislation. It is only the PSC that is affected.

The PSC suffers a deemed employment income tax charge. They have to:

- Treat the income from relevant engagements arising in a tax year as if it were paid out as salary to the employee.
- Account for the income tax and NIC on the notional salary.
- Only expenses typically allowed to employees, plus a flat rate 5% deduction, can be deducted from the notional salary. The rules regarding which expenses can be deducted by an employee are more stringent than those applying to companies.

Note that the AAT reference material set out in section 7 below includes some information about the IR35 legislation.

5 Test your understanding

Test your understanding 7

AB Ltd

The following details relate to AB Ltd.

Year ended	*31 Dec 2015*	*31 Dec 2016*
	£	£
Adjusted trading profit/(loss)	19,000	(67,000)
Bank interest received	2,000	1,000
Chargeable gains	4,000	4,000
Qualifying charitable donation	10,000	

Required:

Assuming AB Ltd uses its loss as early as possible, what is the amount of loss carried forward at 31 December 2016?

A £62,000

B £47,000

C £42,000

D £37,000

Test your understanding 8

Eldorado (Birmingham) Limited

Eldorado (Birmingham) Limited prepares accounts annually to 31 August in each year. The company commenced to trade on 1 September 2014.

The results for the first few years were as follows:

	2015	*2016*	*2017*
	£	£	£
Trading profits/(loss)	18,000	(81,000)	(6,000)
Chargeable gain	3,000		
Property income	22,000	22,000	22,000

Required:

Show how relief is obtained for the trading losses, assuming that relief is claimed as soon as possible.

Test your understanding 9

Read the following statements and state whether they are true or false.

1 Capital losses can only be offset against chargeable gains in the year of the loss, and then against chargeable gains in future years.

2 Trading losses carried forward can be set against trading profits from the same trade in any future year in which it is beneficial to do so.

3 Trading losses can be deducted from other income and chargeable gains of the current accounting period.

4 Where trading losses have been relieved against the total profits of the loss making period, any losses remaining must then be offset against the total profits of the previous 12 months.

6 Summary

Losses often appear in assessments.

The rules depend on the type of loss:

- trading losses – current year and carry back relief against total profits before qualifying charitable donations, carry forward against trading profits only
- capital losses – current year against chargeable gains only, carry forward against chargeable gains only.

Small and medium sized enterprises (SMEs) can claim extra tax relief on allowable R&D costs.

230% of the cost of qualifying R&D can be deducted as an allowable expense.

Qualifying R&D must be revenue expenditure that contributes to seeking an advance in science or technology.

If the deduction of the R&D tax relief creates a loss the loss can be surrendered for a cash sum = to 14.5% of the loss.

If a company is determined to be a PSC then any income from relevant engagements will be subject to a deemed employment charge.

7 AAT reference material

Corporation tax – losses

- Can elect to set trading losses against current accounting period total profits. Qualifying charitable donations will remain unrelieved.
- If the above election is made, can also carry back trading loss to set against total profits within the previous 12 months.
- Trading losses are automatically carried forward to set against the first available profits of the same trade if not utilised by the above two claims.
- If there is a choice of loss relief, firstly consider the rate of loss relief then the timing of relief.

Set out the use of the losses in a loss memorandum.

Current tax reliefs and other tax issues

Research and Development (R&D) Tax Credits for Small and Medium Sized Companies

A small or medium sized enterprise (SME) is a company with less than 500 employees with either:

- an annual turnover under €100 million, or
- a balance sheet under €86 million.

The SME tax relief scheme

From 1 April 2015, the tax relief on allowable R&D costs is 230%.

R&D tax credits

If a company makes a loss, it can choose to receive R&D tax credits instead of carrying forward a loss. The amount of tax credit is limited to the total of PAYE and National Insurance contribution liabilities of the company.

Costs that qualify for R&D tax relief

To qualify as R&D, any activity must contribute directly to seeking an advance in science or technology or must be a qualifying indirect activity.

Intermediaries (IR35) legislation

IR35 legislation prevents personal service companies ("PSC") being used to disguise permanent employment.

The rules apply where the relationship between the worker and the client, would be considered to be an employment relationship if the existence of the PSC was ignored.

If the rules apply, a **deemed employment income tax charge** is charged on the PSC.

The **deemed employment income tax charge** is calculated based upon the actual payments made to the PSC by the client.

Test your understanding answers

Test your understanding 1

Banks Ltd

The correct answer is D.

Explanation

D is the correct answer. When you are asked to use the loss 'as early as possible' it means the loss is set off against total profits before qualifying charitable donations in the current year and then total profits before qualifying charitable donations in the preceding 12 months.

A current year claim must be made before a carry back claim, as follows:

		£
Trading loss		120,000
Less: Utilised	– Current year offset	(3,000)
	– Carry back claim	(52,000)
Available to carry forward		65,000

Test your understanding 2

Uncut Undergrowth Ltd

	Year ended 30 Jun 2015	6 months to 31 Dec 2015	Year ended 31 Dec 2016
	£	£	£
Trading profit	35,000	25,000	Nil
Non-trade interest	–	15,000	22,000
Property income	25,000	–	–
Chargeable gains (W1)	Nil	–	Nil
Total profits	60,000	40,000	22,000
Less: Loss relief			
– Current year relief			(22,000)
– Carry back relief (W2)	(30,000)	(40,000)	
	30,000	Nil	Nil
Less: Qualifying charitable donation	(1,000)	Wasted	Wasted
Taxable total profits	29,000	Nil	Nil

Balances carried forward

- There is a trading loss at 31 December 2016 to carry forward of £258,000 (W2).
- Capital losses of £10,000 available for carry forward (W1).

Workings:

(W1) Net chargeable gains

	£
Year ended 31 December 2016	
Chargeable gain	30,000
Losses b/f (£40,000)	(30,000)
Net chargeable gain	Nil
Losses c/f (£40,000 – £30,000)	10,000

(W2) Trading losses

	£
Loss for 12 months to 31 December 2016	350,000
Current year relief	(22,000)
Carry back relief – 6 months to 31 December 2015	(40,000)
– 12 months to 30 June 2015 (£60,000 × 6/12)	(30,000)
Carry forward at 31 December 2016	258,000

Test your understanding 3

Potter Limited

Years ended 30 September	**2016**	**2017**
	£	£
Trading profit	Nil	94,000
Less: Losses b/f (£35,000 – £32,700)	–	(2,300)
	Nil	91,700
Non-trade interest	11,400	8,400
Property income	21,300	21,400
Total profits	32,700	121,500
Less: Loss relief – Current year	(32,700)	
	Nil	121,500
Less: Qualifying charitable donation	(Wasted)	(500)
Taxable total profits	Nil	121,000

Test your understanding 4

Coriander Ltd – Corporation tax computations

Year ended 31 December	**2014**	**2015**	**2016**
	£	£	£
Trading profit	37,450	Nil	20,000
Less: Loss relief b/f			(20,000)[(3)]
			Nil
Non-trade interest	1,300	1,400	1,600
Chargeable gains			
(£12,000 – £5,000 b/f)	Nil		7,000
Total profits	38,750	1,400	8,600
Less: Loss relief			
– Current year		(1,400)[(1)]	
– Carry back	(38,750)[(2)]		
	Nil	Nil	8,600
Less: QCD	Wasted	Wasted	(3,000)
Taxable total profits	Nil	Nil	5,600
QCD wasted	3,000	3,000	

Loss memorandum

		£
Trading loss in the year ended 31 December 2015		81,550
(1)	Current period relief	(1,400)
(2)	Carry back relief – year ended 31 December 2014	(38,750)
		41,400
(3)	Carry forward against trading profits – year ended 31 December 2016	(20,000)
Loss to carry forward at 31 December 2016		21,400

Test your understanding 5

1	False	Trading losses can only be relieved by carry back after a claim for current year relief has been made.
2	False	Trading losses are deducted from other income before deducting qualifying charitable donations. Any excess QCDs remaining unrelieved are wasted.
3	True	Trading losses carried forward must be set off against the first available future trading profit from the same trade.
4	False	Capital losses cannot be offset against other income. They can only be set against chargeable gains.

Test your understanding 6

1	False	If the company incurs £42,000 of qualifying R&D expenditure it can deduct a total of £96,600 (£42,000 × 230%).
2	False	An SME must have less than 500 employees.
3	True	The company has a trade profit of £21,000 before R&D. The R&D deduction is £80,500 (£35,000 × 230%). This gives a trading loss of £59,500 (£21,000 – £80,500).

Test your understanding 7

AB Ltd

The correct answer is D.

Explanation

Year ended 31 December		**2015**	**2016**
		£	£
Trading income		19,000	Nil
Interest income		2,000	1,000
Chargeable gains		4,000	4,000
Total profits		25,000	5,000
Less: Loss relief	– Current year		(5,000)
	– 12 month carry back	(25,000)	
Taxable total profits		Nil	Nil

Note: Loss relief is given before qualifying charitable donations are deducted. As a result the qualifying charitable donation in 2015 is wasted.

Loss memorandum

		£
Year ended 31 December 2016		67,000
Less:	Current year offset – y/e 31 Dec 2016	(5,000)
	Carry back – 12 months to y/e 31 Dec 2015	(25,000)
Loss carried forward at 31 December 2016		37,000

Test your understanding 8

Eldorado (Birmingham) Limited

Corporation tax computations

Year to 31 August	**2015**	**2016**	**2017**
	£	£	£
Trading profit	18,000	Nil	Nil
Property income	22,000	22,000	22,000
Chargeable gain	3,000	–	–
Total profits	43,000	22,000	22,000
Less Loss relief:			
– Current year		(22,000)	(6,000)
– Carry back	(43,000)		
Taxable total profits	Nil	Nil	16,000

Loss memorandum

	£		£
Loss – y/e 31 Aug 2016	81,000	Loss – y/e 31 Aug 2017	6,000
Offset: Current year	(22,000)	Offset: Current year	(6,000)
Carry back	(43,000)		
Losses carried forward	16,000		Nil

The losses carried forward can only be offset against future trading profits of the same trade.

Test your understanding 9

1	True	Capital losses can only be offset against chargeable gains of the current and future periods.
2	False	Trading losses carried forward must be set off against the first available trading profit from the same trade as soon as it arises.
3	True	Trading losses can be offset against the total profits of the loss making accounting period; total profits includes income and chargeable gains.
4	False	Where trading losses have been relieved against the total profits of the loss making period, a company can choose to offset any losses remaining against the total profits of the previous 12 months but it is not obliged to do so.

7 Payment and administration – companies

Introduction

This chapter looks at the payment and administration aspects of corporation tax (see Chapter 13 for sole traders and partnerships).

ASSESSMENT CRITERIA

Tax return filing deadlines (3.1)

Payment rules for limited companies: amounts and dates (3.1)

Penalties for late filing of tax returns and failing to notify chargeability (3.2)

Late payment interest and surcharges (3.2)

The enquiry window and penalties for incorrect returns (3.2)

What records need to be maintained by a business, how long these records need to be maintained and the penalties for failing to keep these records (4.3)

CONTENTS

1 Corporation tax self-assessment (CTSA)

1.1 Scope

Corporation tax self-assessment (CTSA) requires companies to submit a tax return for each CAP and a self-assessment of any tax payable.

1.2 Filing the return

A company is required to file a return (form CT600) when it receives a notice requiring it to do so.

All companies must file their returns online.

A company which is chargeable to tax, but which does not receive a notice requesting a return, must notify HMRC within 12 months of the end of the accounting period.

Failure to notify may result in a penalty. The penalty is calculated in broadly the same way as penalties for incorrect returns (see below) and is a maximum of 100% of the tax outstanding.

The return must include a calculation (self-assessment) of the corporation tax payable for the accounting period covered by the return.

The return must be made within:

- 12 months of the end of the period of account or, if later
- three months from the date of the notice requiring the return.

Long periods of account

The return filing date is based on the period of account (which may be more than 12 months long).

For a set of accounts of more than 12 months long, there will be two CAPs, two corporation tax computations and therefore two returns to file.

However, both returns will have the same filing date; 12 months after the end of the period of account.

Example

Edgar Ltd has prepared a set of accounts for the 15 months ended 31 March 2017.

Identify the period(s) for which return(s) must be completed and the filing date(s).

Solution

The period of account is the period for which accounts are drawn up (i.e. 15 months to 31 March 2017).

	Periods for returns	*Filing date*
(i)	First 12 months	
	– 12 months ended 31 December 2016	31 March 2018
(ii)	Balance	
	– 3 months ended 31 March 2017	31 March 2018

Penalties for late filing

Failure to submit a return by the due date will result in a penalty.

The system operates as follows:

• Less than 3 months overdue	£100
• Delay of more than three months	£200
• Delay of more than six months	£200 plus 10% of tax due
• Delay of more than 12 months	£200 plus 20% of tax due

If the return is late three times in a row then the £100 penalty is increased to £500 and the £200 penalty to £1,000.

A penalty will not be charged if the taxpayer has a reasonable excuse for the late filing, for example a serious illness. A lack of knowledge of the tax system is not a reasonable excuse.

Note that many of the details about dates, time limits and penalties are contained in the AAT reference material set out below in section 8. You should refer to this throughout this chapter.

Example

Flat Ltd received a notice to file Form CT600 for the year ended 30 June 2015 on 31 August 2015. The company submitted the corporation tax return on 28 February 2017 and paid its corporation tax liability of £35,000.

What are the maximum penalties that can be charged in respect of the late filing of the return?

Solution

The corporation tax return was due to be filed on 30 June 2016, 12 months after the end of the period of account. The return was filed more than six months but less than 12 months late.

A fixed penalty of £200 will be charged plus 10% of any tax still outstanding. In this case that will be an additional penalty of £3,500 (£35,000 × 10%) making a total due of £3,700.

Test your understanding 1

Payment and administration

Read the following statements and state whether they are true or false.

1 Companies must file their corporation tax returns before they pay their corporation tax.

2 The filing date for a company which prepares accounts for the 11 months to 28 February 2017 is 28 February 2018.

3 DEF Ltd filed its corporation tax return for the year ended 31 March 2017 on 19 May 2018. The latest date that it can amend the return is 19 May 2019.

4 The maximum penalty for not filing a corporation tax return on time is £100.

1.3 Amending the return

A company can amend a return within 12 months of the filing due date.

HMRC can amend a return to correct obvious errors and anything else which they believe to be incorrect by reference to the information they hold within:

- nine months of the date it was filed, or
- nine months of the filing of an amendment.

If the company disagrees with HMRC's amendment it may reject it.

This rejection should be made within:

- the normal time limit for amendments or
- if this time limit has expired, within three months of the date of correction.

1.4 Recovery of overpaid tax

A company may claim a repayment of tax within four years of the end of an accounting period. An appeal against HMRC's decision on such a claim must be made within 30 days.

A company is not allowed to make such a claim if its return was made in accordance with a generally accepted accounting practice which prevailed at the time.

1.5 Interest on late payments of corporation tax

Interest is charged automatically on late paid corporation tax:

- from the due date
- to the date of payment.

Where there is an amendment to the self-assessment interest runs:

- from the date the tax would have been payable had it been correctly self-assessed in the first place.

Interest paid on late payments of corporation tax is allowable as a deduction from non-trade interest income.

1.6 Interest on overpaid corporation tax

If corporation tax is overpaid HMRC will pay interest:

- from the later of the normal due date (see below) and the date of overpayment
- to the date it is refunded.

Interest received on overpaid corporation tax is assessable as non-trade interest income.

Detailed computations of interest will not be required in the assessment (such as daily calculations), but the principles must be understood.

1.7 Penalties for incorrect returns

A penalty will be charged where:

- an inaccurate return is submitted to HMRC or
- the company fails to notify HMRC where an under assessment of tax is made by them.

The percentage depends on the reason for the error.

Taxpayer behaviour	**Maximum penalty % of tax lost**
Mistake	No penalty
Failure to take reasonable care	30%
Deliberate understatement	70%
Deliberate understatement with concealment	100%

The penalties may be reduced at HMRC discretion where the taxpayer discloses information to HMRC. The reduction depends on the circumstances of the penalty and whether the taxpayer discloses the information before HMRC discover the error (unprompted disclosure) or afterwards (prompted disclosure).

	Minimum penalties	
Taxpayer behaviour	**Unprompted disclosure % of tax lost**	**Prompted disclosure % of tax lost**
Failure to take reasonable care	Nil	15
Deliberate understatement	20	35
Deliberate understatement with concealment	30	50

 **Example**

State the maximum and minimum penalties that may be levied on each of the following companies which have submitted incorrect tax returns.

L Ltd Accidentally provided an incorrect figure even though the return was checked carefully. The company notified HMRC of the error three days after submitting the return.

S Ltd Was unable to check the return due to staff being on holiday. The return included a number of errors. The return was checked thoroughly the following week and the company provided HMRC with the information necessary to identify the errors.

J Ltd Deliberately understated its tax liability and attempted to conceal the incorrect information that had been provided. HMRC have identified the understatement and J Ltd is helping them with their enquiries.

Solution

Penalties for incorrect tax returns are a percentage of the under declared tax.

L Ltd No penalty is charged where a taxpayer has been careful and has made a genuine mistake.

S Ltd The maximum percentage for failing to take reasonable care is 30%. The minimum percentage for unprompted disclosure is nil.

J Ltd The maximum percentage for a deliberate understatement with concealment is 100%. The minimum percentage for prompted disclosure of information (where the taxpayer provides information in response to HMRC identifying the error) in respect of deliberate understatement with concealment is 50%.

2 HM Revenue and Customs' (HMRC) compliance checks

2.1 Basic rules

HMRC have the right to enquire into a company's tax return under their compliance check powers. This may be a random check or because they have reason to believe that income or expenses have been misstated in the tax return.

Where a return is submitted on time, notice must normally be given within a year of the actual filing date.

Where a return is submitted late HMRC can give notice of a compliance check (also referred to as an enquiry) within a year of the 31 January, 30 April, 31 July or 31 October following the actual date of delivery of the return.

HMRC may also demand that the company produce documents for inspection. If the company fails to do so, a penalty of £300, plus up to £60 a day, may be imposed.

A compliance check (enquiry) ends when HMRC give notice that it has been completed and notify what amendments they believe to be necessary.

Example

CTS Ltd has produced accounts for the year ended 30 June 2016. The company filed its return on 1 April 2017.

What is the latest date by which HMRC must give notice of a compliance check (enquiry)?

How would your answer differ if CTS Ltd had filed its return on 1 September 2017?

Solution

HMRC must give notice within a year of the actual filing date. The actual filing date is 1 April 2017; therefore notice must be given by 1 April 2018.

If the company had filed its return on 1 September 2017, (i.e. after the due filing date of 30 June 2017) HMRC would need to give notice by 31 October 2018 (i.e. 12 months after 31 October following the actual date of delivery of the return).

2.2 Discovery assessments

A discovery assessment may be issued if HMRC believe that insufficient tax has been collected.

The taxpayer can appeal to the Tribunal against a discovery assessment.

2.3 Appeals procedure

The taxpayer can request an informal review of a disputed decision.

Alternatively, a formal appeal may be made to the Tax Tribunal.

Appeals from the Tax Tribunal on a point of law (but not on a point of fact) may be made to the Court of Appeal and from there to the Supreme Court.

The Tax Tribunal is independent of HMRC.

3 Record keeping requirements

A company and its tax adviser must keep records to assist in dealings with and support evidence given to HMRC.

Companies must keep records until the latest of:

- six years from the end of the accounting period
- the date any enquiries are completed
- the date after which enquiries may not be commenced.

Failure to keep records can lead to a penalty of up to £3,000 for each accounting period affected.

4 Payment of corporation tax

4.1 Payment date

All payments of corporation tax must be made electronically.

Companies must normally pay corporation tax within 9 months and one day of the end of the chargeable accounting period (CAP).

A company with a year ended 31 January 2017 must pay corporation tax by 1 November 2016.

Note that Edgar Ltd (in an earlier example) which had a long period of account of the 15 months ended 31 March 2017 would have two payment dates.

Edgar Ltd would pay corporation tax for:

- CAP 1 = 12 months ended 31 December 2016, by 1 October 2017
- CAP 2 = 3 months ended 31 March 2017, by 1 January 2018.

From this we can see that a company with a long period of account can have:

- two separate payment dates
- but one common filing date.

Note that the payment dates are earlier than the filing date.

This normal payment date rule does not however apply to large companies (see below).

4.2 Payment by instalments

Large companies are required to make quarterly payments on account of their corporation tax liability.

A 'large' company is one with augmented profits of more than £1,500,000. This figure is time apportioned for short accounting periods and may have to be divided between 51% group companies.

Augmented profits are the company's taxable total profits plus its dividend income. Dividends received from 51% group companies are ignored when calculating augmented profits.

Two companies are 51% group companies if:

- one is a 51% subsidiary of the other, or
- both are 51% subsidiaries of the same company.

Broadly a 51% subsidiary is one where more than 50% of the shares are owned.

Therefore, a company with two other 51% group companies will be required to pay its corporation tax in instalments if its augmented profits exceed £500,000 (£1,500,000 ÷ 3).

Exceptions to the rule

A company is not required to make quarterly instalment payments in the first period in which it becomes large, unless its profits exceed £10 million.

This £10 million limit is also shared between 51% group companies and time apportioned for short CAPs.

In addition, a company does not have to make quarterly instalment payments if its CT liability does not exceed £10,000.

Payment amounts and pay days

The quarterly payments should be based on the actual corporation tax liability for the current year.

The first payment is made on the 14th day of the seventh month of the accounting period.

The other quarterly payments are due on the 14th day of months 10, 13 and 16.

Note that the payments begin during the accounting period itself, not afterwards. So you must begin counting months from the start of the accounting period.

Example

State the instalment payment dates for a company with a 12 month accounting period ending on 28 February 2017.

Solution

The payments on account are due on:

- 14 September 2016
- 14 December 2016
- 14 March 2017
- 14 June 2017

Each payment due is a quarter of the corporation tax liability for the year.

Therefore estimates of the corporation tax liability for the year need to be made at each payment date.

At least the first three (and probably all four instalments) usually have to be estimated in practice.

The first instalment payment would be a quarter of the best estimate at that date.

The second payment would require a revised estimate to which an amount is added or deducted for any under or over payment in respect of the first instalment and so on.

HMRC may expect to see some proof that the estimates were made with care.

A penalty may be imposed where a company deliberately makes insufficient quarterly payments.

Test your understanding 2

Russell plc prepares accounts to 31 December each year and its taxable total profits for the year ended 31 December 2016 are £1,600,000.

Russell plc has no subsidiaries, receives no dividend income and its taxable total profits for the year ended 31 December 2015 were £720,000.

Which one of the following statements is correct with respect to Russell plc's corporation tax liability for the year ended 31 December 2016?

A The liability is payable
– in 4 equal instalments beginning on 14 July 2016

B The liability is payable
– in 4 equal instalments beginning on 14 July 2017

C The liability is payable on 1 October 2017

D The liability is payable on 31 December 2017

4.3 Interest

Companies should revise the estimate of their corporation tax liability every quarter. It is a good idea to keep records showing how the estimate has been calculated. This will help to justify the size of a payment if HMRC should dispute the amount paid.

Interest runs from the due date on any underpayments or overpayments.

Interest paid by the company is a deductible expense. Interest received by the company is taxable income. Both are dealt with under the loan relationship rules as non-trade interest.

Penalties may be charged if a company deliberately fails to pay instalments of a sufficient size.

5 Approach to preparing written answers

5.1 Written advice to clients

There will be a written task in the assessment that could cover a number of syllabus areas including those dealing with filing dates, payments of tax, penalties and interest for companies or individuals (see Chapter 13).

For the AQ2013 syllabus, the chief assessor wrote a guidance document to assist learners with written answers in personal tax. However, much of the guidance is relevant for business tax and is likely to continue to be relevant under the AQ2016 assessment.

Some of the key points from the advice are set out below.

Firstly, it's important you understand that the software in which you are answering the task is not Microsoft Word. So there's no:

- spell checker
- grammar checker
- automatic correcting of typos.

You **must** proofread what you've written and correct any obvious spelling and grammatical errors.

There's often a mark for presentation of the answer, and the assessor is looking for whether the way you've presented your work would be acceptable in the workplace. This mark is independent of the technical answer, and what we look for is whether a client would find the answer acceptable from a visual perspective.

Before you start to type:

You must read the question in detail. We've noticed that learners often scan read a question, decide what it's about in an instant and then write the answer without giving any thought or consideration to the details. You should:

- read through once to get the general feel of the question
- read through again, slower this time, concentrating on key words or phrases
- plan your answer, ensuring all key areas are covered
- decide the structure of your answer, considering where you'll use things like an email, a memo or bullet points
- type up your answer
- proof read your answer, correcting any errors.

Too many times it would seem that learners only follow the fifth of these points. If you do this it **will** affect your marks.

Consider exactly who you're writing to. Most likely it will be a client, so this needs to influence your approach.

Remember, if the client is writing to you for advice, they don't know the answer. We often see learners give half answers which the assessor will understand, but which a client would not. As a result, they lose marks.

Similarly, be sure to avoid:

- abbreviations
- technical jargon
- SMS/text message speak.

Test your understanding 3

Space plc, which has taxable total profits of £2 million annually, is preparing its budget for the year ending 31 March 2017. It does not have any dividend income.

Required:

(a) Prepare a plan of projected corporation tax payments based on its results for the year, stating the amounts due and the due dates.

(b) Advise of any other administrative requirements for corporation tax purposes.

Approach to the question

Step 1: Calculate the corporation tax liability.

Step 2: Consider the impact of the instalment system on this large company.

Step 3: Consider the *returns* required, and the impact of late payments.

6 Test your understanding

Test your understanding 4

ABC Ltd

ABC Ltd has four 51% group companies. In the year to 31 March 2016 its profits were £200,000. In the year to 31 March 2017 it sold its factory and had profits of £3 million.

When is the corporation tax for the year to 31 March 2017 due?

A The liability is payable in 4 equal instalments beginning on 14 October 2016

B The liability is payable in 4 equal instalments beginning on 14 October 2017

C The liability is payable on 1 January 2018

D The liability is payable on 31 March 2018

Test your understanding 5

Wendy Windows plc

Wendy Windows plc has augmented profits above £1,500,000 every year and has taxable total profits in the year ended 31 January 2017 of £2,400,000.

Required:

Calculate the corporation tax liability of Wendy Windows plc for the accounting period to 31 January 2017 and state when this liability is due for payment.

7 Summary

There are numerous deadlines and penalties under CTSA.

The key points are:

- A company must file a return within
  - 12 months of the end of its period of account or
  - if later, three months from the date of the notice from HMRC.
- Failure to submit a return on time results in an immediate penalty of £100.
- The company can amend a return within 12 months of the due filing date.
- HMRC can conduct a compliance check (enquiry) into a return provided they give written notice within a year of the actual filing date.
- Companies must keep records for six years from the end of the accounting period. Failure to do so can result in a penalty of up to £3,000.
- The due date for corporation tax is nine months and one day after the end of the accounting period.
- Companies with augmented profits of more than £1,500,000 (adjusted for short accounting periods and 51% group companies) must pay their liability in quarterly instalments, commencing on the 14th day of the seventh month of the accounting period.

8 AAT reference material

Corporation tax – payment and administration

Payment dates

- Small companies (annual profits less than £1.5 million): 9 months + 1 day after end of the accounting period (CAP).
- Large companies (annual profits greater than £1.5 million) must estimate year's tax liability and pay 25% of the year's liability:
  - 6 months and 14 days after start of CAP
  - 9 months and 14 days after start of CAP
  - 14 days after end of CAP
  - 3 months and 14 days after end of CAP.
- Estimate must be revised for each quarter. Penalties may be charged if company deliberately fails to pay sufficient instalments.
- No instalments due for first year company is large unless profits are greater than £10 million.
- 51% group companies share the annual profit limit of £1.5 million equally.

Interest on late payments

- Interest charged daily on late payment. Overpayment of tax receives interest from HMRC. Interest is taxable/tax allowable as interest income.

Filing the return

- Filed on the later of 12 months after end of CAP or 3 months after the notice to deliver a tax return has been issued.
- Late filing penalties are: less than 3 months late: £100; greater than 3 months late: £200; greater than 6 months late: 10% of tax due per return; greater than 12 months late: 20% of tax due per return.
- Company must notify HMRC it is within scope of corporation tax within 3 months of starting to trade.
- Company can amend return within 12 months of the filing date.

Enquiries and other penalties

- HMRC must notify company of enquiry within 12 months of submission of return.
- Basis of enquiry – random or HMRC believe income/expenses misstated.
- Penalty for failure to produce enquiry documents: £300 + £60 per day.
- Penalty for failure to keep proper records is up to £3,000. Records must be retained for six years after the end of the relevant accounting period.
- Penalties for incorrect returns are the same as for sole traders and partners – see sole traders and partners link.

Test your understanding answers

Test your understanding 1

Payment and administration

1	False	The due date for the payment of the corporation tax falls before the due filing date. Companies may need to estimate the payment of corporation tax that is due.
2	True	The filing date is 12 months from the end of the period of account regardless of the length of the accounting period.
3	False	The latest date that DEF Ltd can amend its return is 31 March 2019 (i.e. 12 months after the due filing date not the actual filing date).
4	False	The immediate penalty for late filing of £100. There can then be additional penalties once the delay exceeds three months.

Test your understanding 2

Russell plc

The correct answer is C.

Explanation

C is the correct answer because even though Russell plc has augmented profits of more than £1,500,000 for the year ended 31 December 2016, it is large for the first time and its profits are below £10 million.

Russell plc did not have augmented profits of more than £1,500,000 in the previous year and therefore (given its profits do not exceed £10 m) will not have to pay instalments for the year ended 31 December 2016.

Russell plc's corporation tax liability will be due within 9 months and 1 day of the end of the accounting period (i.e. by 1 October 2017).

Test your understanding 3

(a) Space plc

Projected corporation tax payments – y/e 31 Mar 2017

Taxable total profits and augmented profits	£2,000,000
Corporation tax liability (at 20%)	£400,000.00

The accounting period will be subject to quarterly instalments as the company is large and was large in the previous year.

The liability for the year ended 31 March 2017 should be settled by four equal instalments of £100,000 (£400,000 ÷ 4).

		£
Instalment 1	14 October 2016	100,000.00
Instalment 2	14 January 2017	100,000.00
Instalment 3	14 April 2017	100,000.00
Instalment 4	14 July 2017	100,000.00

(b) Administrative requirements

(1) A return, including statutory accounts and computations, must be submitted online by 31 March 2018 (i.e. within 12 months of the accounting period end otherwise penalties will be charged).

(2) Late payments of tax will give rise to interest charges, which will be deductible from non-trade interest income.

Test your understanding 4

ABC Ltd

The correct answer is A.

Explanation

ABC Ltd is a large company in the year to 31 March 2017.

It must pay its corporation tax in instalments even though it was not a large company in the year to 31 March 2016. This is because its profits in the year to 31 March 2017 exceed £2 million (i.e. £10 million × 1/5 (four 51% group companies)).

The tax is due on:

14 October 2016, 14 January 2017, 14 April 2017 and 14 July 2017.

Test your understanding 5

Wendy Windows plc

Corporation tax liability and payment dates

	£
Corporation tax due:	
FY2014 (£2,400,000 × 2/12 × 21%)	84,000.00
FY2015 (£2,400,000 × 10/12 × 20%)	400,000.00
Corporation tax liability	484,000.00
Due date of instalments:	
14 August 2015 (£484,000.00 × ¼)	121,000.00
14 November 2015	121,000.00
14 February 2016	121,000.00
14 May 2016	121,000.00
	484,000.00

Sole traders and partnerships – principles of taxation

Introduction

In Chapters 2 to 7 we have considered how we tax the profits and gains of one type of business entity – a company.

In the next few chapters we look at how we tax the profits of sole traders and partnerships (unincorporated businesses).

This chapter is an introduction to the main differences in the method of dealing with the tax affairs of these business entities.

CONTENTS

1 Sole trader

1.1 No separate legal entity

A sole trader is an individual who has set up his/her own business. The business is not a separate legal entity.

1.2 Types of tax payable

The individual who sets up as a sole trader pays:

- income tax, on income including adjusted trading profits; and
- capital gains tax, on chargeable gains.

Example

Which of the following business entities is a sole trader?

(a) Fred Flint, haulage contractor.

(b) Fred Flint Ltd, haulage contractor.

Solution

(a) Fred Flint is a sole trader. Fred pays income tax on his adjusted trading profit and capital gains tax on his gains.

(b) Fred Flint Ltd is a company (a separate legal entity). The company pays corporation tax on income and gains.

2 Partnerships

2.1 No separate legal entity

A partnership is a group of individuals carrying on in business together. The business is not a separate legal entity.

2.2 Types of tax payable

Each partner individually pays:

- income tax, on his share of the partnership's adjusted trading profit in addition to his other personal income.

A partnership is effectively a collection of sole traders working together, each responsible for his own tax liability.

The allocation of partnership profits is considered further in Chapter 10.

3 Summary

Sole traders and partnerships:

- DO NOT pay corporation tax
- DO pay income tax and capital gains tax
- ARE NOT separate legal entities.

Taxable trade profits for unincorporated businesses

Introduction

The assessment may include a task that looks at the taxable trading profits of a sole trader or partner (unincorporated businesses).

There are some differences in the computation of adjusted trading profits and capital allowances for unincorporated businesses compared to companies.

ASSESSMENT CRITERIA

Apply rules relating to deductible and non-deductible expenditure (1.1)

Classify expenditure as either revenue or capital expenditure (1.1)

Adjust accounting profit and losses for tax purposes (1.1)

Identify the types of capital allowances (1.3)

Calculate capital allowances including adjustment for private usage (1.3)

Accurately complete self-employed tax returns (1.6)

Know what the badges of trade are and how they evolved (4.3)

CONTENTS

1 Adjusted trading profits for individuals

1.1 Badges of trade

We are now concerned with taxing the profits of a trade of an individual.

Statute law defines a 'trade' as including any venture in the nature of trade. This is not particularly helpful in practice and it has been necessary for the Courts to decide in a number of cases whether or not an activity is a trade.

In 1954 a Royal Commission summarised the existing case law relevant to 'trade' by identifying six attributes or 'badges' of trade. The mnemonic 'SOFIRM' as shown below may help you to remember them!

- **Subject matter (S)**

  Assets are generally acquired either for personal use, or as an investment, or as inventory used in a trade (i.e. stock) or as a non-current asset (i.e. fixed asset) used in a trade.

  An investment may be income generating (e.g. shares) or for pleasure (e.g. a painting). If an asset is clearly neither acquired as an investment or for the use of the owner or his family or friends, the inference of trading arises.

- **Length of ownership (O)**

  The shorter the period of ownership the more likely this is indicative of a trade.

- **Frequency of transactions (F)**

  The more frequent a transaction the more likely a trade is being conducted.

- **Improvements/Supplementary work (I)**

  An asset bought and enhanced in some way before sale is more likely to be a trading asset than a similar asset simply bought and sold without improvement.

- **Circumstances of realisation (R)**

  It can be argued that the forced sale of an asset to relieve a cash flow crisis is less likely to be a disposal in the course of a trade.

- **Motive (M)**

  The presence of a profit motive is indicative of a trade.

In borderline cases it is necessary to look at all the 'badges' together and not give undue weight to any particular test.

Note that these six badges are listed in the AAT reference material included in section 7 below.

In addition to the original 6 badges of trade mentioned above, HMRC guidance adds that the following are also considered to indicate trading. You can use the mnemonic 'FAST' to help you to remember these:

- **Finance (F)**

  Where the taxpayer took out a loan to buy the asset which they expect to repay from the proceeds of sale.

- **Method of acquisition (A)**

  Where the taxpayer acquired the asset by way of purchase rather than receiving it as a gift or by inheritance.

- **Existence of similar trading transactions (ST)**

  Where the transactions are similar to those of an existing trade carried on by the taxpayer.

Remember that no one factor is conclusive. All factors must be considered and an overall view taken.

Example

James Aslett renovates classic cars as a 'hobby' in his spare time and exhibits them at classic car events. He has accepted the occasional offer to sell and usually makes a profit if the time he has spent is ignored.

Explain whether you think James will be treated as trading in cars by HMRC.

Solution

- The situation has to be measured against the 'badges of trade'.
- A car could be a trading asset or an investment or for personal use so the 'subject matter' test is inconclusive.
- If James owns the cars for only a brief period and is constantly buying, renovating and selling, perhaps even advertising, there comes a point where the hobby becomes a trade.

1.2 Professions and vocations

The profits made by a self-employed person from a profession or vocation, such as accountancy, are taxed in the same way as the profits of a trade.

2 Adjustment of trading profits

2.1 Comparison between individuals and companies

The starting point in determining the amount of taxable trading profits is the net profit as shown in the accounts, but this must be adjusted for tax purposes in a similar way to companies.

We have already seen in Chapter 3 in the context of a company how to adjust the accounting profits to find the adjusted trading profits for tax purposes. The first part of this chapter will concentrate on approaching the topic from an individual trader's perspective.

Taxable trading profits for an individual comprise adjusted trading profits (Chapter 3) less capital allowances (Chapter 4) for an accounting period in much the same way as it does for a company.

This chapter covers the minor adjustments needed to the rules seen earlier in the context of companies.

Outline pro forma for adjustment of profits computation

		Section	£	£
Net profit per accounts				X
Add:	Disallowable expenditure	2.2	X	
	Income not included in the accounts but taxable as trading income	2.3	X	
			——	X
				——
				X
Less:	Income included in the accounts but not taxable as trading income	2.4	X	
	Expenditure not in the accounts but allowable as a trading deduction	2.5	X	
			——	(X)
				——
Adjusted trading profit (before deducting capital allowances)				X
				——

The same profit adjustment rules for companies apply for individual (or 'sole') traders but with minor adjustments explained as follows.

Note that the AAT reference material set out in section 7 below lists some of the more common adjustments.

2.2 Disallowable expenditure differences

Adjustments for private expenditure

Any private expenditure of the owner of the business deducted in the accounts should be disallowed. This would include any payment of the trader's income tax or national insurance liabilities.

There will sometimes be an estimated proportion of business use, for example with motor expenses or telephone expenses. If this is the case, only the private element should be disallowed and therefore added back.

Under self-assessment the trader has to be prepared to justify his estimate of the private element if HMRC enquire into his self-assessment return.

Salary to proprietor

The salary or drawings paid to the owner is the equivalent of a dividend paid by a company. It is an appropriation of profit, not a business expense, and must therefore be added back to profit.

Example

Gordon has his own business as a motor dealer. His accounts for the year ended 31 December 2016 show the following results:

	£	£
Gross profit		80,000
Less: Expenses		
Salaries	30,000	
Motor expenses	3,000	
Allowable expenses	22,000	
		(55,000)
Net profit per accounts		25,000

Included in motor expenses is £1,000 relating to the cost of running Gordon's car which is used 60% for business purposes and included in salaries is Gordon's 'salary' of £20,000.

Calculate Gordon's adjusted trading profit.

	£
Net profit per accounts	25,000
Add: Disallowable expenses	
Gordon's 'salary'/drawings	20,000
Private motor expenses (£1,000 × 40%)	400
Adjusted trading profit	45,400

Note: Do not add back salaries or private motor expenses of employees. These are allowable expenses for the business (just as they are in a company's computation).

Bad debts/Irrecoverable debts

We saw in Chapter 3 that as companies are required to produce their accounts in accordance with internationally accepted accounting practice, any provisions for irrecoverable debts (bad debts) included within the accounts are specific in nature and therefore allowable for tax purposes.

The accounts of an unincorporated business however are not bound by the Companies Act requirements and therefore may contain *general* provisions which are not allowable for tax purposes.

Movements in general provisions, for example the *general* bad debt provision, are not allowable. An increase in a general provision must be added back, and a decrease in a general provision must be deducted, to arrive at adjusted trading profits.

Movements in *specific* provisions are allowable and do not need adjusting for in calculating the adjusted trading profits.

Note that movements in any other general provisions charged to the statement of profit or loss should also be disallowed (e.g. inventory/stock provisions).

 **Example**

The bad debts account of Greg, an interior designer, for the year ended 30 June 2016 appears as follows:

	£		£
Written off:		Balance brought down:	
Trade	274	Specific provision	185
Former employee	80	General provision	260
Balance carried down:		Recoveries – trade	23
Specific provision	194	Profit and loss account	305
General provision	225		
	773		773

Show the adjustment required in computing the adjusted trading profit.

Solution

The first stage is to establish a breakdown of the statement of profit or loss charge of £305.

Remember that this figure comprises amounts written off and recovered, and movements in provisions.

Statement of profit or loss charge:

	£	**Allowable?**
Increase in specific provision (£194 – £185)	9	✓
Decrease in general provision (£225 – £260)	(35)	×
Trade debt written off	274	✓
Former employee loan written off	80	×
Recoveries – trade	(23)	✓
	305	

The movement in the general provision and the amount owed by the former employee are both disallowed. In this case, the movement in the general provision is a *decrease, so* the adjustment made is to *deduct* it from the profit per the accounts.

The adjustments required to compute the adjusted trading profit are therefore as follows:

		£
Add:	Former employee, debt written off	80
Less:	Decrease in general provision	(35)

Charitable donations

An unincorporated business may make charitable donations. These fall into three categories:

- Small and to a local charity – allowed as trade expenses.
- Donations via the gift aid scheme – these are not allowed as a trade expense but the trader will get relief for the payment via their personal income tax computation. This relief is not tested in the business tax assessment.
- Other charitable donations – not allowed as a trade expense and no other relief is available.

For a company all charitable donations that are not relieved as trade expenses are given relief as qualifying charitable donations and are deducted from total profits.

2.3 Income not included in the accounts but taxable as trading income

This category does not exist for the adjustment of profits for a company.

The most common example is goods taken by the owner for his own use. The proprietor must be taxed on the profit he would have made if the goods had been sold at market value (i.e. at retail or wholesale price as appropriate).

If the cost of sales in the statement of profit or loss has not been reduced for the goods taken for own use then the amount to be added back to arrive at the adjusted profit will be the *selling price*.

If the cost of sales has been reduced by the cost of the goods taken for own use, then the amount added back will be the *profit.*

 **Example**

Sammy operates a toy store and has taken goods for his own use costing £500 during the year ended 31 December 2016. An adjustment has already been made to reflect the cost of the goods taken.

What is the increase to net profit required if:

(a) Sammy operates a mark-up basis of pricing of 40%; or alternatively

(b) Sammy operates on a gross profit margin of 40%?

Read the requirement carefully in the assessment. These will give different results.

Solution

(a) Mark-up means that the cost of the goods represents 100% and that sales value is therefore 140%.

	%
Sales	140
Less: Cost	(100)
Profit	40

The profit is therefore (40% of £500) = £200.

(b) Where a gross profit margin is supplied, sales represent 100% of the value.

If the profit is 40% of sales then the cost of goods is 60%.

	%
Sales	100
Less: Cost	(60)
Profit	40

Therefore the profit element is (£500 × $^{40}/_{60}$) = £333.

Example

Mr Bean has taken £500 of goods from inventory. An adjustment has been made in the accounts for the cost of the goods taken.

An extract from the statement of profit or loss shows the following:

	£	£
Sales		450,000
Opening inventory	160,000	
Purchases	210,000	
Closing inventory	(120,000)	
Cost of sales		(250,000)
Gross profit		200,000

Explain the adjustments needed if the net profit shown in the accounts is £90,000.

Solution

The increase to net profit for the profit element of goods for own use must be calculated by reference to the correct relationship between cost and gross profit.

If cost of goods used is £500 and £250,000 of costs generates £200,000 of profit then:

Profit element = £500 × $\frac{200}{250}$ = £400

Therefore the net profit is adjusted as follows:

	£
Net profit	90,000
Add: Increase in profit for goods for own use	400
Adjusted profit	90,400

2.4 Income included in the accounts but not taxable as trading income

The following are examples of amounts which may be included in the statement of profit or loss, but which are not taxable as trading income. Hence they should be deducted when calculating taxable trading profits.

- Income taxed in another way (e.g. rent, interest receivable).
- Income exempt from income tax (e.g. interest received on delayed tax repayments).
- Profits on sales of non-current assets.

These adjustments are essentially the same as those for companies.

2.5 Expenditure not in the accounts but allowable

This category of adjustment does not arise for companies.

Any business expense not charged in the accounts but paid for or borne privately by the proprietor can be deducted as a business expense.

For example, where a home telephone is used for business calls the cost of the business calls can be deducted (although it is more common for the whole amount to be charged to the statement of profit or loss, in which case the private portion should be disallowed).

Test your understanding 1

Capone (1)

Capone is in business as a wine merchant and has prepared accounts to 30 June 2016. His statement of profit or loss was:

	£	£
Sales		183,658
Cost of sales		(119,379)
Gross profit		64,279
Dividend income		300
		64,579
Salaries	9,740	
Rent and business rates	9,860	
Repairs to premises	2,620	
Motor expenses	740	
Depreciation	4,150	
Bad and doubtful debts	6,030	
Sundry expenses	770	
Salary		
– Capone	14,000	
– Wife, as secretary	1,450	
		(49,360)
Net profit		15,219

The following information is given:

Repairs to premises	£
Alterations to flooring in order to install new bottling machine	1,460
Redecoration	1,160
	2,620

Bad and doubtful debts account

	£		£
Trade debts written off	1,300	Provision brought forward	
Loan to ex-employee		– General	1,850
written off	400	– Specific	580
Provisions carried forward		Statement of profit or loss	6,030
– General	5,200		
– Specific	1,560		
	8,460		8,460

Sundry expenses	£
Fine re breach of Customs bonding regulations	250
Subscription to Wine Retail Trade Association	50
Miscellaneous allowable expenses	470
	770

During the year Capone had withdrawn goods from inventory for his own consumption. The cost of this inventory was £455. The business makes a uniform gross profit of 35% on selling price. No entry had been made in the books in respect of the goods taken.

Required:

Compute Capone's adjusted trading profit before capital allowances for the period ended 30 June 2016, giving reasons for the adjustments made.

Note: Reasons for the adjustments are unlikely to be required in the assessment. It is likely that an adjustment of profits question will involve dragging items of expenditure to the appropriate part of the adjustment of profits calculation or choosing the correct adjustment from a few options.

However, understanding why adjustments are made will help you to remember them better.

3 Capital allowances for individuals

3.1 The general rules

The capital allowance rules for plant and machinery (Chapter 4) have already been explained in detail for companies. The modifications needed to apply these rules for sole traders are explained below.

3.2 Private use assets

Any asset used partly *by the proprietor/owner* for private purposes must be given a separate column in the capital allowances working. Such assets cannot be covered by a short life asset election.

The AIA, WDA or FYA on the asset is based on its full cost. However, the allowance actually *claimed* will be reduced for private use. Only the proportion relating to business use can be claimed.

Note that if applicable, the business can choose the expenditure against which the AIA is matched. It will be most beneficial for the AIA to be allocated against the general pool expenditure rather than any private use asset as only the business proportion of any AIA available can be claimed.

However note that in the assessment the assets most commonly used for private purposes are cars, which are not eligible for the AIA.

On disposal, a balancing adjustment will be calculated. However, the balancing adjustment will be similarly reduced for private use. Only the business proportion can be claimed or is taxable.

The following example demonstrates this.

Example

Gerard is a trader preparing accounts for calendar years.

In May 2016 he bought a motor car for £7,200 which has CO_2 emissions of 125 g/km. He sold this car in February 2018 for £5,000 replacing it with a car costing £18,800 which has a CO_2 emission rate of 170 g/km.

Gerard uses his cars for both business and private purposes and estimates an 80% business use proportion.

Show the capital allowances and balancing adjustments on the cars for the years ended 31 December 2016, 2017 and 2018.

Solution

This example involves two private use cars.

Each car will have a separate column, as a private use asset.

The first stage is to calculate the allowances in the normal way. Then multiply these allowances by 80%, the business use proportion, to find the allowances that can be claimed.

On disposal, the balancing allowance or charge will be calculated as usual, and again multiplied by 80% to find the actual amount to be deducted or added back to adjusted trading profits.

The answer is therefore as follows:

Gerard – Capital allowances

	Private use Car 1		Private use Car 2		Allowances
	£		£		£
Year ended 31 December 2016					
Additions	7,200				
WDA at 18%	(1,296) ×	80%			1,037
TWDV carried forward	5,904				
Year ended 31 December 2017					
WDA at 18%	(1,063) ×	80%			850
TWDV carried forward	4,841				
Year ended 31 December 2018					
Additions			18,800		
Disposal proceeds	(5,000)				
	(159)				
Balancing charge	159 ×	80%			(127)
WDA at 8% (note)			(1,504) ×	80%	1,203
TWDV carried forward			17,296		
Total allowances					1,076

Note: Gerard's new car has emissions of more than 130 g/km and so the WDA is 8%.

Test your understanding 2

Ernest

Ernest prepares accounts to 31 March annually. On 1 April 2016 he had a qualifying general pool balance of plant and machinery brought forward of £24,000.

The following transactions took place in the year to 31 March 2017.

15 April 2016	Purchased car for £16,000 (wholly business usage)
30 April 2016	Sold plant for £3,200 (original cost £4,800)
16 July 2016	Purchased car for £9,200 (wholly business usage)
17 August 2016	Purchased car for £9,400 (30% private usage by Ernest)

In the following year to 31 March 2018, Ernest sold for £8,100 the car originally purchased on 17 August 2016. The car originally purchased on 15 April 2016 was sold for £9,400 on 9 March 2018. There were no other transactions.

All cars purchased had CO_2 emissions between 76 and 130 g/km.

Assume the rates of allowances for the tax year 2016/17 continue into the future.

Required:

Compute the capital allowances and balancing adjustments for the years ended 31 March 2017 and 31 March 2018.

3.3 The impact of the length of the accounting period (sole traders)

As we have seen, capital allowances are computed for accounting periods and deducted in calculating taxable trading profits.

The writing down allowances calculated so far were all for 12 month accounting periods.

Where the accounting period is more or less than 12 months' long, the AIA and WDA must be scaled up or down accordingly. You must perform this calculation to the nearest month.

Note the important difference between companies and sole traders. A company cannot have a chargeable accounting period greater than 12 months, but a sole trader can. Therefore the WDA is scaled up where there is a long period of account for a sole trader.

Remember however that first year allowances are given in full regardless of the length of the accounting period. They are never scaled up or down according to the length of the accounting period.

Capital allowances for periods which are not twelve months long are very popular in the assessment and you should always watch out for them.

Example

Ken started to trade on 1 January 2016, and on that day he purchased three cars for the use of his employees at a total cost of £21,900 and plant which cost £22,000. All the cars had CO_2 emissions of 120 g/km.

Calculate the allowances due for his first two accounting periods on the assumption that he prepares his first accounts to:

(i) 31 December 2016

(ii) 31 October 2016

(iii) 31 March 2017

and annually on those dates thereafter.

Assume the rates of allowances for the tax year 2016/17 continue into the future.

Solution

(i) **First accounts – 12 months to 31 December 2016**

		General pool	Allowances
	£	£	£
12 months to 31 December 2016			
Additions:			
No AIA: Cars		21,900	
Qualifying for AIA:			
Plant	22,000		
Less: AIA	(22,000)		22,000
		Nil	
		21,900	
WDA (18%)		(3,942)	3,942
TWDV c/f		17,958	
Total allowances			25,942
12 months to 31 December 2017			
WDA (18%)		(3,232)	3,232
TWDV c/f		14,726	

(ii) **First accounts – 10 months to 31 October 2016**

		General pool	Allowances
	£	£	£
10 months to 31 October 2016			
Additions:			
No AIA: Cars		21,900	
Qualifying for AIA:			
Plant	22,000		
Less: AIA (Note)	(22,000)		22,000
		Nil	
		21,900	
WDA (18% × 10/12)		(3,285)	3,285
TWDV c/f		18,615	
Total allowances			25,285
12 months to 31 October 2017			
WDA (18%)		(3,351)	3,351
TWDV c/f		15,264	

Note: Maximum AIA = (£200,000 × 10/12) = £166,667.

(iii) **First accounts – 15 months to 31 March 2017**

		General pool	Allowances
	£	£	£
15 months to 31 March 2017			
Additions:			
No AIA: Cars		21,900	
Qualifying for AIA:			
Plant	22,000		
Less AIA (Note)	(22,000)		22,000
		Nil	
		21,900	
WDA (18% × 15/12)		(4,928)	4,928
TWDV c/f		16,972	
Total allowances			26,928
12 months to 31 March 2018			
WDA (18%)		(3,055)	3,055
TWDV c/f		13,917	

Note: Maximum AIA = (£200,000 × 15/12) = £250,000.

Test your understanding 3

Anjula commenced trading on 1 May 2016 and prepares her first set of accounts to 31 August 2017.

On 2 June 2016 she purchased equipment costing £2,500 and a car costing £6,200 with carbon dioxide emissions of 125 g/km and 100% business use.

What are the capital allowances available for the period ended 31 August 2017?

A £8,700

B £3,988

C £2,088

D £3,616

4 Income tax return – self-employment

4.1 Self-employment supplementary pages

An individual may be required to complete a tax return.

There is a main return (SA100) and several supplementary pages to be completed as appropriate. One of the sets of supplementary pages consists of four pages on self-employment (SA103).

4.2 Page SEF 2

This page records the expenses of the business. The detailed section on expenses need only be completed if the annual turnover of the business is at least £83,000. Otherwise it is only necessary to enter a total expenses figure in Box 31.

- The left hand column includes all expenses shown in the accounts (analysed as appropriate).
- The right hand column shows the disallowable expenditure included within the expenses figures.

It is possible that boxes in both columns could include the same figure; for example, if depreciation in the accounts is £3,000 then:

- Box 29 will show £3,000; and
- Box 44 will show £3,000.

Usually the boxes will show different figures; for example, if wages and salaries of £50,000 included the owner's drawings of £20,000 then:

- Box 19 will show £50,000; and
- Box 34 will show £20,000.

Note that this page **only** records expenses and does not include adjustments for:

- goods for own use
- income included in the accounts but not taxable as trading income
- capital allowances.

The following is important in connection with the completion of forms in the assessment.

- When completing the form in the assessment, figures must be entered in the correct boxes.
- You will be asked to complete just one page of any form.
- Commas need not be entered for numbers of four digits or more.
- You do not need to fill in every box, only relevant ones.

Business expenses

Please read the 'Self-employment (full) notes' before filling in this section.

Total expenses	Disallowable expenses
If your annual turnover was below £83,000, you may just put your total expenses in box 31	Use this column if the figures in boxes 17 to 30 include disallowable amounts
17 Cost of goods bought for resale or goods used £ .00	32 £ .00
18 Construction industry – payments to subcontractors £ .00	33 £ .00
19 Wages, salaries and other staff costs £ .00	34 £ .00
20 Car, van and travel expenses £ .00	35 £ .00
21 Rent, rates, power and insurance costs £ .00	36 £ .00
22 Repairs and renewals of property and equipment £ .00	37 £ .00
23 Phone, fax, stationery and other office costs £ .00	38 £ .00
24 Advertising and business entertainment costs £ .00	39 £ .00
25 Interest on bank and other loans £ .00	40 £ .00
26 Bank, credit card and other financial charges £ .00	41 £ .00
27 Irrecoverable debts written off £ .00	42 £ .00
28 Accountancy, legal and other professional fees £ .00	43 £ .00
29 Depreciation and loss/profit on sale of assets £ .00	44 £ .00
30 Other business expenses £ .00	45 £ .00
31 Total expenses (total of boxes 17 to 30) £ .00	46 Total disallowable expenses (total of boxes 32 to 45) £ .00

SA103F 2016 Page SEF 2

Test your understanding 4

Capone (2)

Complete page 2 of the self-employment supplementary pages (below) for the relevant expenses for Capone in test your understanding 1.

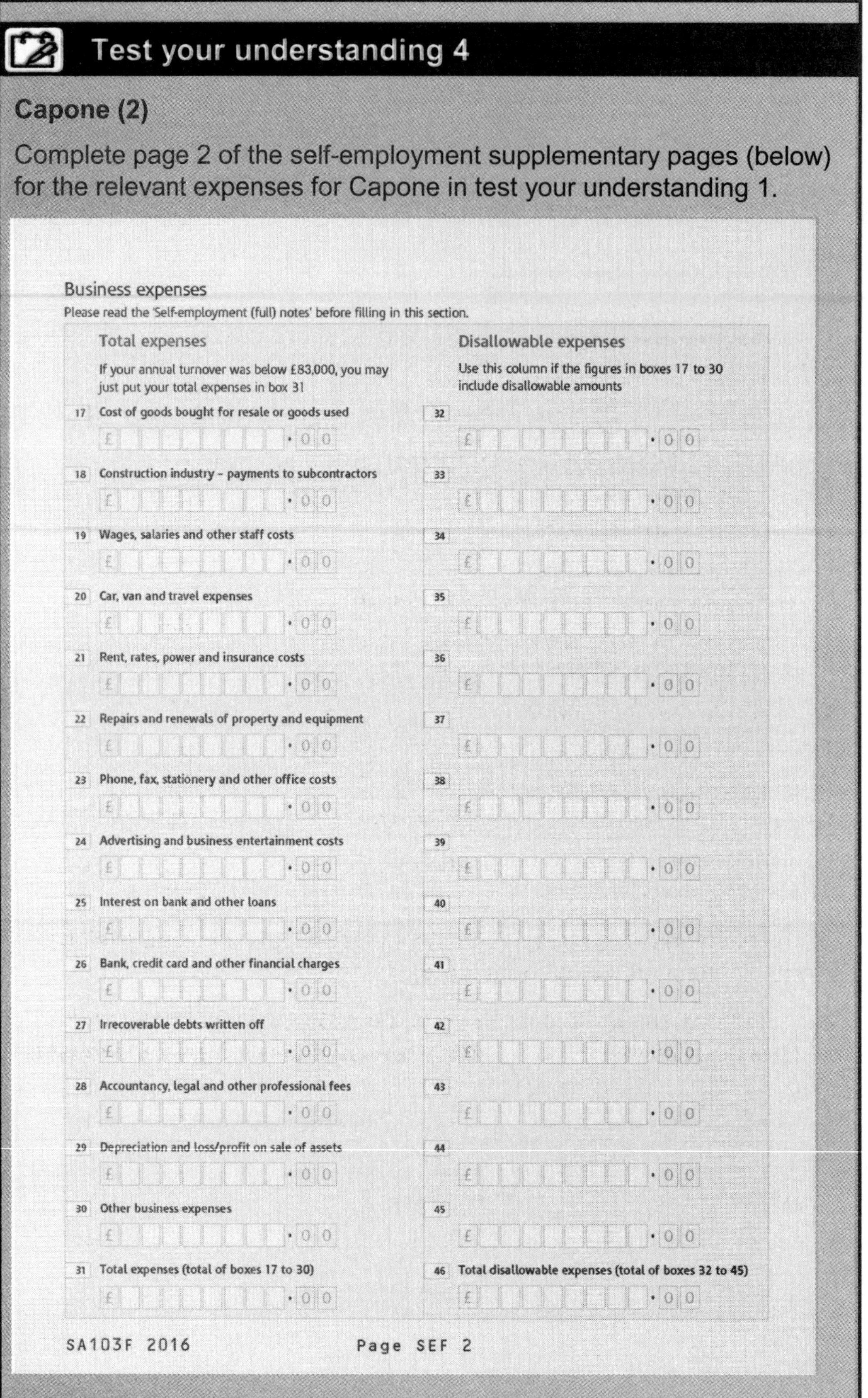

Business expenses

Please read the 'Self-employment (full) notes' before filling in this section.

Total expenses	Disallowable expenses
If your annual turnover was below £83,000, you may just put your total expenses in box 31	Use this column if the figures in boxes 17 to 30 include disallowable amounts
17 Cost of goods bought for resale or goods used £ .00	32 £ .00
18 Construction industry – payments to subcontractors £ .00	33 £ .00
19 Wages, salaries and other staff costs £ .00	34 £ .00
20 Car, van and travel expenses £ .00	35 £ .00
21 Rent, rates, power and insurance costs £ .00	36 £ .00
22 Repairs and renewals of property and equipment £ .00	37 £ .00
23 Phone, fax, stationery and other office costs £ .00	38 £ .00
24 Advertising and business entertainment costs £ .00	39 £ .00
25 Interest on bank and other loans £ .00	40 £ .00
26 Bank, credit card and other financial charges £ .00	41 £ .00
27 Irrecoverable debts written off £ .00	42 £ .00
28 Accountancy, legal and other professional fees £ .00	43 £ .00
29 Depreciation and loss/profit on sale of assets £ .00	44 £ .00
30 Other business expenses £ .00	45 £ .00
31 Total expenses (total of boxes 17 to 30) £ .00	46 Total disallowable expenses (total of boxes 32 to 45) £ .00

SA103F 2016 Page SEF 2

5 Test your understanding

Test your understanding 5

Patrick

Patrick is a self-employed businessman. The following expenses are charged in Patrick's statement of profit or loss for the year to 31 December 2016:

	£	✓ or ×
Patrick's business travelling expenses	5,175	
Christmas presents for staff	250	
Entertaining overseas suppliers	2,750	
Entertaining UK customers	2,300	
Gifts to customers that carry the business name:		
– Boxes of chocolates costing £5.00 each	125	
– Calendars costing £1.50 each	150	
Donation to national charity	50	
Donation to local political party	100	
Subscription to chamber of commerce	25	
A gift to a member of staff upon marriage	45	
Patrick's squash club subscription	250	
Advertising in trade press	280	

Patrick often uses his squash club as a place to take customers since several of them are keen squash players.

Mark each expense with either a ✓ (if the expense is allowable and requires no adjustment) or × (if the expense is disallowable and must be added back).

Test your understanding 6

Georgina

Georgina runs a business which she started on 1 September 2016 and prepares her first set of accounts to 31 May 2017.

On 1 October 2016, she purchased a car with carbon dioxide emissions of 127 g/km for £10,500 which she uses 30% for business purposes.

What are the capital allowances available to her for the period ended 31 May 2017?

A £567

B £1,418

C £1,890

D £425

Test your understanding 7

Adam

Adam's business accounts for the year to 31 March 2017 include the following items.

For each item state what adjustments, if any, are required?

1 Motor expenses for a car used by an employee, private use estimated at 30%.

2 Motor expenses for a car used by Adam, private use estimated at 30%.

3 Overdraft interest on the business bank account.

4 Bank interest received on the business deposit account.

5 Goods taken by Adam which he paid for at cost.

The choices available are:

A None

B Add back full amount

C Deduct full amount

D Add back 30%

E Add back selling price

F Add back profit

Test your understanding 8

Manuel Costa (1)

Manuel Costa is a self-employed wholesale clothing distributor. His summarised accounts for the year ended 30 June 2016 are as follows:

	£	£
Sales		400,000
Opening inventory	40,000	
Purchases	224,000	
	264,000	
Closing inventory	(32,000)	
Cost of sales		(232,000)
Gross profit		168,000
Wages and National Insurance (Note 1)	84,655	
Motor car running expenses		
(Manuel's car) (Note 2)	2,000	
Lighting and heating	4,250	
Rent and business rates	31,060	
Repairs and renewals (all allowable)	3,490	
Legal expenses (Note 3)	1,060	
Depreciation	3,510	
Sundry expenses (all allowable)	5,770	
		(135,795)
Net profit		32,205

Notes to the accounts

(1) Wages

Included in wages are Manuel's drawings of £300 per week, his National Insurance contributions of £146 for the year and wages and National Insurance contributions in respect of his wife totalling £11,750. His wife worked full-time in the business as a secretary.

(2) Motor car running expenses

Manuel estimates that one-third of his mileage is private. Included in the charge is £65 for a speeding fine incurred by Manuel whilst delivering goods to a customer.

(3) Legal expenses

	£
Defending action in respect of alleged faulty goods	330
Defending Manuel in connection with speeding offence	640
Debt collection	90
	1,060

(4) Capital allowances on plant and machinery for the year to 30 June 2016 are £2,480.

Required:

Calculate the taxable trade profits for the accounting period to 30 June 2016.

Test your understanding 9

Manuel Costa (2)

Following on from Activity 8, you are required to complete page SEF 2 (disallowable expenses) for Manuel Costa's tax return for 2016/17.

Business expenses

Please read the 'Self-employment (full) notes' before filling in this section.

	Total expenses If your annual turnover was below £83,000, you may just put your total expenses in box 31		Disallowable expenses Use this column if the figures in boxes 17 to 30 include disallowable amounts
17	Cost of goods bought for resale or goods used £ .00	32	£ .00
18	Construction industry – payments to subcontractors £ .00	33	£ .00
19	Wages, salaries and other staff costs £ .00	34	£ .00
20	Car, van and travel expenses £ .00	35	£ .00
21	Rent, rates, power and insurance costs £ .00	36	£ .00
22	Repairs and renewals of property and equipment £ .00	37	£ .00
23	Phone, fax, stationery and other office costs £ .00	38	£ .00
24	Advertising and business entertainment costs £ .00	39	£ .00
25	Interest on bank and other loans £ .00	40	£ .00
26	Bank, credit card and other financial charges £ .00	41	£ .00
27	Irrecoverable debts written off £ .00	42	£ .00
28	Accountancy, legal and other professional fees £ .00	43	£ .00
29	Depreciation and loss/profit on sale of assets £ .00	44	£ .00
30	Other business expenses £ .00	45	£ .00
31	Total expenses (total of boxes 17 to 30) £ .00	46	Total disallowable expenses (total of boxes 32 to 45) £ .00

SA103F 2016 Page SEF 2

Test your understanding 10

Freda Jones

Freda Jones supplies furniture and furnishings. Her summarised accounts for the year ended 31 December 2016 are as follows:

	£	£
Sales of furniture and furnishings (Note 1)		300,000
Cost of sales		(200,000)
		100,000
Design fees		85,000
Gross profit		185,000
Wages and National Insurance (Note 2)	75,000	
Rent and business rates	18,250	
Miscellaneous expenses (all allowable)	12,710	
Taxation (Freda's income tax)	15,590	
Depreciation	2,540	
Lease rental on car (Freda's car) (Note 3)	8,400	
Motor car running expenses (Freda's car) (Note 4)	2,500	
Lighting and heating	1,750	
		(136,740)
Net profit		48,260

Notes to the accounts

(1) Cost of sales has been reduced by £1,000 reimbursed by Freda for furnishings taken from inventory. This reimbursement represented cost price.

(2) Wages include Freda's drawings of £1,000 per month and her National Insurance contributions of £146 for the year.

(3) Lease rental on car. Freda's car was a BMW costing £50,000 with CO_2 emissions of 150 g/km. The lease was entered into on 1 July 2016.

(4) Motor car running expenses. Freda estimates that one-half of her mileage is private.

(5) Capital allowances for the year to 31 December 2016 are £1,200.

Required:

Calculate the taxable trade profits for the accounting period to 31 December 2016.

 Test your understanding 11

Hudson

Hudson has been carrying on a manufacturing business in a South London suburb since 1 April 2012 preparing accounts to 31 March each year.

He decided to retire on 31 October 2017, and drew up his final set of accounts for the 7 month period to 31 October 2017.

The balance on the general capital allowances pool as at 1 April 2016 was £6,500.

The following plant was acquired for cash on the dates shown:

1 May 2016	New plant costing	£10,858
1 June 2016	Second hand plant costing	£1,000

On 10 July 2016, Hudson bought a car costing £16,000 through his business. Three-quarters of his usage of the car was for business purposes and one-quarter for private purposes. The car has CO_2 emissions of 125 g/km.

No sale of plant took place during these periods, but at 31 October 2017, when the business closed down, all the plant was sold for £2,450 (no one item realising more than its original cost), and the motor car was disposed of to a dealer, who gave Hudson £14,000 for it.

Required:

Calculate the capital allowances for Hudson for the final two accounting periods to 31 October 2017.

Assume the rates of allowances for the tax year 2016/17 continue into the future.

Test your understanding 12

Ethan

Ethan prepares accounts to 31 March annually. In the year to 31 March 2017, he bought three cars for use in his business as follows:

11 May 2016	Purchased car for £17,000 (wholly business usage)
21 June 2016	Purchased car for £8,800 (wholly business usage)
16 September 2016	Purchased car for £11,600 (30% private usage by Ethan)

All the cars have CO_2 emissions between 76 and 130 g/km.

He had never previously acquired any plant and machinery for his business.

In the following year to 31 March 2018, Ethan sold for £9,700 the car originally purchased on 16 September 2016. The car originally purchased on 11 May 2016 was sold for £10,000 on 12 June 2017. There were no other transactions.

Required:

Compute the capital allowances and balancing adjustments for the years ended 31 March 2017 and 31 March 2018.

Assume the rates of allowances for the tax year 2016/17 continue into the future.

Test your understanding 13

Raj

On 1 May 2016, Raj began a small manufacturing business in a rented factory.

He subsequently purchased the following machinery:

		£
2 November 2016	Machinery	20,000
1 February 2017	Car (20% private use by Raj with CO_2 emissions 180 g/km)	16,000
1 February 2017	New tool grinder	6,000
2 October 2017	Car for salesman (with CO_2 emissions 120 g/km)	11,600

Accounts are prepared to 31 March in each year.

Required:

Compute the capital allowances for each accounting period up to 31 March 2018.

Assume the rates of allowances for the tax year 2016/17 continue into the future.

6 Summary

Sole traders must adjust their accounting profits in the same way as companies:

- add back disallowable expenditure
- deduct allowable expenditure which is not shown in the accounts
- deduct income shown in the accounts not taxable as trading income
- add income taxable as trading income which is not shown in the accounts.

The main adjustments applying to individuals but not companies are the disallowance of the proprietor's salary and private expenses, and the adjustment of goods taken for the proprietor's own use.

Capital allowances are then deducted from the adjusted trading profits to give the taxable trading profits. The capital allowances must be restricted for the proprietor's own use of business assets.

7 AAT reference material

The badges of trade

6 Badges of Trade

- Subject matter
- Ownership
- Frequency of transactions
- Improvement expenditure
- Reason for sale
- Motive for profit

Adjustment of profits – sole traders, partnerships and companies

Pro forma for adjustment of profits

	£	£
Net profit as per accounts		X
Add: Expenses charged in the accounts that are not allowable as trading expenses	X	
		X
Less: Income included in the accounts which is not assessable as trading income	X	
		(X)
Adjusted profit/(loss)		X

Disallowed expenses

- Expenses that fail the remoteness test so not "wholly and exclusively" for trading purposes.
- Fines on the business or fraud by directors/owners.
- Qualifying charitable donations (such as Gift Aid donations) will be allowed for companies. Political donations are never allowable.

- Capital expenditure, e.g. purchase of equipment included in profit and loss account.
- Depreciation. Capital allowances granted instead.
- Costs of bringing newly acquired second-hand assets to useable condition.
- Legal and professional expenses relating to capital items or breaking the law.
- Customer entertaining. Staff entertaining can be allowable.
- Customer gifts, unless gift incorporates business advertising, cost is less than £50 per annum per customer, and gift is not food, drink, tobacco or cash vouchers.

Non-assessable income

- Income taxed in any other way, e.g. interest or property income for individuals.
- Profits on sale of fixed assets.

Unincorporated businesses – trading income

Trading income calculated for each period of account:

	£
Adjusted accounting profit	X
Less: Capital allowances:	
Plant and machinery	(X)
Plus: Balancing charges	X
Trading income for the period of account	X

Expenses charged in the accounts which are not allowable as trading expenses

- See adjustment of profits – sole traders, partnerships and companies.
- Transactions with the owner of the business. For example:
  - Add back salary paid to owner. Salaries paid to family members do not need to be added back.
  - Private expenditure included in accounts.
  - Class 2 National Insurance contributions.
  - Goods taken for own use.

Private use assets

- Private use assets have separate column in Capital Allowance computation.
- Disallow private use % of WDA/AIA/FYA.

Capital allowances – business cessation

- In the cessation period of account, no WDA/AIA/FYA.
- Include additions and disposals as normal. Any asset taken over by owner, treat as a disposal at market value. Balancing adjustment made (balancing charge or balancing allowance).

Test your understanding answers

Test your understanding 1

Capone (1)

Adjusted trading profit for 12 months ended 30 June 2016

Expenditure charged but not allowable

Most of the required adjustments will be under this heading.

Start at the top of the statement of profit or loss and work down considering the admissibility of each item in turn and reading any relevant notes.

Do not flit from item to item at random since this is a sure way to overlook something.

If you do not know for certain whether any particular item is allowable or not, do not waste time thinking too much about it – take an informed guess; more often than not you will guess right.

Remember the main rule of allowability – the expenditure must be 'incurred wholly and exclusively for the purposes of the trade', in this case the trade of a wine merchant.

The adjustments under this heading are as follows:

	£	**Reason**
Net profit per accounts	15,219	
Repairs to premises – floor alterations	1,460	Capital cost
Depreciation	4,150	Capital cost
Bad and doubtful debts		
General provision increase	3,350	An appropriation
Loan to ex-employee written off	400	Not wholly and exclusively
Sundry expenses		
Fine	250	Not wholly and exclusively
Salary – Capone	14,000	Appropriation

Notes:

(1) A company could treat the ex-employee loan write-off as a non-trade interest expense under the loan relationship rules. No such relief is available for a sole trader incurring a similar loss.

(2) It is assumed that Capone's wife's salary can be justified as a business expense.

Income credited but not taxable as trading income

It is fairly likely that all credit items will either be assessed as a type of non-trading income or will be capital items or will not be taxable.

The adjustment under this heading is as follows:

	£	**Reason**
Dividend income	300	Taxed as dividend income

Income not credited but assessable

An adjustment under this heading will normally arise because goods have been taken for the proprietor's own use. Legal precedent has established that this 'sale' is to be brought to account for tax purposes at full market price, i.e. (£455 × $^{100}/_{65}$) = £700.

The £700 will be an addition to the profits per the accounts in calculating adjusted trading profits, i.e. an adjustment on the plus side of the computation.

Capone

Adjustment of profits for 12 months ended 30 June 2016

	+	–
	£	£
Net profit per accounts	15,219	
Repairs – alterations to flooring	1,460	
Depreciation	4,150	
Bad and doubtful debts		
General provision increase	3,350	
Loan to ex-employee written off	400	
Sundry expenses		
Fine	250	
Salary – Capone	14,000	
Dividends		300
Goods withdrawn by Capone (£455 × $\frac{100}{65}$)	700	
	39,529	300
	(300)	
Adjusted trading profit (before capital allowances)	39,229	

Test your understanding 2

Ernest

Capital allowances computation – plant and machinery

	General pool	Private use asset		Allowances
	£	£		£
Year ended 31 March 2017				
TWDV b/f at 1 April 2016	24,000			
Additions: No AIA: Cars				
15 April 2016	16,000			
16 July 2016	9,200			
17 August 2016		9,400		
Disposals				
30 April 2016	(3,200)			
	46,000			
WDA (18%)	(8,280)	(1,692)	× 70%	9,464
TWDV c/f	37,720	7,708		
Total allowances				9,464
Year ended 31 March 2018				
Disposals				
Car proceeds	(9,400)	(8,100)		
Balancing charge		(392)	× 70%	(274)
	28,320			
WDA 18%	(5,098)			5,098
TWDV at 31 March 2018	23,222			
Total allowances				4,824

Test your understanding 3

Anjula

The correct answer is B.

Explanation

B is the correct answer because:

- the equipment attracts 100% AIA
- the car attracts a WDA of 18% pro-rated up by 16/12 as the first accounting period is 16 months long.

The calculation is therefore:

	£
AIA	2,500
WDA (£6,200 × 18% × 16/12)	1,488
Total allowances	3,988

Test your understanding 4

Capone (2)

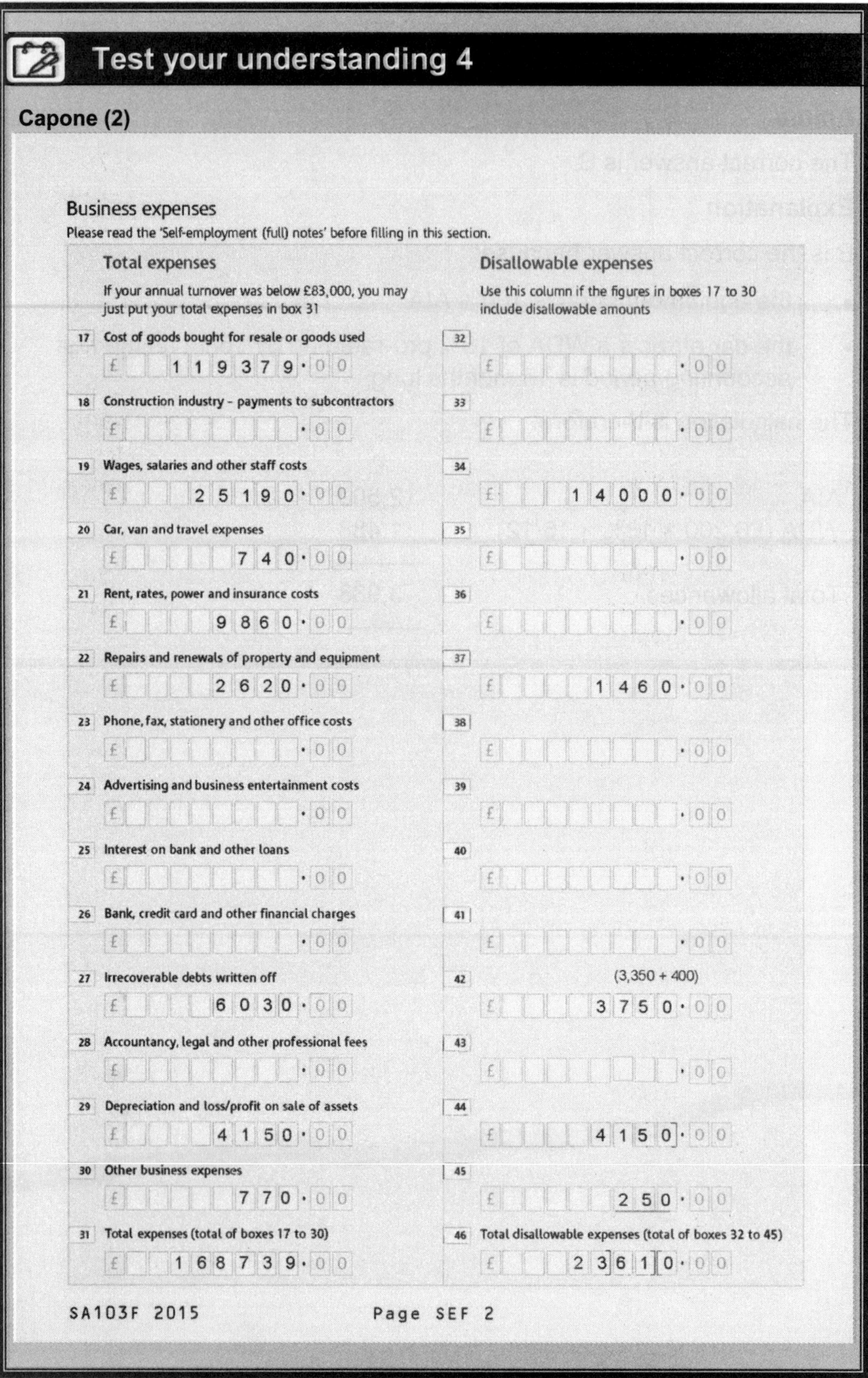

Business expenses

Please read the 'Self-employment (full) notes' before filling in this section.

Box	Total expenses If your annual turnover was below £83,000, you may just put your total expenses in box 31	£	Box	Disallowable expenses Use this column if the figures in boxes 17 to 30 include disallowable amounts	£
17	Cost of goods bought for resale or goods used	119379.00	32		.00
18	Construction industry – payments to subcontractors	.00	33		.00
19	Wages, salaries and other staff costs	25190.00	34		14000.00
20	Car, van and travel expenses	740.00	35		.00
21	Rent, rates, power and insurance costs	9860.00	36		.00
22	Repairs and renewals of property and equipment	2620.00	37		1460.00
23	Phone, fax, stationery and other office costs	.00	38		.00
24	Advertising and business entertainment costs	.00	39		.00
25	Interest on bank and other loans	.00	40		.00
26	Bank, credit card and other financial charges	.00	41		.00
27	Irrecoverable debts written off	6030.00	42	(3,350 + 400)	3750.00
28	Accountancy, legal and other professional fees	.00	43		.00
29	Depreciation and loss/profit on sale of assets	4150.00	44		4150.00
30	Other business expenses	770.00	45		250.00
31	Total expenses (total of boxes 17 to 30)	168739.00	46	Total disallowable expenses (total of boxes 32 to 45)	23610.00

SA103F 2015 Page SEF 2

Test your understanding 5

Patrick

The correct answer is:

	£	✓ or ✗
Patrick's business travelling expenses	5,175	✓
Christmas presents for staff	250	✓
Entertaining overseas suppliers	2,750	✗
Entertaining UK customers	2,300	✗
Gifts to customers that carry the business name:		
– Boxes of chocolates costing £5.00 each	125	✗
– Calendars costing £1.50 each	150	✓
Donation to national charity	50	✗
Donation to local political party	100	✗
Subscription to chamber of commerce	25	✓
A gift to a member of staff upon marriage	45	✓
Patrick's squash club subscription	250	✗
Advertising in trade press	280	✓

✓ = allowable ✗ = add back as disallowable expense

Test your understanding 6

Georgina

The correct answer is D.

Explanation

D is the correct answer because the car attracts a WDA at 18%, pro-rated for the short 9 month accounting period and adjusted for private use, as follows:

9 months ended 31 May 2017	Private use car		Allowances
	£		£
Addition – no AIA	10,500		
WDA (18% × 9/12)	(1,418)	× 30%	425
TWDV c/f	9,082		

Test your understanding 7

Adam

The correct answers are as follows:

1 A These are fully allowable from the business point of view and, as they have already been deducted in the accounts, no adjustment is required. The employee may be assessed on the private use as a taxable benefit.

2 D 30% of the motor expenses should be added back as the private use is by the owner of the business.

3 A This is an allowable trade expense and, as it has already been deducted in the accounts, no adjustment is required.

4 C Bank interest is not taxed as trading profits, therefore deduct in full.

5 F Add back the profit that would have been made had Adam paid the full selling price.

Test your understanding 8

Manuel Costa (1)

Adjustment of profits for 12 months ended 30 June 2016

	£
Net profit per accounts	32,205
Manuel's drawings (£300 × 52)	15,600
Manuel's NIC	146
Speeding fine	65
Motor expenses (1/3 of balance) (£2,000 – £65) × $^1/_3$	645
Legal expenses in connection with speeding offence	640
Depreciation	3,510
	52,811
Less: Capital allowances	(2,480)
Taxable trade profits	50,331

Test your understanding 9

Manuel Costa (2)

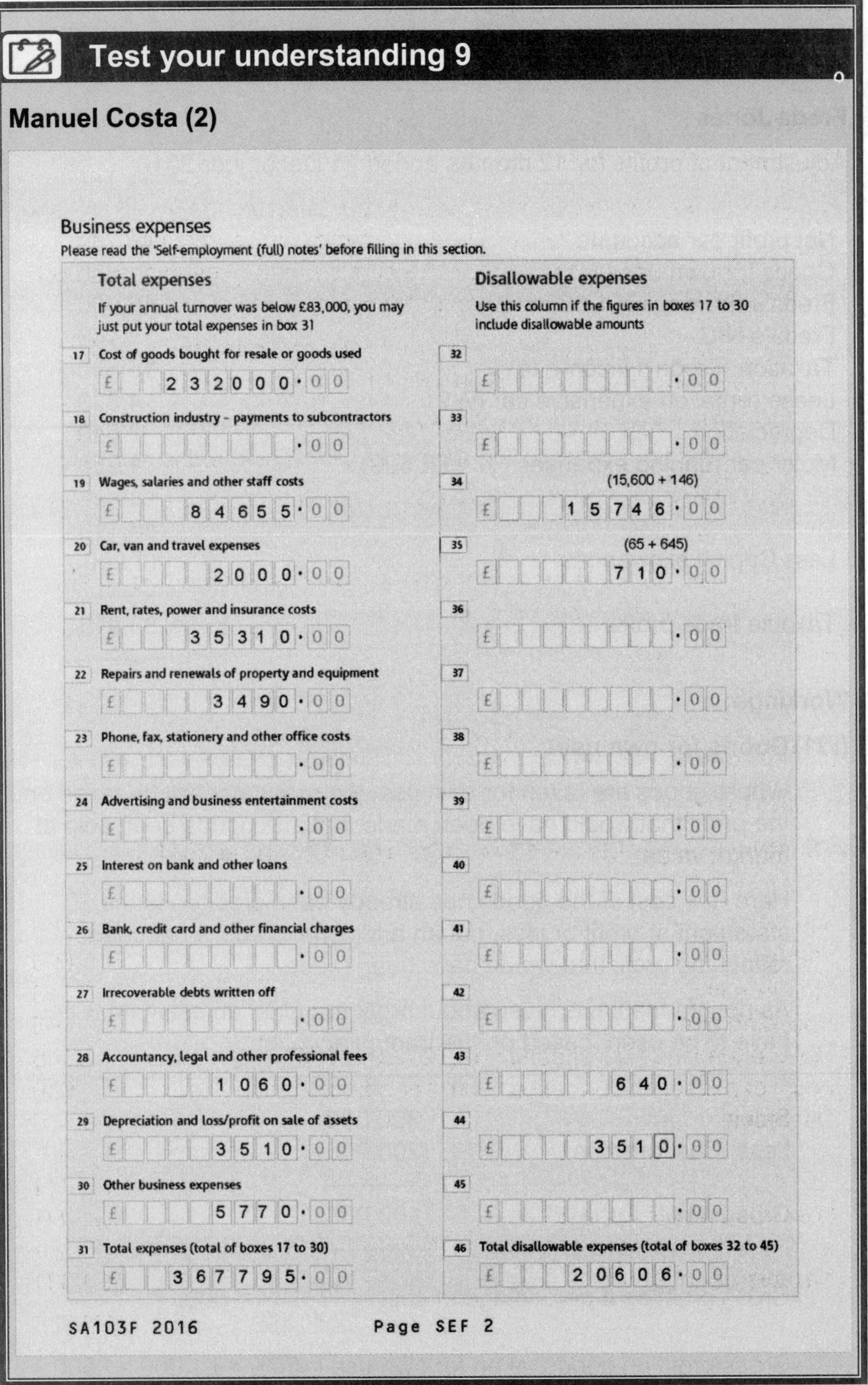

Business expenses

Please read the 'Self-employment (full) notes' before filling in this section.

Total expenses If your annual turnover was below £83,000, you may just put your total expenses in box 31		Disallowable expenses Use this column if the figures in boxes 17 to 30 include disallowable amounts	
17 Cost of goods bought for resale or goods used	£ 232000.00	32	£ .00
18 Construction industry – payments to subcontractors	£ .00	33	£ .00
19 Wages, salaries and other staff costs	£ 84655.00	34 (15,600 + 146)	£ 15746.00
20 Car, van and travel expenses	£ 2000.00	35 (65 + 645)	£ 710.00
21 Rent, rates, power and insurance costs	£ 35310.00	36	£ .00
22 Repairs and renewals of property and equipment	£ 3490.00	37	£ .00
23 Phone, fax, stationery and other office costs	£ .00	38	£ .00
24 Advertising and business entertainment costs	£ .00	39	£ .00
25 Interest on bank and other loans	£ .00	40	£ .00
26 Bank, credit card and other financial charges	£ .00	41	£ .00
27 Irrecoverable debts written off	£ .00	42	£ .00
28 Accountancy, legal and other professional fees	£ 1060.00	43	£ 640.00
29 Depreciation and loss/profit on sale of assets	£ 3510.00	44	£ 3510.00
30 Other business expenses	£ 5770.00	45	£ .00
31 Total expenses (total of boxes 17 to 30)	£ 367795.00	46 Total disallowable expenses (total of boxes 32 to 45)	£ 20606.00

SA103F 2016 Page SEF 2

Test your understanding 10

Freda Jones

Adjustment of profits for 12 months ended 31 December 2016

	£
Net profit per accounts	48,260
Goods for own use (W1)	500
Freda's drawings (£1,000 × 12)	12,000
Freda's NIC	146
Taxation (Freda's income tax)	15,590
Lease rental on expensive car (W2)	4,830
Depreciation	2,540
Motor car running expenses (½ × £2,500)	1,250
	85,116
Less Capital allowances	(1,200)
Taxable trade profits	83,916

Workings:

(W1) Goods for own use

Where goods are taken for own use, the proprietor will be taxed on the profit that would have been made, had the goods been sold at market value.

Here, the cost of the goods has already been credited to the statement of profit or loss, but an additional credit is needed to reflect the profit that would have been made.

As no information is given about profit margins, an estimate will have to be used, based on the trading account.

	£
Sales	300,000
Less: Cost of sales	(200,000)
Gross profit	100,000

Gross profit as a percentage of cost = $\frac{100,000}{200,000}$ = 50%

Gross profit on goods taken for own use = 50% × £1,000 = £500

(W2) Lease rental on high emission car

Amount to be disallowed is 15% of hire charges:

Disallowed amount = 15% × £8,400 = £1,260

The car is also used privately so in addition to the disallowable amount calculated above, the private use element of the balance must also be disallowed.

Balance of expenditure £8,400 – £1,260 = £7,140

Private use element £7,140 × 1/2 = £3,570

Total amount disallowed:

	£
High emission element	1,260
Private use element	3,570
	4,830

Alternative calculation:

Amount allowed = (£8,400 × 85% × 50%) = £3,570

Amount to be added back = (£8,400 – £3,570) = £4,830

Test your understanding 11

Hudson

Capital allowances computation

		General pool	Private use asset		Allowances
	£	£	£		£
Year ended 31 March 2017					
TWDV b/f		6,500			
Addition – No AIA			16,000		
Addition qualifying for AIA:					
– New plant	10,858				
– Second hand plant	1,000				
	11,858				
Less: AIA	(11,858)				11,858
		Nil			
WDA @ 18%		(1,170)	(2,880)	× 75%	3,330
TWDV c/f		5,330	13,120		
Total allowances					15,188
7 months ended 31 Oct 2017					
Disposal proceeds		(2,450)	(14,000)		
Balancing allowance		2,880			2,880
Balancing charge			(880)	× 75%	(660)
Total allowances					2,220

Note: No WDAs are given in the final accounting period.

Test your understanding 12

Ethan

Capital allowances computation

	General pool	Private use asset	Allowances
	£	£	£
Year ended 31 March 2017			
Additions not qualifying for AIA			
11 May 2016	17,000		
21 June 2016	8,800		
16 September 2016		11,600	
	25,800		
WDA (18% × £25,800)	(4,644)		4,644
WDA (18% × 11,600) (Note 1)		(2,088)	1,462
TWDV c/f	21,156	9,512	
Total allowances			6,106
Year ended 31 March 2018			
Disposals	(10,000)	(9,700)	
	11,156	(188)	
Balancing charge (Note 2)		188	(132)
WDA (18% × £11,156)	(2,008)		2,008
TWDV c/f	9,148		
Total allowances			1,876

Notes:

(1) Business portion of WDA = (£2,088 × 70%) = £1,462

(2) Business portion of charge = (£188 × 70%) = £132

Test your understanding 13

Raj

Capital allowances computation

		General pool	Private use asset		Allowances
	£	£	£		£
11 m/e 31 March 2017					
Additions not qualifying for AIA					
Car			16,000		
Additions qualifying for AIA					
Machinery	20,000				
Tool grinder	6,000				
	26,000				
Less: AIA (Note)	(26,000)				26,000
		Nil			
WDA (8% × 11/12 × £16,000)			(1,173)	× 80%	938
TWDV c/f		Nil	14,827		
Total allowances					26,938
Year ended 31 March 2018					
Additions not qualifying for AIA					
Car		11,600			
		11,600			
WDA (18% × £11,600)		(2,088)			2,088
WDA (8% × £14,827)			(1,186)	× 80%	949
TWDV c/f		9,512	13,641		
Total allowances					3,037

Partnership profit allocation

Introduction

Some of the tasks in the assessment will relate to either a sole trader or a partnership (i.e. an unincorporated business).

Both are given the same tax treatment with one extra step for partnerships, which is covered in this chapter.

ASSESSMENT CRITERIA

Apportion profits between a maximum of four partners (1.4)

Allocate profits between the partners (1.4)

Accurately complete partnership tax returns (1.6)

CONTENTS

1 Allocation of profits

1.1 Computation of taxable trade profits

There is no difference between a sole trader and a partnership when applying the rules for computing the adjustment of the profits of a partnership.

A partnership is merely treated for tax purposes as a collection of sole traders.

Each partner is assessed on his share of partnership profits as if he were a sole trader earning those profits.

1.2 Division of profits between partners

Profits are allocated according to the profit sharing arrangements during the *accounting period* in which profits are earned.

Example

Andrew and Bernard have been in business for many years, drawing up their accounts to 31 December each year, and sharing profits in the ratio of 2:1.

The partnership's taxable trade profits for the year ended 31 December 2016 were £37,500.

Show how these profits are allocated to partners.

Solution

Year ended 31 December 2016	**Total**	**Andrew**	**Bernard**
Profits split (2:1)	£37,500	£25,000	£12,500

Test your understanding 1

John and Kyle

John and Kyle began in partnership on 6 April 2016 and have taxable trading profits for the year to 5 April 2017 of £24,047.

They have agreed to share profits and losses in the ratio of 3:2.

Calculate each partner's share of the taxable profits for the year ended 5 April 2017.

Example

Vivienne, Caroline, Nathan and Marie started business on 1 January 2016. They shared profits as follows:

Interest on fixed capital	10%
Salaries	
Vivienne	£3,000 per annum
Caroline	£4,000 per annum
Nathan	£4,000 per annum
Marie	£3,000 per annum
Share of balance	
Vivienne	50%
Caroline	20%
Nathan	10%
Marie	20%

Capital account balances were as follows:

Vivienne	£10,000
Caroline	£5,000
Nathan	£5,000
Marie	£5,000

The taxable trade profits of the partnership for the year ended 31 December 2016 were £100,000.

Show how these profits are allocated to the partners.

Solution

Profits are allocated as follows:

	Total	**V**	**C**	**N**	**M**
	£	£	£	£	£
Interest on capital					
(10% × capital)	2,500	1,000	500	500	500
Salaries	14,000	3,000	4,000	4,000	3,000
Balance (50:20:10:20)	83,500	41,750	16,700	8,350	16,700
Total taxable profits	100,000	45,750	21,200	12,850	20,200

It is important to realise that the whole profit of £100,000 is classed as taxable trade profits.

Even though there is reference to salaries and interest, this is merely a means of allocation. For example, Vivienne is now treated as having taxable trade profits of £45,750; she is not regarded as having received interest income or employment income.

2 Change in profit sharing arrangements

2.1 Principle of allocating profits

Where there is a change in the profit sharing arrangements during the accounting period, the period must be split into two or more parts (depending on the number of changes), with a separate division among the partners for each part.

Example

Rosie, Fran and Gilly have been in business for many years.

During the year ended 31 December 2016, their taxable trade profits were £94,000. Profits were shared as follows:

	Rosie	**Fran**	**Gilly**
	£	£	£
To 30 June 2016			
Salary (per annum)	10,000	6,100	–
Balance	1	1	1
To 31 December 2016			
Salary (per annum)	Nil	Nil	Nil
Balance	2	1	1

Show how the profits would be allocated between the partners.

Solution

Beware, the salaries are quoted per annum; if a change occurs during an accounting period the salary must be time apportioned.

Year ended 31 December 2016

	Total	Rosie	Fran	Gilly
	£	£	£	£
Period 1 January 2016 – 30 June 2016 (6/12)				
Salary	8,050	5,000	3,050	
Balance (1:1:1)	38,950	12,983	12,983	12,984
(£94,000 × 6/12)	47,000			
Period 1 July 2016 – 31 December 2016 (6/12)				
Balance (2:1:1)	47,000	23,500	11,750	11,750
Total	94,000	41,483	27,783	24,734

The profits are deemed to accrue evenly over time.

Each partner now has their own taxable trade profits for the accounting period.

Test your understanding 2

Read the following statements and state whether they are true or false.

1 A partnership pays tax on the partnership profits.

2 Brian and Mary trade in partnership sharing profits equally and preparing accounts to 31 December. If they want to change their profit shares to 1/3:2/3 on 1 July 2016 they need to prepare accounts to 30 June 2016.

3 Partners' salaries and interest on capital are deductible in computing adjusted trading profit.

The AAT reference material set out in section 8 includes brief details on partnership allocations. It also includes mention of basis periods which are dealt with in Chapter 11.

3 Partnership changes

3.1 Principle of allocating profits

Where there is a change in the partnership during the accounting period, the period must be split into two or more parts (depending on the number of changes), exactly as for a change in the profit share arrangement.

A change in the partnership may occur when a new partner is admitted.

 **Example**

Charles and David began to trade in partnership with effect from 1 July 2013, preparing accounts to 30 June each year and sharing profits equally.

On 1 January 2015, Edward joined the partnership. Profits were then split in the ratio 2:2:1.

The tax adjusted trading profits of the partnership were as follows:

	£
Year ended 30 June 2014	70,000
Year ended 30 June 2015	73,200
Year ended 30 June 2016	74,000

Show the profit allocation for each partner for each accounting period.

Solution

Allocate accounting period profits to partners according to profit share, splitting the accounting period where appropriate.

	Total	**C**	**D**	**E**
	£	£	£	£
Year ended 30 June 2014 (1:1)	70,000	35,000	35,000	–
Year ended 30 June 2015				
1 July 2014 – 31 Dec 2014 (1:1) $\frac{6}{12}$	36,600	18,300	18,300	–
1 Jan 2015 – 30 June 2015 (2:2:1) $\frac{6}{12}$	36,600	14,640	14,640	7,320
	73,200	32,940	32,940	7,320
Year ended 30 June 2016 (2:2:1)	74,000	29,600	29,600	14,800

A change in the partnership may also occur when a partner leaves the partnership or dies.

 **Example**

Fred, George and Harry began to trade in partnership with effect from 1 July 2013, preparing accounts to 30 June each year and sharing profits equally.

On 31 October 2016 George died. Profits and losses were then split in the ratio 3:2.

The tax adjusted trading profits of the partnership were as follows:

	£
Year ended 30 June 2014	60,000
Year ended 30 June 2015	85,200
Year ended 30 June 2016	75,000
Year ended 30 June 2017	75,600

Show the profit allocation for each partner for each accounting period.

Solution

Allocate accounting period profits to partners according to profit share, splitting the accounting period where appropriate.

	Total	**F**	**G**	**H**
	£	£	£	£
Year ended 30 June 2014 (1:1:1)	60,000	20,000	20,000	20,000
Year ended 30 June 2015 (1:1:1)	85,200	28,400	28,400	28,400
Year ended 30 June 2016 (1:1:1)	75,000	25,000	25,000	25,000
Year ended 30 June 2017				
1 July 2016 – 31 Oct 2017 (1:1:1) $\frac{4}{12}$	25,200	8,400	8,400	8,400
1 Nov 2017 – 30 June 2018 (3:2) $\frac{8}{12}$	50,400	30,240	–	20,160
	75,600	38,640	8,400	28,560

The assessor has confirmed that in the assessment there will be a maximum of four partners in any one scenario.

The assessment could test changes to a partnership agreement and/or changes to the members of a partnership.

Test your understanding 3

Michael, Nick and Liz (1)

Michael Peters and Nick Wyatt commenced business as printers on 1 October 2013, preparing accounts to 30 September each year and sharing profits equally.

On 1 January 2015, Liz Stretton was admitted to the partnership and profits continued to be shared equally.

On 30 June 2016, Nick retired. Profits continued to be shared equally.

On 31 December 2017 the partnership was dissolved.

The adjusted profits of the partnership, after deducting capital allowances, were as follows:

	£
Year ended 30 September 2014	30,000
Year ended 30 September 2015	36,000
Year ended 30 September 2016	42,500
Year ended 30 September 2017	40,000
Three months to 31 December 2017	17,500

Required:

Show the allocation of profits to each partner for all accounting periods.

4 Partnership interest income

4.1 Allocation of partnership interest income

Interest received by a partnership must be deducted in the partnership adjustment of profits computation as it is not trading income.

The income must however be assessed on the partners.

The interest is therefore apportioned between the partners according to the profit sharing ratio applicable to the balance of trading income, on the date the interest is received.

Each partner then includes his share of the interest in his personal income tax return.

5 Partnership tax return

5.1 Partnership tax return

Although the partnership does not pay its own tax liability, there is still a requirement to file a tax return for the partnership. One partner will be nominated by the other members of the partnership to complete and submit the return.

The return covers details of the partnership income and related information. It also includes a partnership statement, which shows each partner's share of profits, losses and income. Each individual partner will then enter this information on their own personal tax return.

The partnership return consists of 8 pages, broken down as follows:

- Page 1 – There is no information to complete on the first page, which simply sets out the partners' responsibilities.
- The long form return (4 pages) – Pages 2 to 5.
- The short form return (2 pages) – Pages 6 and 7.
- Page 8 – Other information relevant to the partnership.

In an assessment you will only be required to complete the short form return.

5.2 Partnership tax return: Page 6

This page is the first page of the 'partnership statement (short)', which will be used by the individual partners to make entries on their personal tax returns.

Information is transferred from the remainder of the return and then allocated between the partners.

The tax adjusted trading profit of the partnership is put in Box 11, or the trading loss is inserted in Box 12.

It is possible that the partnership will also have received interest income. If so, this needs to be entered in Box 22. This interest will not necessarily have been taxed (as stated in the narrative on the return), however these rules have changed under Finance Act 2016 and a new version of the tax return is not yet available.

The short statement caters for up to 3 partners when page 7 is used but in the assessment you will only have to complete one partner's information on page 6.

You should complete Boxes 6 – 10 for individual partner details with the information provided in the assessment, if applicable, regarding the name, address, unique taxpayer reference, NI number and date appointed or ceased as a partner.

The trading profit or loss should then be apportioned between the partners according to the profit sharing agreement, and entered in Boxes 11 or 12 on each partner's statement.

The partnership may have received payments under the Construction Industry Scheme (CIS). Any tax deducted from such payments should be entered in Box 24 for the partnership with the appropriate amounts entered in Box 24 for each of the individual partners.

You do not need to give any further information if the split is a simple profit sharing ratio, but if any partner is entitled to a salary or interest on capital, this should be explained in Box 3.116 – 'additional information' on page 5 of the long form return. This explanation on the long form return will not be required in the assessment.

Any interest received by the partnership will be apportioned between the partners according to the profit sharing ratio on the date of receipt of the interest, and entered in Box 22 on each partner's statement.

You should ignore the text which says 'Copy this figure to box …' as this is only relevant when completing the partner's individual income tax returns.

5.3 Completing the tax return

The following is important in connection with the completion of forms in the assessment.

- When completing the form in the assessment, figures must be entered in the correct boxes.
- Commas need not be entered for numbers of four digits or more.
- You do not need to fill in every box, only relevant ones.

Page 6 is shown overleaf.

PARTNERSHIP STATEMENT (SHORT) for the year ended 5 April 2017

Please read these instructions before completing the Statement

Use these pages to allocate partnership income if the only income for the relevant return period was trading and professional income or taxed interest and alternative finance receipts from banks and building societies. Otherwise you must download or ask the SA Orderline for the 'Partnership Statement (Full)' pages to record details of the allocation of all the partnership income. Go to **www.gov.uk/self-assessment-forms-and-helpsheets**

Step 1 Fill in boxes 1 to 29 and boxes A and B as appropriate. Get the figures you need from the relevant boxes in the Partnership Tax Return. Complete a separate Statement for each accounting period covered by this Partnership Tax Return and for each trade or profession carried on by the partnership.

Step 2 Then allocate the amounts in boxes 11 to 29 attributable to each partner using the allocation columns on this page and page 7, read the Partnership Tax Return Guide, go to www.gov.uk/self-assessment-forms-and-helpsheets
If the partnership has more than 3 partners, please photocopy page 7.

Step 3 Each partner will need a copy of their allocation of income to fill in their personal tax return.

PARTNERSHIP INFORMATION

If the partnership business includes a trade or profession, enter here the accounting period for which appropriate items in this statement are returned.

Start **1** / /

End **2** / /

Nature of trade **3**

MIXED PARTNERSHIPS

Tick here if this Statement is drawn up using Corporation Tax rules **4**

Tick here if this Statement is drawn up using tax rules for non-residents **5**

Individual partner details

6 Name of partner

Address

Postcode

Date appointed as a partner (if during 2015–16 or 2016–17) **7** / /

Partner's Unique Taxpayer Reference (UTR) **8**

Date ceased to be a partner (if during 2015–16 or 2016–17) **9** / /

Partner's National Insurance number **10**

Partnership's profits, losses, income, tax credits, etc	Tick this box if the items entered in the box had foreign tax taken off		Partner's share of profits, losses, income, tax credits, etc	Copy figures in boxes 11 to 29 to boxes in the individual's **Partnership (short)** pages as shown below
• **for an accounting period ended in 2016–17**	▼			
from box 3.83 Profit from a trade or profession	A	11 £	Profit 11 £	Copy this figure to box 8
from box 3.82 Adjustment on change of basis		11A £	11A £	Copy this figure to box 10
from box 3.84 Loss from a trade or profession	B	12 £	Loss 12 £	Copy this figure to box 8
from box 10.4 Business Premises Renovation Allowance		12A £	12A £	Copy this figure to box 15
• **for the period 6 April 2016 to 5 April 2017***				
from box 7.9A UK taxed interest and taxed alternative finance receipts		22 £	22 £	Copy this figure to box 28
from box 3.97 CIS deductions made by contractors on account of tax		24 £	24 £	Copy this figure to box 30
from box 3.98 Other tax taken off trading income		24A £	24A £	Copy this figure to box 31
from box 7.8A Income Tax taken off		25 £	25 £	Copy this figure to box 29
from box 3.117 Partnership charges		29 £	29 £	Copy this figure to box 4, 'Other tax reliefs' section on page Ai 2 in your personal tax return

* if you are a 'CT Partnership' see the Partnership Tax Return Guide

SA800 2016 PARTNERSHIP TAX RETURN: PAGE 6

Test your understanding 4

Michael, Nick and Liz (2)

Following on from TYU 3, complete page 6 of the partnership return in respect of the year ended 30 September 2016 for Michael.

PARTNERSHIP STATEMENT (SHORT) for the year ended 5 April 2017

Please read these instructions before completing the Statement

Use these pages to allocate partnership income if the only income for the relevant return period was trading and professional income or taxed interest and alternative finance receipts from banks and building societies. Otherwise you must download or ask the SA Orderline for the 'Partnership Statement (Full)' pages to record details of the allocation of all the partnership income. Go to **www.gov.uk/self-assessment-forms-and-helpsheets**

Step 1 Fill in boxes 1 to 29 and boxes A and B as appropriate. Get the figures you need from the relevant boxes in the Partnership Tax Return. Complete a separate Statement for each accounting period covered by this Partnership Tax Return and for each trade or profession carried on by the partnership.

Step 2 Then allocate the amounts in boxes 11 to 29 attributable to each partner using the allocation columns on this page and page 7, read the Partnership Tax Return Guide, go to www.gov.uk/self-assessment-forms-and-helpsheets
If the partnership has more than 3 partners, please photocopy page 7.

Step 3 Each partner will need a copy of their allocation of income to fill in their personal tax return.

PARTNERSHIP INFORMATION
If the partnership business includes a trade or profession, enter here the accounting period for which appropriate items in this statement are returned.

Start **1** / /

End **2** / /

Nature of trade **3**

MIXED PARTNERSHIPS

Tick here if this Statement is drawn up using Corporation Tax rules **4**

Tick here if this Statement is drawn up using tax rules for non-residents **5**

Individual partner details

6 Name of partner

Address

Postcode

Date appointed as a partner (if during 2015–16 or 2016–17) **7** / /

Partner's Unique Taxpayer Reference (UTR) **8**

Date ceased to be a partner (if during 2015–16 or 2016–17) **9** / /

Partner's National Insurance number **10**

Partnership's profits, losses, income, tax credits, etc	Tick this box if the items entered in the box had foreign tax taken off		Partner's share of profits, losses, income, tax credits, etc	Copy figures in boxes 11 to 29 to boxes in the individual's **Partnership (short)** pages as shown below
• **for an accounting period ended in 2016–17**				
from box 3.83 Profit from a trade or profession	A	11 £	Profit 11 £	Copy this figure to box 8
from box 3.82 Adjustment on change of basis		11A £	11A £	Copy this figure to box 10
from box 3.84 Loss from a trade or profession	B	12 £	Loss 12 £	Copy this figure to box 8
from box 10.4 Business Premises Renovation Allowance		12A £	12A £	Copy this figure to box 15
• **for the period 6 April 2016 to 5 April 2017***				
from box 7.9A UK taxed interest and taxed alternative finance receipts		22 £	22 £	Copy this figure to box 28
from box 3.97 CIS deductions made by contractors on account of tax		24 £	24 £	Copy this figure to box 30
from box 3.98 Other tax taken off trading income		24A £	24A £	Copy this figure to box 31
from box 7.8A Income Tax taken off		25 £	25 £	Copy this figure to box 29
from box 3.117 Partnership charges		29 £	29 £	Copy this figure to box 4, 'Other tax reliefs' section on page Ai 2 in your personal tax return

* if you are a 'CT Partnership' see the Partnership Tax Return Guide

SA800 2016 PARTNERSHIP TAX RETURN: PAGE 6

6 Test your understanding

Test your understanding 5

Lindsay, Tricia and Kate (1)

Lindsay and Tricia have been in partnership for many years, running a dry cleaning business. They prepare their accounts to 31 March each year. Their profit sharing ratio has always been 3:2.

On 1 August 2016, Kate joined the partnership and the profit sharing ratio was changed to 4:3:2 for Lindsay, Tricia and Kate.

For the year ended 31 March 2017, the trading profit was £150,000.

The division of profit would be calculated as:

	Total	Lindsay	Tricia	Kate
	£	£	£	£
Period to [ ]	1	2	3	
Period to [ ]	4	5	6	7

Options

1	A	£150,000
	B	£75,000
	C	£50,000
	D	£100,000
2	A	£30,000
	B	£20,000
	C	£45,000
	D	£90,000
3	A	£30,000
	B	£20,000
	C	£60,000
	D	£40,000

4	A	£150,000
	B	£75,000
	C	£50,000
	D	£100,000
5	A	£33,333
	B	£22,222
	C	£66,667
	D	£44,445
6	A	£22,222
	B	£25,000
	C	£33,333
	D	£44,445
7	A	£16,667
	B	£22,222
	C	£33,333
	D	£44,445

Test your understanding 6

Anne, Betty, Chloe and Diana

Anne and Betty have been in partnership since 1 January 2004 sharing profits equally.

On 30 June 2015, Betty resigned as a partner and was replaced on 1 July 2015 by Chloe. Diana was admitted as a partner on 1 April 2016. Profits were shared equally throughout.

The partnership's taxable trade profits are as follows:

		£
Year ended	31 December 2015	60,000
Year ended	31 December 2016	72,000

Required:

Show the allocation of the taxable trade profits between the partners for each of the years to 31 December 2015 and 2016.

Test your understanding 7

Bert and Harold

Bert and Harold have traded in partnership for several years. Their accounts for the year ended 30 September 2016 show taxable trade profits of £16,500.

Bert and Harold changed their profit-sharing ratio on 1 July 2016. The old profit-sharing ratio applies until 30 June 2016, and the new ratio applies from 1 July 2016.

	Bert	**Harold**
Old ratio:		
Salaries p.a.	£3,000	£2,000
Share of balance	3/5	2/5
New ratio:		
Salaries p.a.	£6,000	£4,000
Share of balance	2/3	1/3

Required:

Show the allocation of the taxable trade profits between the partners for the year to 30 September 2016.

Test your understanding 8

Peter and Nathan Flannery

Brothers Peter and Nathan Flannery have traded in partnership as Superhero Supplies for many years, trading in books and comics.

Their tax adjusted trading profits for the year ended 31 March 2017 are £130,400, and the partnership received interest of £16,210.

Peter and Nathan have always shared the profits of their business in the ratio 4:3.

Required:

Complete page 6 of the partnership tax return in respect of the year ended 31 March 2017 for the partnership as a whole and for Peter.

PARTNERSHIP STATEMENT (SHORT) for the year ended 5 April 2017

Please read these instructions before completing the Statement

Use these pages to allocate partnership income if the only income for the relevant return period was trading and professional income or taxed interest and alternative finance receipts from banks and building societies. Otherwise you must download or ask the SA Orderline for the 'Partnership Statement (Full)' pages to record details of the allocation of all the partnership income. Go to **www.gov.uk/self-assessment-forms-and-helpsheets**

Step 1 Fill in boxes 1 to 29 and boxes A and B as appropriate. Get the figures you need from the relevant boxes in the Partnership Tax Return. Complete a separate Statement for each accounting period covered by this Partnership Tax Return and for each trade or profession carried on by the partnership.

Step 2 Then allocate the amounts in boxes 11 to 29 attributable to each partner using the allocation columns on this page and page 7, read the Partnership Tax Return Guide, go to www.gov.uk/self-assessment-forms-and-helpsheets
If the partnership has more than 3 partners, please photocopy page 7.

Step 3 Each partner will need a copy of their allocation of income to fill in their personal tax return.

PARTNERSHIP INFORMATION
If the partnership business includes a trade or profession, enter here the accounting period for which appropriate items in this statement are returned.

Start **1** / /

End **2** / /

Nature of trade **3**

MIXED PARTNERSHIPS

Tick here if this Statement is drawn up using Corporation Tax rules **4**

Tick here if this Statement is drawn up using tax rules for non-residents **5**

Individual partner details

6 Name of partner

Address

Postcode

Date appointed as a partner (if during 2015–16 or 2016–17) **7** / /

Partner's Unique Taxpayer Reference (UTR) **8**

Date ceased to be a partner (if during 2015–16 or 2016–17) **9** / /

Partner's National Insurance number **10**

Partnership's profits, losses, income, tax credits, etc		Tick this box if the items entered in the box had foreign tax taken off		Partner's share of profits, losses, income, tax credits, etc		Copy figures in boxes 11 to 29 to boxes in the individual's **Partnership (short)** pages as shown below
• **for an accounting period ended in 2016–17**		▼				
from box 3.83	Profit from a trade or profession	**A**	**11** £	Profit	**11** £	Copy this figure to box 8
from box 3.82	Adjustment on change of basis		**11A** £		**11A** £	Copy this figure to box 10
from box 3.84	Loss from a trade or profession	**B**	**12** £	Loss	**12** £	Copy this figure to box 8
from box 10.4	Business Premises Renovation Allowance		**12A** £		**12A** £	Copy this figure to box 15
• **for the period 6 April 2016 to 5 April 2017***						
from box 7.9A	UK taxed interest and taxed alternative finance receipts		**22** £		**22** £	Copy this figure to box 28
from box 3.97	CIS deductions made by contractors on account of tax		**24** £		**24** £	Copy this figure to box 30
from box 3.98	Other tax taken off trading income		**24A** £		**24A** £	Copy this figure to box 31
from box 7.8A	Income Tax taken off		**25** £		**25** £	Copy this figure to box 29
from box 3.117	Partnership charges		**29** £		**29** £	Copy this figure to box 4, 'Other tax reliefs' section on page Ai 2 in your personal tax return

* If you are a 'CT Partnership' see the Partnership Tax Return Guide

SA800 2016 PARTNERSHIP TAX RETURN: PAGE 6

Test your understanding 9

Lindsay, Tricia and Kate (2)

For Lindsay in Test your understanding 5, complete page 6 in the partnership return in respect of the year ended 31 March 2017.

PARTNERSHIP STATEMENT (SHORT) for the year ended 5 April 2017

Please read these instructions before completing the Statement

Use these pages to allocate partnership income if the only income for the relevant return period was trading and professional income or taxed interest and alternative finance receipts from banks and building societies. Otherwise you must download or ask the SA Orderline for the 'Partnership Statement (Full)' pages to record details of the allocation of all the partnership income. Go to **www.gov.uk/self-assessment-forms-and-helpsheets**

Step 1 Fill in boxes 1 to 29 and boxes A and B as appropriate. Get the figures you need from the relevant boxes in the Partnership Tax Return. Complete a separate Statement for each accounting period covered by this Partnership Tax Return and for each trade or profession carried on by the partnership.

Step 2 Then allocate the amounts in boxes 11 to 29 attributable to each partner using the allocation columns on this page and page 7, read the Partnership Tax Return Guide, go to www.gov.uk/self-assessment-forms-and-helpsheets
If the partnership has more than 3 partners, please photocopy page 7.

Step 3 Each partner will need a copy of their allocation of income to fill in their personal tax return.

PARTNERSHIP INFORMATION

If the partnership business includes a trade or profession, enter here the accounting period for which appropriate items in this statement are returned.

Start **1** / /

End **2** / /

Nature of trade **3**

MIXED PARTNERSHIPS

Tick here if this Statement is drawn up using Corporation Tax rules **4**

Tick here if this Statement is drawn up using tax rules for non-residents **5**

Individual partner details

6 Name of partner

Address

Postcode

Date appointed as a partner (if during 2015–16 or 2016–17) **7** / /

Partner's Unique Taxpayer Reference (UTR) **8**

Date ceased to be a partner (if during 2015–16 or 2016–17) **9** / /

Partner's National Insurance number **10**

Partnership's profits, losses, income, tax credits, etc	Tick this box if the items entered in the box had foreign tax taken off		**Partner's share of profits, losses, income, tax credits, etc**	Copy figures in boxes 11 to 29 to boxes in the individual's **Partnership (short)** pages as shown below
• for an accounting period ended in 2016–17				
from box 3.83 Profit from a trade or profession	A	11 £	Profit 11 £	Copy this figure to box 8
from box 3.82 Adjustment on change of basis		11A £	11A £	Copy this figure to box 10
from box 3.84 Loss from a trade or profession	B	12 £	Loss 12 £	Copy this figure to box 8
from box 10.4 Business Premises Renovation Allowance		12A £	12A £	Copy this figure to box 15
• for the period 6 April 2016 to 5 April 2017*				
from box 7.9A UK taxed interest and taxed alternative finance receipts		22 £	22 £	Copy this figure to box 28
from box 3.97 CIS deductions made by contractors on account of tax		24 £	24 £	Copy this figure to box 30
from box 3.98 Other tax taken off trading income		24A £	24A £	Copy this figure to box 31
from box 7.8A Income Tax taken off		25 £	25 £	Copy this figure to box 29
from box 3.117 Partnership charges		29 £	29 £	Copy this figure to box 4, 'Other tax reliefs' section on page Al 2 in your personal tax return

* if you are a 'CT Partnership' see the Partnership Tax Return Guide

SA800 2016 PARTNERSHIP TAX RETURN: PAGE 6

7 Summary

The taxable trade profits of a partnership are apportioned between the partners in accordance with the profit sharing arrangements during the accounting period.

Where there are salaries and interest on capital these should be dealt with first, and then any balance shared out using the profit sharing ratio.

Interest income is apportioned according to the profit sharing ratio on the date the interest is received.

8 AAT reference material

Partnerships

- Each partner is taxed like a sole trader on their share of the partnership profits
- First step is to share accounting profits between partners:
  - Allocate the correct salaries and interest on capital for the period to each partner.
  - Divide the remaining profit for each set of accounts between the partners based upon the profit sharing arrangement.
  - You may need to split the period if there is a change such as a partner joining or leaving.
- Opening year and cessation rules apply to partners individually when they join or leave the partnership.
- Allocate the profit for each partner to the correct tax year using usual basis period rules.
- Basis periods for continuing partners are unaffected by joiners or leavers.
- Each partner enters their share of profits for a tax year in the partnership pages of their own tax return.

Test your understanding answers

 Test your understanding 1

John and Kyle

Year ending 5 April 2017	**Total**	**John**	**Kyle**
	£	£	£
Profits split (3:2)	24,047	14,428	9,619

Test your understanding 2

1	False	The partnership is not a separate legal entity from the partners. It is the partners who pay tax on their share of the partnership profits.
2	False	The profits are time apportioned to the period before and after 30 June, and then allocated using the profit sharing ratio in each period.
3	False	Salaries and interest must be added back in calculating adjusted trading profit as they are not actually salaries and interest. They merely represent a method chosen by the partners of allocating profits between them.
		They are taken into account in apportioning the profit between the partners, but the partners are assessed to their total share of trading profits of the partnership as trading income.

Test your understanding 3

Michael, Nick and Liz (1)

	Total	Michael	Nick	Liz
	£	£	£	£
y/e 30 September 2014	30,000	15,000	15,000	
y/e 30 September 2015				
1 October 2014 – 31 December 2014	9,000	4,500	4,500	
1 January 2015 – 30 September 2015	27,000	9,000	9,000	9,000
	36,000	13,500	13,500	9,000
y/e 30 September 2016				
1 October 2015 – 30 June 2016	31,875	10,625	10,625	10,625
1 July 2016 – 30 September 2016	10,625	5,313	–	5,312
	42,500	15,938	10,625	15,937
y/e 30 September 2017	40,000	20,000		20,000
Period ending 31 December 2017	17,500	8,750		8,750

Test your understanding 4

Michael, Nick and Liz (2)

PARTNERSHIP STATEMENT (SHORT) for the year ended 5 April 2017

Please read these instructions before completing the Statement

Use these pages to allocate partnership income if the only income for the relevant return period was trading and professional income or taxed interest and alternative finance receipts from banks and building societies. Otherwise you must download or ask the SA Orderline for the 'Partnership Statement (Full)' pages to record details of the allocation of all the partnership income. Go to **www.gov.uk/self-assessment-forms-and-helpsheets**

Step 1 Fill in boxes 1 to 29 and boxes A and B as appropriate. Get the figures you need from the relevant boxes in the Partnership Tax Return. Complete a separate Statement for each accounting period covered by this Partnership Tax Return and for each trade or profession carried on by the partnership.

Step 2 Then allocate the amounts in boxes 11 to 29 attributable to each partner using the allocation columns on this page and page 7, read the Partnership Tax Return Guide, go to www.gov.uk/self-assessment-forms-and-helpsheets
If the partnership has more than 3 partners, please photocopy page 7.

Step 3 Each partner will need a copy of their allocation of income to fill in their personal tax return.

PARTNERSHIP INFORMATION
If the partnership business includes a trade or profession, enter here the accounting period for which appropriate items in this statement are returned.

Start **1** 01 / 10 / 15

End **2** 30 / 09 / 16

Nature of trade **3** Printers

MIXED PARTNERSHIPS

Tick here if this Statement is drawn up using Corporation Tax rules **4**

Tick here if this Statement is drawn up using tax rules for non-residents **5**

Individual partner details

6 Name of partner Michael Peters
Address

Postcode

Date appointed as a partner (if during 2015–16 or 2016–17) **7** / /

Partner's Unique Taxpayer Reference (UTR) **8**

Date ceased to be a partner (if during 2015–16 or 2016–17) **9** / /

Partner's National Insurance number **10**

Partnership's profits, losses, income, tax credits, etc	Tick this box if the items entered in the box had foreign tax taken off		**Partner's share of profits, losses, income, tax credits, etc**	Copy figures in boxes 11 to 29 to boxes in the individual's **Partnership (short)** pages as shown below
• **for an accounting period ended in 2016–17**				
from box 3.83 Profit from a trade or profession	A	11 £ 42,500	Profit 11 £ 15,938	Copy this figure to box 8
from box 3.82 Adjustment on change of basis		11A £	11A £	Copy this figure to box 10
from box 3.84 Loss from a trade or profession	B	12 £	Loss 12 £	Copy this figure to box 8
from box 10.4 Business Premises Renovation Allowance		12A £	12A £	Copy this figure to box 15
• **for the period 6 April 2016 to 5 April 2017***				
from box 7.9A UK taxed interest and taxed alternative finance receipts		22 £	22 £	Copy this figure to box 28
from box 3.97 CIS deductions made by contractors on account of tax		24 £	24 £	Copy this figure to box 30
from box 3.98 Other tax taken off trading income		24A £	24A £	Copy this figure to box 31
from box 7.8A Income Tax taken off		25 £	25 £	Copy this figure to box 29
from box 3.117 Partnership charges		29 £	29 £	Copy this figure to box 4, 'Other tax reliefs' section on page Ai 2 in your personal tax return

* if you are a 'CT Partnership' see the Partnership Tax Return Guide

SA800 2016 PARTNERSHIP TAX RETURN: PAGE 6

Test your understanding 5

Lindsay, Tricia and Kate (1)

The correct answers are as follows:

First period to: 31 July 2016

(1) C

(2) A

(3) B

Second period to: 31 March 2017

(4) D

(5) D

(6) C

(7) B

Explanation:

The split of partnership profits will be as follows:

	Total	Lindsay	Tricia	Kate
	£	£	£	£
Year ending 31 March 2017				
1 April 2016 – 31 July 2016 (4m)	50,000	30,000	20,000	
1 Aug 2016 – 31 March 2017 (8m)	100,000	44,445	33,333	22,222
	150,000	74,445	53,333	22,222

Test your understanding 6

Anne, Betty, Chloe and Diana

	Total	Anne	Betty	Chloe	Diana
	£	£	£	£	£
Year ended 31 Dec 2015					
1 Jan 2015 – 30 Jun 2015					
$\frac{6}{12}$ × £60,000	30,000	15,000	15,000		
1 Jul 2015 – 31 Dec 2015					
$\frac{6}{12}$ × £60,000	30,000	15,000		15,000	
	60,000	30,000	15,000	15,000	
Year ended 31 Dec 2016					
1 Jan 2016 – 31 Mar 2016					
$\frac{3}{12}$ × £72,000	18,000	9,000		9,000	
1 Apr 2016 – 31 Dec 2016					
$\frac{9}{12}$ × £72,000	54,000	18,000		18,000	18,000
	72,000	27,000		27,000	18,000

Test your understanding 7

Bert and Harold

Allocation of taxable trade profits

The profit-sharing ratio was changed on 1 July 2016 which is 9 months into the accounting period. The profits will therefore be time-apportioned for allocation as follows:

Old ratio £16,500 × $\frac{9}{12}$ = £12,375

New ratio £16,500 × $\frac{3}{12}$ = £4,125

Allocation of taxable trade profits

	Total	**Bert**	**Harold**
	£	£	£
1 Oct 2015 to 30 Jun 2016			
Salaries ($\frac{9}{12}$)	3,750	2,250	1,500
Balance (3:2)	8,625	5,175	3,450
	12,375	7,425	4,950
1 Jul 2016 to 30 Sep 2016			
Salaries ($\frac{3}{12}$)	2,500	1,500	1,000
Balance (2:1)	1,625	1,083	542
	4,125	2,583	1,542
Total allocation	16,500	10,008	6,492

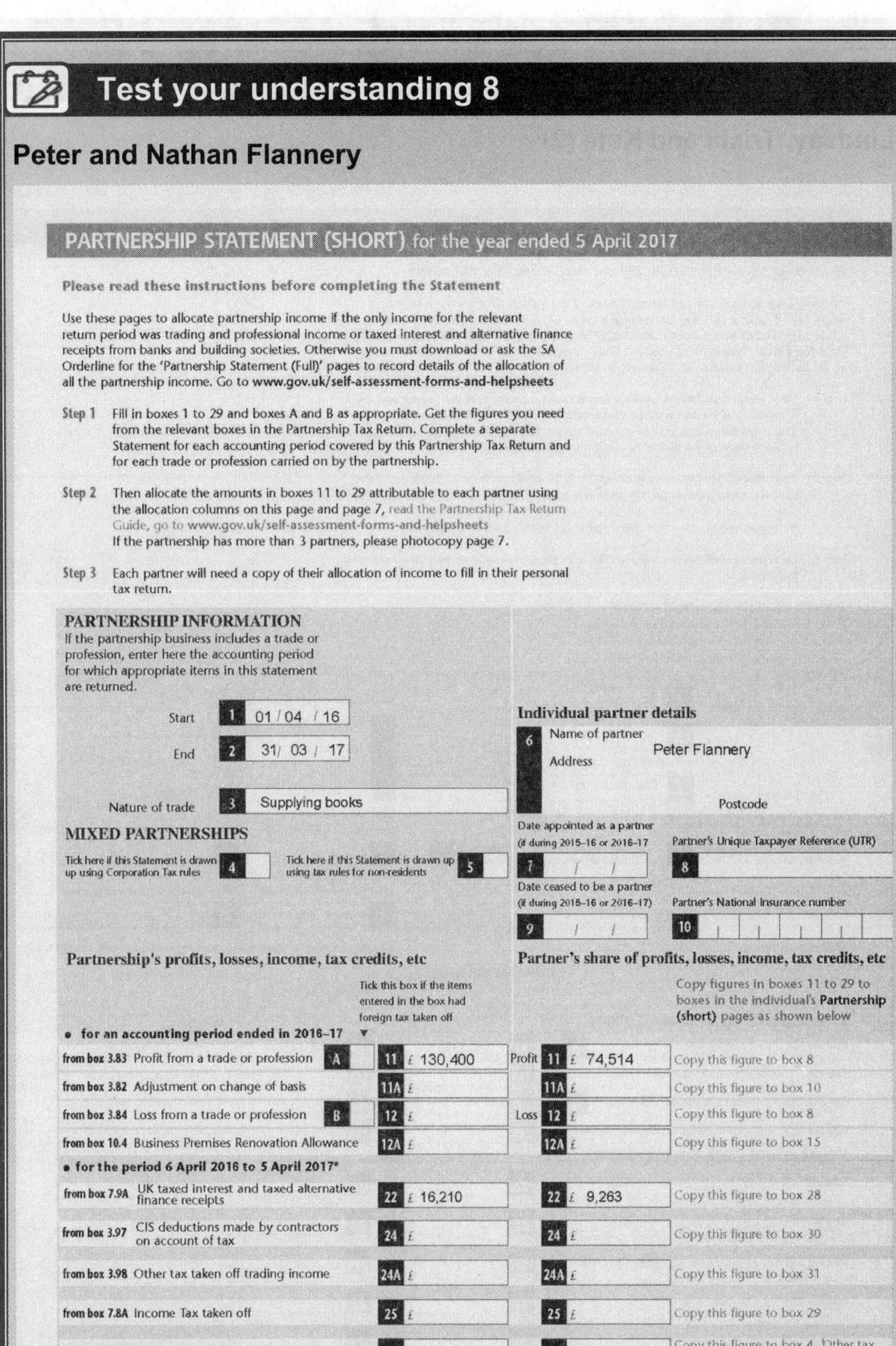

Test your understanding 8

Peter and Nathan Flannery

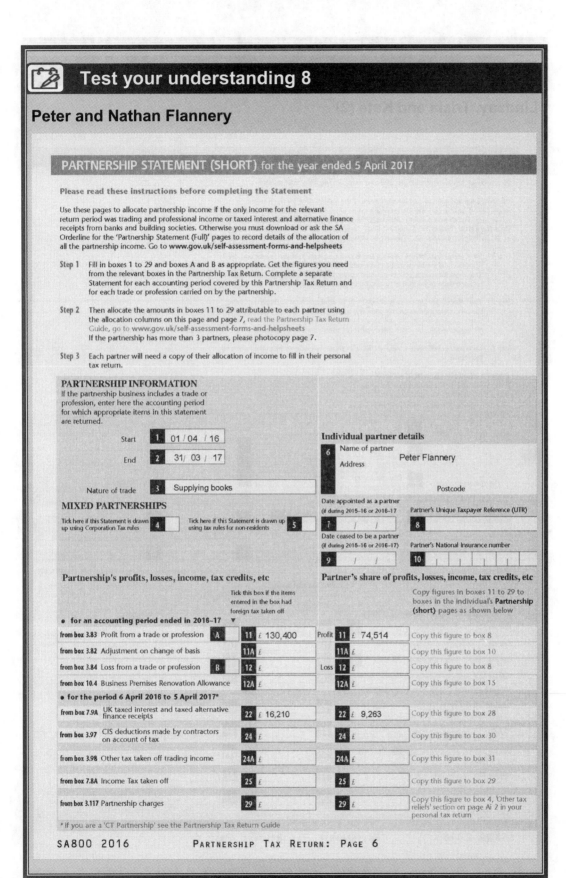

PARTNERSHIP STATEMENT (SHORT) for the year ended 5 April 2017

Please read these instructions before completing the Statement

Use these pages to allocate partnership income if the only income for the relevant return period was trading and professional income or taxed interest and alternative finance receipts from banks and building societies. Otherwise you must download or ask the SA Orderline for the 'Partnership Statement (Full)' pages to record details of the allocation of all the partnership income. Go to **www.gov.uk/self-assessment-forms-and-helpsheets**

Step 1 Fill in boxes 1 to 29 and boxes A and B as appropriate. Get the figures you need from the relevant boxes in the Partnership Tax Return. Complete a separate Statement for each accounting period covered by this Partnership Tax Return and for each trade or profession carried on by the partnership.

Step 2 Then allocate the amounts in boxes 11 to 29 attributable to each partner using the allocation columns on this page and page 7, read the Partnership Tax Return Guide, go to www.gov.uk/self-assessment-forms-and-helpsheets
If the partnership has more than 3 partners, please photocopy page 7.

Step 3 Each partner will need a copy of their allocation of income to fill in their personal tax return.

PARTNERSHIP INFORMATION
If the partnership business includes a trade or profession, enter here the accounting period for which appropriate items in this statement are returned.

Start **1** 01 / 04 / 16

End **2** 31/ 03 / 17

Nature of trade **3** Supplying books

MIXED PARTNERSHIPS

Tick here if this Statement is drawn up using Corporation Tax rules **4**

Tick here if this Statement is drawn up using tax rules for non-residents **5**

Individual partner details

6 Name of partner: Peter Flannery
Address
Postcode

Date appointed as a partner (if during 2015–16 or 2016–17) **7** / /

Partner's Unique Taxpayer Reference (UTR) **8**

Date ceased to be a partner (if during 2015–16 or 2016–17) **9** / /

Partner's National Insurance number **10**

Partnership's profits, losses, income, tax credits, etc	Tick this box if the items entered in the box had foreign tax taken off		Partner's share of profits, losses, income, tax credits, etc	Copy figures in boxes 11 to 29 to boxes in the individual's **Partnership (short)** pages as shown below
• **for an accounting period ended in 2016–17**				
from box 3.83 Profit from a trade or profession	A	11 £ 130,400	Profit 11 £ 74,514	Copy this figure to box 8
from box 3.82 Adjustment on change of basis		11A £	11A £	Copy this figure to box 10
from box 3.84 Loss from a trade or profession	B	12 £	Loss 12 £	Copy this figure to box 8
from box 10.4 Business Premises Renovation Allowance		12A £	12A £	Copy this figure to box 15
• **for the period 6 April 2016 to 5 April 2017***				
from box 7.9A UK taxed interest and taxed alternative finance receipts		22 £ 16,210	22 £ 9,263	Copy this figure to box 28
from box 3.97 CIS deductions made by contractors on account of tax		24 £	24 £	Copy this figure to box 30
from box 3.98 Other tax taken off trading income		24A £	24A £	Copy this figure to box 31
from box 7.8A Income Tax taken off		25 £	25 £	Copy this figure to box 29
from box 3.117 Partnership charges		29 £	29 £	Copy this figure to box 4, 'Other tax reliefs' section on page Ai 2 in your personal tax return

* If you are a 'CT Partnership' see the Partnership Tax Return Guide

SA800 2016 PARTNERSHIP TAX RETURN: PAGE 6

Test your understanding 9

Lindsay, Tricia and Kate (2)

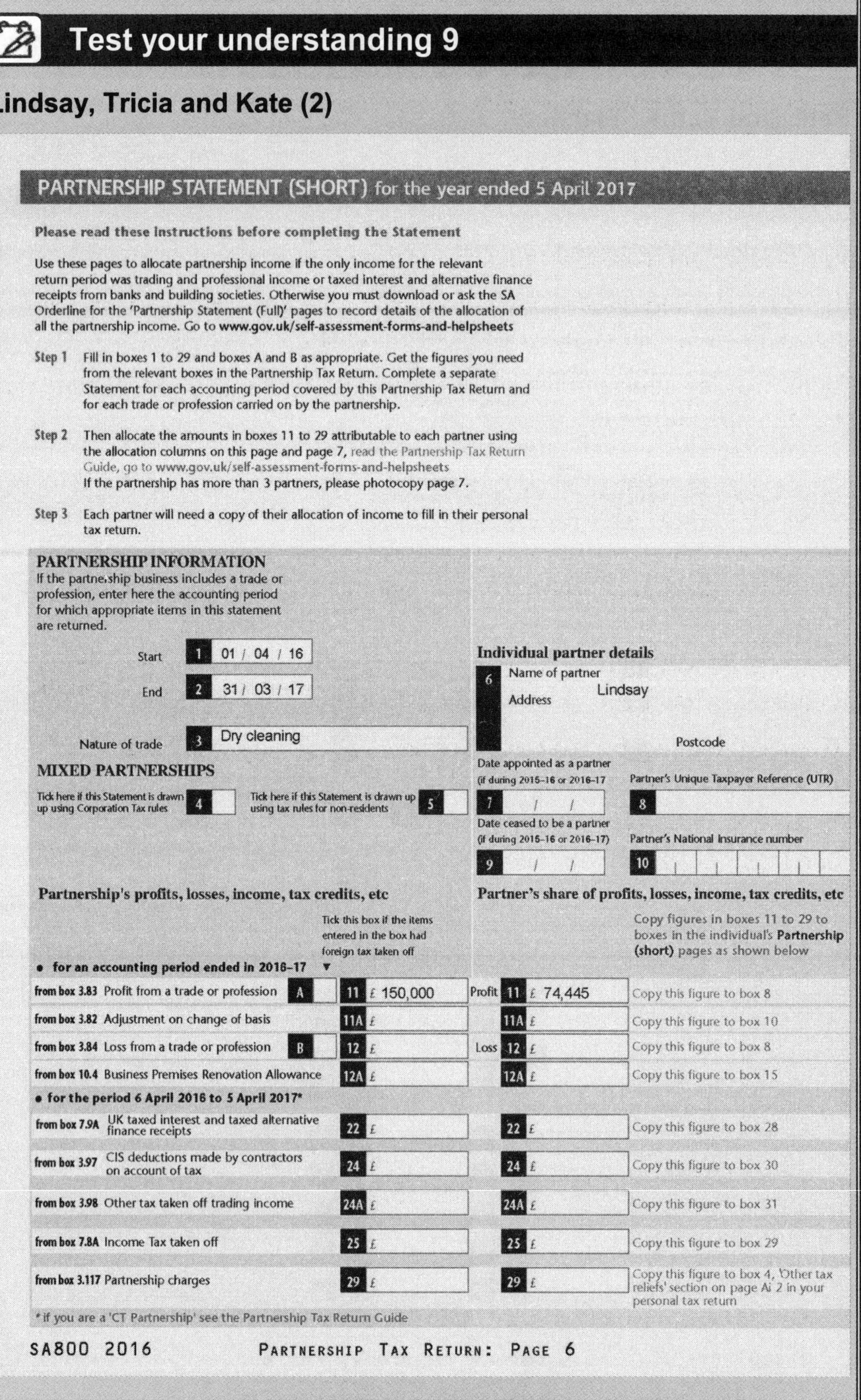

PARTNERSHIP STATEMENT (SHORT) for the year ended 5 April 2017

Please read these instructions before completing the Statement

Use these pages to allocate partnership income if the only income for the relevant return period was trading and professional income or taxed interest and alternative finance receipts from banks and building societies. Otherwise you must download or ask the SA Orderline for the 'Partnership Statement (Full)' pages to record details of the allocation of all the partnership income. Go to **www.gov.uk/self-assessment-forms-and-helpsheets**

Step 1 Fill in boxes 1 to 29 and boxes A and B as appropriate. Get the figures you need from the relevant boxes in the Partnership Tax Return. Complete a separate Statement for each accounting period covered by this Partnership Tax Return and for each trade or profession carried on by the partnership.

Step 2 Then allocate the amounts in boxes 11 to 29 attributable to each partner using the allocation columns on this page and page 7, read the Partnership Tax Return Guide, go to www.gov.uk/self-assessment-forms-and-helpsheets
If the partnership has more than 3 partners, please photocopy page 7.

Step 3 Each partner will need a copy of their allocation of income to fill in their personal tax return.

PARTNERSHIP INFORMATION
If the partnership business includes a trade or profession, enter here the accounting period for which appropriate items in this statement are returned.

Start **1** 01 / 04 / 16

End **2** 31 / 03 / 17

Nature of trade **3** Dry cleaning

MIXED PARTNERSHIPS

Tick here if this Statement is drawn up using Corporation Tax rules **4** ☐

Tick here if this Statement is drawn up using tax rules for non-residents **5** ☐

Individual partner details

6 Name of partner: Lindsay
Address
Postcode

Date appointed as a partner (if during 2015–16 or 2016–17) **7** / /

Partner's Unique Taxpayer Reference (UTR) **8**

Date ceased to be a partner (if during 2015–16 or 2016–17) **9** / /

Partner's National Insurance number **10**

Partnership's profits, losses, income, tax credits, etc — Tick this box if the items entered in the box had foreign tax taken off

Partner's share of profits, losses, income, tax credits, etc — Copy figures in boxes 11 to 29 to boxes in the individual's **Partnership (short)** pages as shown below

	Foreign tax	Partnership		Partner's share	
• for an accounting period ended in 2016–17					
from box 3.83 Profit from a trade or profession	A	11 £ 150,000	Profit	11 £ 74,445	Copy this figure to box 8
from box 3.82 Adjustment on change of basis		11A £		11A £	Copy this figure to box 10
from box 3.84 Loss from a trade or profession	B	12 £	Loss	12 £	Copy this figure to box 8
from box 10.4 Business Premises Renovation Allowance		12A £		12A £	Copy this figure to box 15
• for the period 6 April 2016 to 5 April 2017*					
from box 7.9A UK taxed interest and taxed alternative finance receipts		22 £		22 £	Copy this figure to box 28
from box 3.97 CIS deductions made by contractors on account of tax		24 £		24 £	Copy this figure to box 30
from box 3.98 Other tax taken off trading income		24A £		24A £	Copy this figure to box 31
from box 7.8A Income Tax taken off		25 £		25 £	Copy this figure to box 29
from box 3.117 Partnership charges		29 £		29 £	Copy this figure to box 4, 'Other tax reliefs' section on page Ai 2 in your personal tax return

* if you are a 'CT Partnership' see the Partnership Tax Return Guide

SA800 2016 PARTNERSHIP TAX RETURN: PAGE 6

Basis periods

Introduction

Sole traders and partners must complete a tax return each year.

There are rules to determine which profits go into each tax return, with special rules for the opening and closing years of a business.

There are also special rules when a business changes its accounting date after the opening years.

ASSESSMENT CRITERIA

Identify the basis periods using the opening year and closing year rules (1.2)

Determine overlap periods and overlap profits (1.2)

Explain the effect on the basis period of a change in accounting date (1.2)

Determine the basis periods for continuing, new or departing partners (1.4)

CONTENTS

1 Tax years

1.1 Tax year

An individual in business will need to complete a tax return for a tax year. A tax year runs from 6 April to the following 5 April.

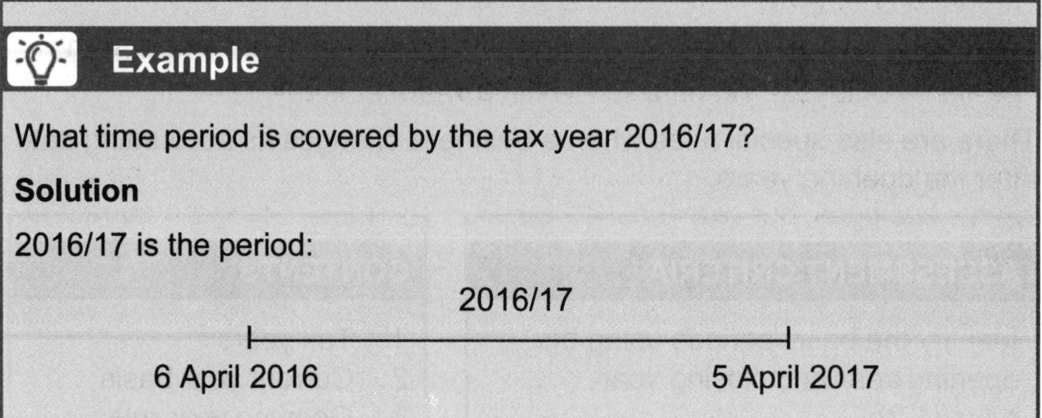

Example

What time period is covered by the tax year 2016/17?

Solution

2016/17 is the period:

We need to determine which taxable trade profits are to be assessed in each tax year.

2 Current year basis

2.1 Ongoing business

The basic rule is that the taxable trade profits assessed in any tax year will be based on the profit for the 12 month period of account ending in that tax year. This is known as the current year basis.

Example

Vivienne prepares accounts to 30 April each year.

Her taxable trade profits after making all necessary adjustments, including capital allowances, were as follows:

	£
Year ended 30 April 2015	20,000
Year ended 30 April 2016	25,000

State in which tax years these profits will be taxed.

Solution

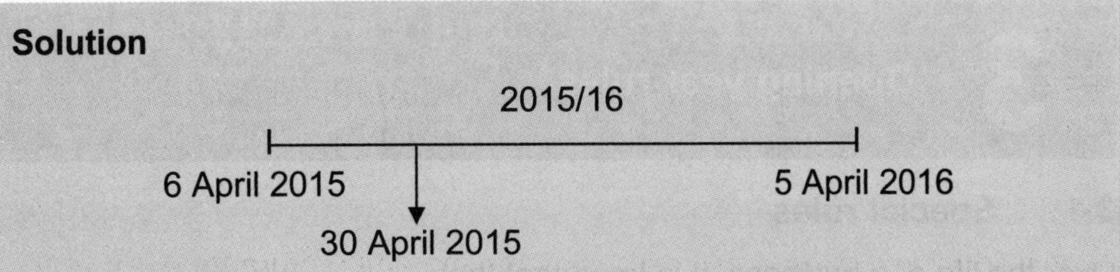

The year ended 30 April 2015 ends in 2015/16 and therefore all of the profits of that year will be taxed in the tax year 2015/16.

The year ended 30 April 2016 ends in 2016/17 and therefore all of the profits of that year will be taxed in the tax year 2016/17.

An individual can choose whichever accounting period end date he wants for his business, but care must be taken to tax the profits in the correct tax year.

Example

In which tax years will the following profits be taxed?

Profits for year ending: 30 April 2017
31 March 2017
30 June 2017
31 January 2017
31 December 2016

Solution

Profits for year ending:	Tax year of assessment
30 April 2017	2017/18
31 March 2017	2016/17
30 June 2017	2017/18
31 January 2017	2016/17
31 December 2016	2016/17

It often helps to draw a diagram showing the beginning and end of the tax year and mark on the accounting period end date to ensure you select the correct tax year.

3 Opening year rules

3.1 Special rules

Over the life of a business, it is important that:

- the total taxable trading profits of the business should be taxed, and
- there should be an assessment for each tax year of trading.

Suppose a business starts trading on 1 July 2016 and prepares accounts up to 30 June 2017.

Although the business starts in 2016/17 there is no accounting period ending in 2016/17, so if the normal 'current year basis' is applied, there would be no tax assessment in 2016/17.

To make sure that there is an assessment in every year the business trades, there are special opening year rules.

These are explained below.

(a) **First tax year**

The first tax year is the tax year in which the business started to trade.

The basis of assessment for the first tax year is *always* the period:

- from the date of commencement
- to the following 5 April.

This is known as the *actual basis of assessment*.

(b) **Second tax year**

In the second tax year, you need to ask the question:

Is there a set of accounts that ends in the second tax year?

If no accounts are prepared to a date ending in the second tax year, the basis of assessment is:

- the actual profits of the second tax year (6 April to 5 April).

If accounts are prepared to a date ending in the second tax year, you need to ask another question:

How long are the accounts that end in the second tax year?

If the accounts are:

- 12 months or more after the business started:
  - the basis of assessment is the profits of the 12 months to the end of that period.
- less than 12 months after the business started:
  - the basis of assessment is the profits of the first 12 months trading.

(c) **Third year**

In the third tax year, the basis of assessment is:

- the profits of the 12 months to the accounting date ending in the third year.

This is usually the **current year basis**.

For the purposes of your assessment, any apportionments of profit are made on a monthly basis (not daily).

There are details of the opening year rules in the AAT reference material set out below in section 9.

The following examples will illustrate the three possibilities for the second tax year.

Example

Lara started in business on 1 November 2014, preparing accounts to 31 October each year.

Her adjusted profits were as follows:

	£
Year ended 31 October 2015	18,000
Year ended 31 October 2016	37,500
Year ended 31 October 2017	44,000

State the taxable trade profits for the first four tax years of trading.

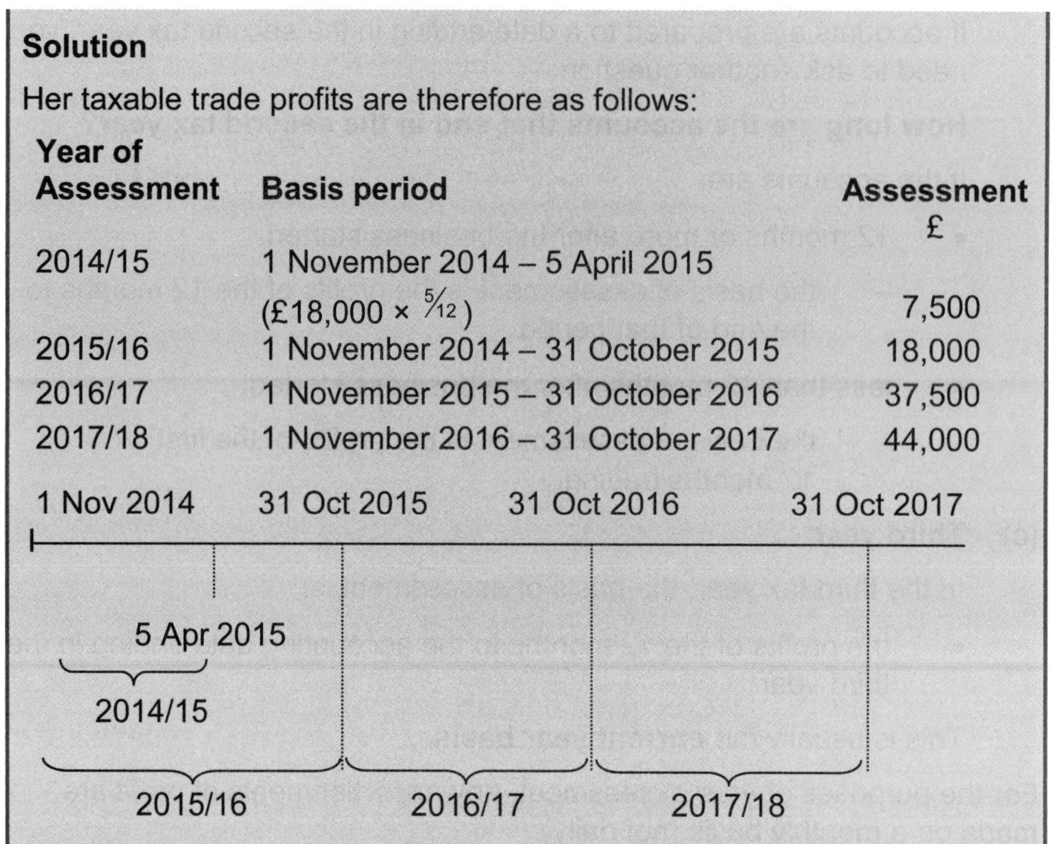

Solution

Her taxable trade profits are therefore as follows:

Year of Assessment	Basis period	Assessment £
2014/15	1 November 2014 – 5 April 2015 (£18,000 × 5/12)	7,500
2015/16	1 November 2014 – 31 October 2015	18,000
2016/17	1 November 2015 – 31 October 2016	37,500
2017/18	1 November 2016 – 31 October 2017	44,000

3.2 Overlap profits

When an individual starts to trade, some profits may be taxed twice. Profits assessed in more than one tax year are called overlap profits.

In the previous example, the following profits are assessed in both 2014/15 and 2015/16:

1 November 2014 to 5 April 2015 = (£18,000 × $^5/_{12}$) = £7,500

However, as stated before, it is very important that over the life of the business, the trader will be taxed on the total taxable profits of the business – and only once.

Therefore, relief for overlap profits is given by deducting them from the final assessment when an individual ceases to trade.

Note that there will be no overlap profits if the trader has a 5 April year end. Since we work to the nearest month for exams, this means that starting business and choosing a 31 March year end will also have no overlap profits.

Example

Edrich started in business on 1 July 2014. He prepared his first set of accounts for the six months ended 31 December 2014 and then for calendar years thereafter.

His adjusted profits were as follows:

	£
Six months ended 31 December 2014	3,100
Year ended 31 December 2015	7,600
Year ended 31 December 2016	8,200
Year ended 31 December 2017	6,400

Show the taxable trade profits for the tax years 2014/15 to 2017/18 inclusive, and calculate the amount of any overlap profits.

Solution

His taxable trade profits are therefore as follows:

Year of assessment	**Basis period**	**Assessment** £
2014/15	1 July 2014 – 5 April 2015	
	£3,100 + (£7,600 × $^{3}/_{12}$)	5,000
2015/16	1 January 2015 – 31 December 2015	7,600
2016/17	1 January 2016 – 31 December 2016	8,200
2017/18	1 January 2017 – 31 December 2017	6,400

There are overlap profits of £1,900 (£7,600 × $^{3}/_{12}$) for the period from 1 January 2015 to 5 April 2015.

Example

Hammond started in business on 1 January 2015. He prepared his first set of accounts for the seven months ended 31 July 2015 and annually to 31 July thereafter.

His adjusted profits were as follows:

	£
Seven months ended 31 July 2015	10,500
Year ended 31 July 2016	33,600
Year ended 31 July 2017	19,800

Show the taxable trade profits for the tax years 2014/15 to 2017/18 inclusive, and calculate the amount of any overlap profits.

Solution

The business commenced on 1 January 2015, which is in 2014/15.

The second tax year is 2015/16 and the accounts ending in that period are those for the seven months to 31 July 2015. This date is less than 12 months after the business started. Therefore the second year assesses the first 12 months trading.

Remember we must tax 12 months of profits in the second year.

Hammond's taxable trade profits are therefore as follows:

Year of Assessment	**Basis period**	**Assessment**
		£
2014/15	1 January 2015 – 5 April 2015 £10,500 × 3/7	4,500
2015/16	1 January 2015 – 31 December 2015 £10,500 + (£33,600 × 5/12)	24,500
2016/17	1 August 2015 – 31 July 2016	33,600
2017/18	1 August 2016 – 31 July 2017	19,800

The overlap profits are:

	£
1 Jan 2015 – 5 April 2015 (£10,500 × 3/7)	4,500
1 Aug 2015 – 31 Dec 2015 (£33,600 × 5/12)	14,000
	18,500

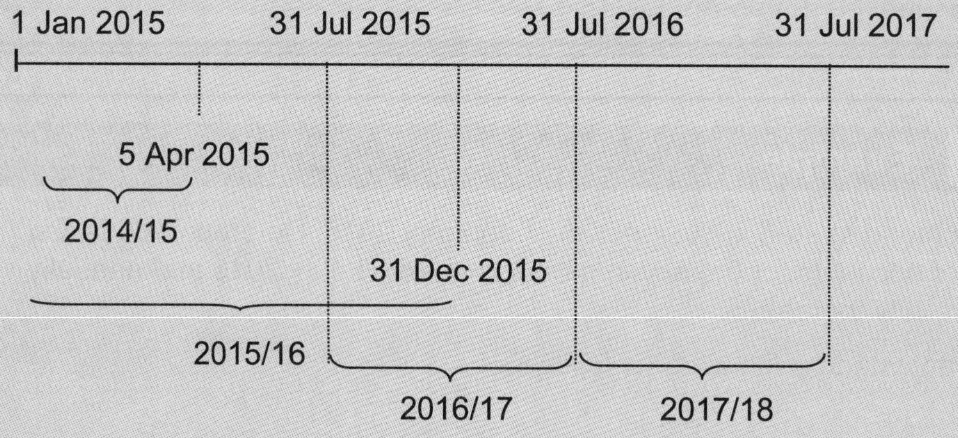

1 Jan 2015 31 Jul 2015 31 Jul 2016 31 Jul 2017

5 Apr 2015

2014/15

31 Dec 2015

2015/16

2016/17 2017/18

Example

Yallop started in business on 1 February 2015. He prepared his first set of accounts for the 18 months to 31 July 2016 and annually to 31 July thereafter.

His adjusted profits were as follows:

	£
18 months ended 31 July 2016	9,000
Year ended 31 July 2017	2,680

Show the taxable trade profits for the tax years 2014/15 to 2017/18 inclusive, and calculate the amount of any overlap profits.

Solution

The taxable trade profits are as follows:

Year of Assessment	**Basis period**	**Assessment**
		£
2014/15	1 February 2015 – 5 April 2015	
	£9,000 × $^{2}/_{18}$	1,000
2015/16	6 April 2015 – 5 April 2016	
	£9,000 × $^{12}/_{18}$	6,000
2016/17	1 August 2015 – 31 July 2016	
	£9,000 × $^{12}/_{18}$	6,000
2017/18	1 August 2016 – 31 July 2017	2,680

The overlap profits are:

1 Aug 2015 – 5 April 2016 (£9,000 × 8/18)	£4,000

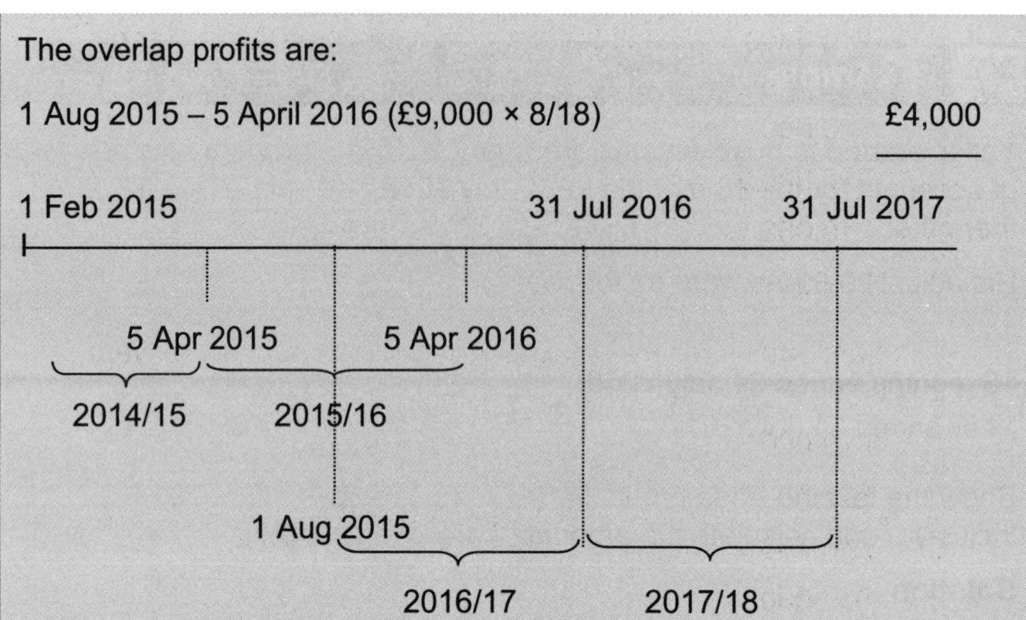

Note: In this example there is an 18 month period of account ending in the third tax year 2016/17.

In the second tax year where there are no accounts ending in that year, the actual profits from 6 April to 5 April are assessed.

In the third tax year, because we must only assess 12 months of profits, we take the last 12 months ending on the accounting date (i.e. 12 m/e 31 July 2016).

Test your understanding 1

Jane

Jane started trading on 1 November 2013. She prepares her accounts to 30 April each year. The adjusted profits were as follows:

	£
Period ended 30 April 2014	12,000
Year ended 30 April 2015	27,000
Year ended 30 April 2016	30,000

1 In which tax year did Jane start trading?

A 2012/13

B 2013/14

C 2014/15

D 2015/16

2 What are Jane's taxable trading profits for the first tax year of trading?

A £25,500

B £12,000

C £10,000

D £9,600

3 What are Jane's taxable trading profits for the second tax year of trading?

A £12,000

B £25,500

C £26,750

D £27,000

4 What are Jane's taxable trading profits for the third tax year of trading?

A £30,000

B £29,750

C £27,000

D £26,750

5 What are Jane's overlap profits? £

6 Her overlap profits are relieved as follows:

A There is no relief for overlap profits

B From the taxable profits of her choice

C From her taxable profits in the first tax year of trade

D From her taxable profits in the final tax year of trade

Test your understanding 2

Robert and Jack

(a) Robert started in business on 1 May 2014.

His first set of accounts was prepared to 30 September 2014 and he then retained 30 September as his year end.

Tax adjusted results in the early years were as follows:

	£
1 May 2014 – 30 September 2014	20,250
Year ended 30 September 2015	29,700
Year ended 30 September 2016	36,450
Year ended 30 September 2017	28,350

(b) Jack started in business on 1 January 2014 and prepared his first set of accounts to 30 April 2015.

He then continued to prepare his accounts to 30 April. The tax adjusted results in the early years were as follows:

	£
1 January 2014 – 30 April 2015	37,800
Year ended 30 April 2016	26,325
Year ended 30 April 2017	29,350

Required:

Show the amounts assessable for all tax years affected by these results and compute any overlap profits.

4 Closing year rules

4.1 Method of assessment

When an individual trader ceases to trade, any profits not yet assessed will be taxed in the tax year in which trading ceases.

The penultimate year (and the years prior to the penultimate year) is assessed on a current year basis. The final tax year assesses those profits that have not yet been assessed.

Note that this could result in the profits of more than one accounting period being assessed in the final tax year, as shown in the next example.

Example

Hutton has been in business for many years, preparing his accounts to 30 June each year. Owing to ill-health, he stopped trading on 31 January 2017.

His adjusted profits were as follows:

	£
Year ended 30 June 2015	12,000
Year ended 30 June 2016	10,000
Seven months ended 31 January 2017	3,640

Show the taxable trade profits for the last two tax years of assessment.

Solution

Step 1: Identify in which tax year the last few accounting periods end.

Accounting period	**Ends in**
Year ended 30 June 2015	2015/16
Year ended 30 June 2016	2016/17
Seven months ended 31 January 2017	2016/17

Step 2: Assess the profits in the tax years shown on the right hand side in step 1.

His taxable trade profits are therefore as follows:

Year of assessment	**Basis period**	**Assessment**
		£
2015/16	1 July 2014 – 30 June 2015	12,000
2016/17	1 July 2015 – 31 January 2017 (£10,000 + £3,640)	13,640

4.2 Overlap profits

As previously stated, over the life of the business, a trader will be taxed on his total taxable profits – and only once.

Therefore relief for overlap profits in the opening years is given by deducting them from the assessment of the final tax year.

Example

Barrington started in business on 1 August 2013, preparing accounts to 31 July each year. He ceased to trade on 31 July 2017, on which date his business was acquired by another firm.

His adjusted profits were as follows:

	£
Year ended 31 July 2014	15,000
Year ended 31 July 2015	23,000
Year ended 31 July 2016	27,000
Year ended 31 July 2017	35,600
Total adjusted profits	100,600

Show the taxable trade profits for the tax years 2013/14 to 2017/18 inclusive and calculate the amount of any overlap profits.

Solution

Step 1: Identify the tax year in which trade commences

In this year profits from the date of commencement to 5 April will be assessed (1 August 2013 is in 2013/14).

Step 2: Deal with the second tax year

The second tax year has a 12 month period ending in it therefore those 12 months profits are assessed.

After this you should be able to identify the amount of the overlap profits.

Step 3: Work out assessments for all years up to year of cessation

All other years will be taxed on the current year basis until the year of cessation.

Step 4: Work out the final year assessment

In the tax year of cessation (2017/18) all profits not yet assessed are taxed.

In this example it is straightforward as all periods are 12 months long.

Step 5: Deduct overlap profits

Finally, deduct from the final assessment the overlap profits.

The taxable trade profits are as follows.

Year of assessment	Basis period	Assessment
		£
2013/14	1 August 2013 – 5 April 2014	
	£15,000 × 8/12	10,000
2014/15	1 August 2013 – 31 July 2014	15,000
2015/16	1 August 2014 – 31 July 2015	23,000
2016/17	1 August 2015 – 31 July 2016	27,000
2017/18	1 August 2016 – 31 July 2017	
	(£35,600 – £10,000)	25,600
Total assessments		100,600

The overlap profits amount to £10,000. This sum is deducted from the assessment for the final tax year (2017/18).

Barrington's aggregate profits over his four years of trading total £100,600 and his aggregate taxable trade profits for the five tax years involved come to exactly the same figure.

5 Change of accounting date

5.1 Effect on basis period

An unincorporated trader or partnership may wish to change its accounting date for commercial or other reasons.

Where a trader who has previously prepared accounts to 30 June changes his accounting date to 30 September, the next set of accounts is going to be for either three months or 15 months.

However, in every tax year (other than the first and final tax years) the trader must be taxed on 12 months' worth of profits. Therefore in the 'year of change' (the first tax year in which accounts are made up to the new date), there will either be new overlap profits created, or some overlap profits brought forward will be offset.

5.2 New date is earlier in the tax year

Where the new accounting date is earlier in the tax year than the old one, for example a change from 31 January 2017 to 30 November 2016, the basis period for the tax year of change will be the **12-month period ending with the new accounting date**.

This will result in some profits being assessed more than once. Overlap profits will therefore arise, which are treated in exactly the same way as overlap profits arising on the commencement of trade.

It is possible to have either a long or short period of account ending on the new date.

 **Example**

(a) Andrea, a sole trader, has always prepared her accounts to 31 March. She decides to change her accounting date to 30 June by preparing accounts for the three month period to 30 June 2016.

Andrea's tax adjusted profits after capital allowances are as follows:

	£
Year ended 31 March 2016	60,000
Three months to 30 June 2016	20,000
Year ended 30 June 2017	85,000

Calculate Andrea's trading income assessments for 2015/16 to 2016/17.

Solution

(a) The accounting date has moved from March to June, i.e. to earlier in the tax year.

The tax year of change is the year in which accounts to the new accounting date are prepared (i.e. 2016/17).

The basis period for the tax year of change is the 12 months to the new accounting date.

Tax year	Basis period	Taxable income
		£
2015/16	Year to 31 March 2016	60,000
2016/17	12-month period to the new accounting date of 30 June 2016:	
	Year to 31 March 2016: (£60,000 × 9/12)	45,000
	Period to 30 June 2016	20,000
		65,000
2017/18	Year to 30 June 2017	85,000

Note: The change in accounting date has created further overlap profits of £45,000, as the 9 months to March 2016 are assessed in both 2015/16 and 2016/17.

(b) Assume that instead of producing a three month set of accounts, Andrea had decided to change her accounting date to 30 June by preparing accounts for the fifteen month period to 30 June 2017 with tax adjusted profits of £105,000.

Calculate Andrea's trading income assessments for 2015/16 to 2016/17 and prove that the result would be virtually the same.

Solution

(b) The tax year of change is 2016/17 as Andrea does not adopt her normal 31 March year end here.

Andrea is allowed to adopt the new accounting date in this year, and the profits assessed are those for the 12 months to the new accounting date – 30 June.

Tax year	Basis period	Taxable income
		£
2015/16	Year to 31 March 2016	60,000
2016/17	12-month period to the new accounting date of 30 June 2016:	
	Year to 31 March 2016: (£60,000 × 9/12)	45,000
	Period to 30 June 2016: (£105,000 × 3/15)	21,000
		66,000
2017/18	Year to 30 June 2017 (£105,000 × 12/15)	84,000

Note: Overlap profits still arise in respect of the 9 months to 31 March 2016 as before equal to £45,000.

5.3 New date is later in the tax year

Where the new accounting date is later in the tax year than the old one the basis period for the tax year of change will be **the period ending with the new accounting date**.

As the resulting basis period may be more than 12 months, a corresponding proportion of any overlap profits that arose upon the commencement of trading are offset against the taxable profits.

Again, it is possible to have either a short accounting period or a long accounting period creating the new date.

Example

Peter, a sole trader, has always prepared his accounts to 30 June.

Peter has overlap profits of £13,500 from the period 1 July 2013 to 5 April 2013.

He has now decided to change his accounting date to 30 September by preparing accounts for the 15 month period to 30 September 2016.

Peter's tax adjusted trading profits after capital allowances are:

	£
Year ended 30 June 2015	24,000
Period ended 30 September 2016	30,000
Year ended 30 September 2017	36,000

Calculate Peter's trading income assessments for 2014/15 to 2017/18.

Solution

The tax year of change is the tax year in which accounts are prepared to the new accounting date (i.e. 2016/17).

As the new accounting date is later in the tax year, the basis period is the period ending with the new accounting date.

Tax year	Basis period	Taxable income £
2015/16	Year to 30 June 2015	24,000
2016/17	Period not yet assessed ending on the new accounting date	
	15-month period to 30 September 2016	30,000
	Less: overlap profits (£13,500 × 3/9)	(4,500)
		25,500
2017/18	Year to 30 September 2017 (£105,000 × 12/15)	36,000

Note: In 2016/17 the period of account not yet assessed and ending with the new accounting date is 15 months. As no assessment can exceed 12 months, Peter is allowed to offset 3 months of his overlap profits.

The remaining 6 months of overlap profits are carried forward as normal and are available for relief, either on a further change in accounting date or on the cessation of trade.

5.4 Conditions for a valid change

(1) The change of accounting date must be notified to HMRC on or before 31 January following the tax year in which the change is to be made.

E.g. if the year of change is 2016/17 then HMRC must be notified by 31 January 2018 (the latest filing date for the 2016/17 tax return).

(2) The first accounts to the new accounting date must not exceed 18 months in length.

The AAT reference material set out in section 9 below contains some details of the change of accounting date rules.

6 Partnerships

6.1 Separate traders

A partnership is treated as a collection of individual traders.

Therefore, if some individuals have been trading in partnership for many years, each will be assessed on his own share of the profits on a current year basis.

6.2 Partners joining

Where an individual joins the partnership, he alone will be assessed using the opening year rules on his share of the partnership profits.

The remaining partners will use the current year basis.

6.3 Partners leaving

Where an individual leaves the partnership, he alone will be assessed using the closing year rules on his share of the partnership profits.

The remaining partners will use the current year basis.

6.4 Procedure for partnerships

The correct procedure to follow for partnerships is:

Step 1: Adjust profits of the accounting period (including calculating capital allowances) for the partnership as a whole.

Step 2: Allocate the profits of the accounting period to the partners using the profit share arrangement.

Step 3: Consider each partner in turn, as if they were sole traders, to determine whether to apply current year basis, opening year rules or closing year rules.

 **Example**

Using the results of the Fred, George and Harry example in Chapter 10 as set out below, calculate the taxable trade profits for each partner for the tax years 2013/14 to 2016/17.

	Total	F	G	H
	£	£	£	£
Year ended 30 June 2014 (1:1:1)	60,000	20,000	20,000	20,000
Year ended 30 June 2015 (1:1:1)	85,200	28,400	28,400	28,400
Year ended 30 June 2016 (1:1:1)	75,000	25,000	25,000	25,000
Year ended 30 June 2017				
1 July 2016 – 31 Oct 2016 (1:1:1) ($^{4}/_{12}$)	25,200	8,400	8,400	8,400
1 Nov 2016 – 30 June 2017 (3:2) ($^{8}/_{12}$)	50,400	30,240	–	20,160
	75,600	38,640	8,400	28,560

Solution

Steps 1 and 2 of the procedure have already been completed above.

Step 3: Determine the basis of assessment for each partner.

- Fred and Harry both commenced in partnership on 1 July 2013, hence apply the opening year rules. The following figures relate to Fred.

Year of assessment	Basis period	Assessment
		£
2013/14	1 July 2013 – 5 April 2014	
	(£20,000 × $^{9}/_{12}$)	15,000
2014/15	Year ended 30 June 2014	20,000
2015/16	Year ended 30 June 2015	28,400
2016/17	Year ended 30 June 2016	25,000
2017/18	Year ended 30 June 2017	38,640

Overlap profits = £15,000

- Harry would be the same as Fred until 2017/18 when his assessment would be £28,560.
- George commenced in partnership on 1 July 2013, and ceased on 31 October 2015, hence apply both opening and closing year rules:

Year of assessment	**Basis period**	**Assessment** £
2013/14	1 July 2013 – 5 April 2014	
	(£20,000 × $\frac{9}{12}$)	15,000
2014/15	Year ended 30 June 2014	20,000
2015/16	Year ended 30 June 2015	28,400
2016/17	1 July 2015 – 31 October 2016	
	(£25,000 + £8,400 – £15,000)	18,400

Overlap profits = £15,000

In the assessment you will probably only need to perform Step 3 for one of the partners.

Test your understanding 3

Adam, Ben and Catrina

Adam, Ben and Catrina have been in partnership since 1 April 2011. The partnership prepares accounts to 31 December each year. On 1 November 2016, Adam retired from the partnership and the profit sharing arrangements were changed from that date onwards.

Which one of the following statements is correct?

A The partnership is deemed to cease on Adam's retirement and the partners will apply the closing year rules to calculate their trading income assessments for the final years.

B The final year of trading for Adam, Ben and Catrina will be 2016/17.

C Ben and Catrina will have to apply the opening year rules to calculate their trading income assessments for 2016/17.

D Adam will apply the closing year rules in order to calculate his trading income assessment for 2016/17.

7 Test your understanding

Test your understanding 4

Xavier

Xavier commenced trading on 1 January 2016 and prepared his first set of accounts to 31 May 2017.

The period of profits which will be taxed in the second tax year is:

A 1 January 2016 to 5 April 2016

B 1 January 2016 to 31 December 2016

C 6 April 2016 to 5 April 2017

D 12 months ended 31 May 2017

Test your understanding 5

Mario

Mario commenced trading on 1 February 2016 and intends to prepare his accounts to 31 May each year. His first set of accounts is prepared to 31 May 2017.

For 2016/17, he will be assessed on trading profits for the 12 month period to 31 May 2017.

A True

B False

Test your understanding 6

Rupert

Rupert commenced in business as a fashion designer on 1 July 2015, and prepared his first set of accounts to 30 April 2017.

His profit for the period, adjusted for taxation, was £33,000.

What is the amount of overlap profit that arises on the commencement of Rupert's trade?

A £18,000

B £16,500

C £4,500

D £Nil

Test your understanding 7

Katrina

Katrina ceased trading on 28 February 2017. Her tax adjusted trading profits for the final periods of trading are as follows:

	£
Year ended 30 June 2015	30,000
Year ended 30 June 2016	27,000
Period ended 28 February 2017	20,000

She has unrelieved overlap profits of £12,000.

What is Katrina's trading income assessment for 2016/17?

A £8,000

B £47,000

C £35,000

D £65,000

Test your understanding 8

James

James started in business on 1 January 2013 and prepared his first set of accounts to 30 April 2014.

He then continued to prepare his accounts to 30 April and his taxable trade profits in the early years were as follows:

	£
1 January 2013 – 30 April 2014	75,600
Year ended 30 April 2015	52,650
Year ended 30 April 2016	56,900

Required:

Show the amounts assessable for all tax years affected by these results and calculate the overlap profits arising.

Test your understanding 9

Avril

Avril commenced trading on 1 January 2014. She prepared accounts to 30 June each year.

Her taxable trade profits for the first few years of trading were:

Period		£
6 months to	30 June 2014	80,000
Year ended	30 June 2015	100,000
Year ended	30 June 2016	110,000

Required:

Calculate the amounts assessable for 2013/14 to 2016/17, and show the overlap profit arising to be carried forward.

Test your understanding 10

Benny

Benny, a fashion designer, decided to commence his own business on 1 July 2014. He prepared accounts on a calendar year basis and his taxable trade profits for the first few periods of trading are as follows:

Period		£
6 months to	31 December 2014	14,000
Year ended	31 December 2015	36,000
Year ended	31 December 2016	28,000

Required:

Show the amounts assessable for 2014/15 to 2016/17, and state the overlap profit to be carried forward.

Test your understanding 11

Elle

Elle prepares accounts to 31 May annually.

Recent taxable trade profits have been as follows:

	£
Year ended 31 May 2015	22,000
Year ended 31 May 2016	26,000

Elle had overlap profits on commencement of the business totalling £5,000.

Required:

Show the assessments for all relevant tax years for the following alternative dates for cessation of trading.

(a) 31 May 2017 with taxable trade profits of £27,000.

(b) 31 January 2017 with taxable trade profits of £22,500.

Test your understanding 12

Bernadette

Bernadette opened a riding school on 1 October 2013.

Accounts were prepared regularly to 30 September and her taxable trade profits are as follows:

		£
Year ended	30 September 2014	21,280
Year ended	30 September 2015	24,688
Year ended	30 September 2016	28,816
Year ended	30 September 2017	30,304

She intends to cease trading on 28 February 2018. The forecast taxable trade profits for the period from 1 October 2017 to 28 February 2018 have been estimated at £16,792.

Required:

Show the assessable amounts for all tax years of the business.

Test your understanding 13

Bay

Bay, who has been carrying on a manufacturing business in a South London suburb since 1 January 2013, decided to retire on 31 October 2016, having reached 65 years of age.

His adjusted profits (before capital allowances) and capital allowances (CAs) over the life of the business are:

		Profits	CAs
		£	£
Year ending	31 December 2013	19,487	4,343
Year ending	31 December 2014	17,840	3,879
Year ending	31 December 2015	16,928	3,310
Period ending	31 October 2016	18,040	1,326

Required:

Compute all the assessable amounts for Bay for the years 2012/13 to 2016/17 inclusive.

Note that you must proceed in the following order:

- deduct the CAs from the adjusted profits
- apply the basis period rules to the profits after deducting CAs.

Test your understanding 14

Ranjit

On 1 November 2014, Ranjit commenced a manufacturing business preparing accounts to 30 September in each year.

The adjusted profits for income tax purposes but before deducting capital allowances and the capital allowances are as follows:

		Profits	**CAs**
		£	£
Period ended	30 September 2015	6,106	3,800
Year ended	30 September 2016	8,845	5,000
Year ended	30 September 2017	19,087	9,950

Required:

Compute the assessable amounts for each of the years affected by the results and calculate the amount of overlap profits.

Test your understanding 15

Violet

Violet, a sole trader, has always prepared her accounts to 30 September.

Violet has six months of overlap profits of £7,200.

She has now decided to change her accounting date to 28 February by preparing accounts for the 17 month period to 28 February 2017.

Violet's tax adjusted trading profits after capital allowances are:

	£
Year ended 30 September 2015	15,600
Period ended 28 February 2017	42,500

Required:

Calculate Violet's trading income assessments for 2015/16 and 2016/17.

Test your understanding 16

Period of assessment

Read the following statements and state whether they are true or false.

1 The basis of assessment is always the 12 months to the accounting date ending in the tax year.

2 If Paul started trading on 1 August 2015 and prepares account to 5 April each year, he will have no overlap profits.

3 When a new partner joins a partnership, he is immediately taxed on his share of the profits of the accounting period ending in the tax year.

Test your understanding 17

John and Edward

John and Edward started trading on 1 April 2016 and made a tax adjusted trading profit for the year ended 31 March 2017 of £60,000. They agreed to split the profits equally.

Joe joined the partnership on 1 January 2017, at which point the profit sharing arrangement was changed and John, Edward and Joe agreed to share profits in the ratio 3:2:1.

What is Joe's trading income assessment for 2016/17?

A £2,500

B £5,000

C £10,000

D £7,500

Test your understanding 18

Richard and Brenda

Richard and Brenda commenced in business on 1 October 2013 as hotel proprietors, sharing profits equally.

On 1 October 2015 their son Michael joined the partnership and from that date each of the partners was entitled to one third of the profits.

Recent profits of the partnership adjusted for income tax are:

	£
Year ended 30 June 2016	50,000
Year ended 30 June 2017	60,000

What amount of profit is assessable on Michael for 2016/17?

A £12,500

B £17,500

C £8,333

D £18,750

8 Summary

As the final step in assessing profits of an individual, we must consider whether to apply the:

- current year basis
- opening year rules (and calculate overlap profits)
- closing year rules (and deduct overlap profits).

There are additional rules to learn where there has been a change of accounting date. The rules ensure that 12 months of profits are subject to tax in all tax years other than the year in which the trade starts and the year in which it stops.

9 AAT reference material

Sole traders – basis periods

Tax year – 2016/17 tax year runs from 6 April 2016 to 5 April 2017

Basis period rules

- First year – runs from start date of trading to the next 5 April.
- Second year and third year:

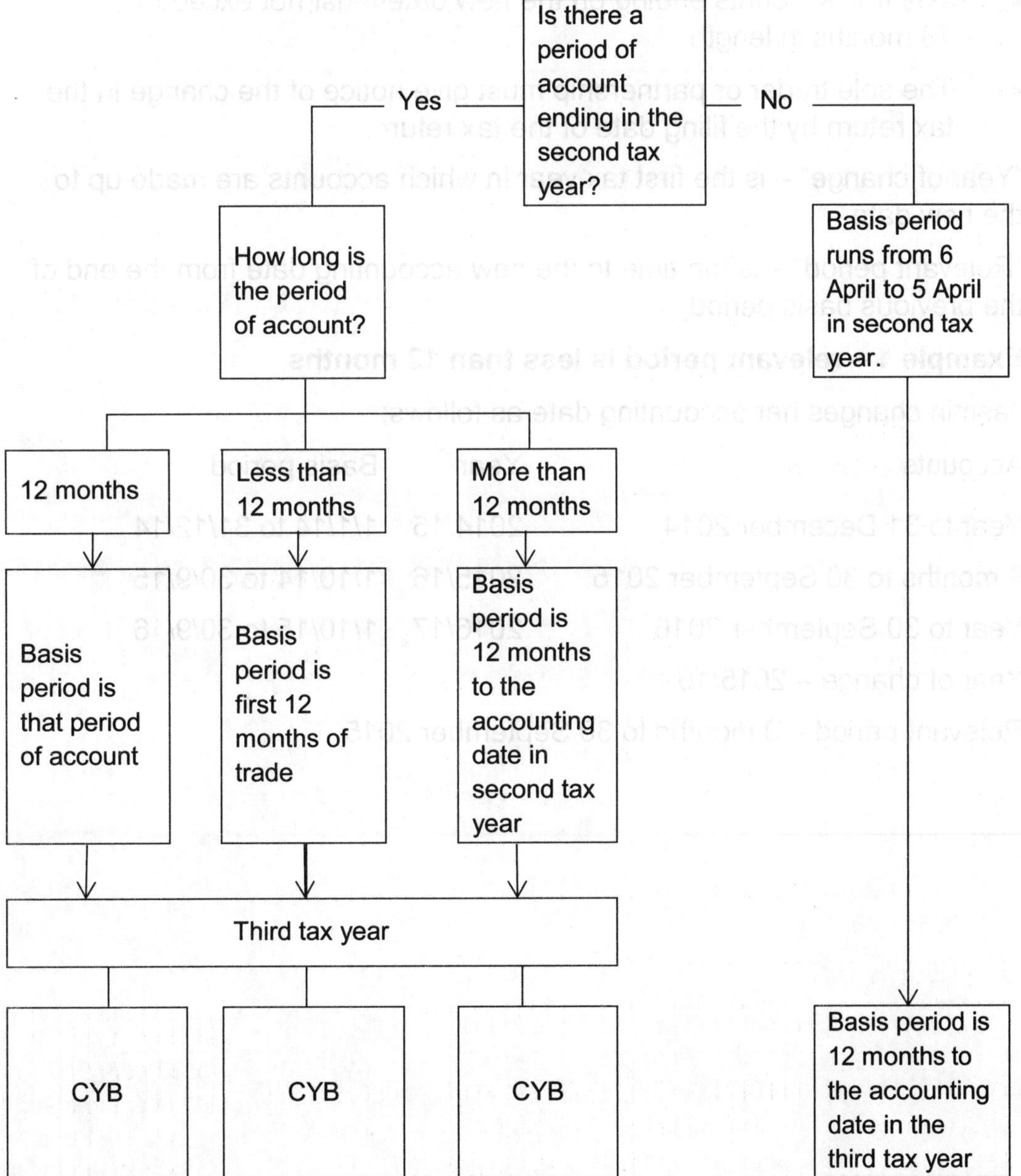

Later years – basis period is the period of account ending in the tax year = Current Year basis (CYB).

Final year – basis period is the period from the end of the basis period for the previous tax year to cessation date.

Overlap profits – opening year rules may lead to profits being taxed twice. Relief is given on cessation of the business.

Sole traders – change of accounting date

For an accounting date change to be recognised for tax purposes the following conditions must be satisfied:

- The first accounts ending on the new date must not exceed 18 months in length.
- The sole trader or partnership must give notice of the change in the tax return by the filing date of the tax return.

"Year of change" – is the first tax year in which accounts are made up to the new date.

"Relevant period" – is the time to the new accounting date from the end of the previous basis period.

Example 1 – relevant period is less than 12 months

Jasmin changes her accounting date as follows:

Accounts	Year	Basis period
Year to 31 December 2014	2014/15	1/1/14 to 31/12/14
9 months to 30 September 2015	2015/16	1/10/14 to 30/9/15
Year to 30 September 2016	2016/17	1/10/15 to 30/9/16

Year of change – 2015/16

Relevant period – 9 months to 30 September 2015

Example 2 – relevant period is greater than 12 months

Vaughan changes his accounting date as follows:

Accounts	Year	Basis period
Year to 31 December 2014	2014/15	1/1/14 to 31/12/14
15 months to 31 March 2016	2015/16	1/1/15 to 31/3/16
Year to 31 March 2017	2016/17	1/4/16 to 31/3/17

Year of change – 2015/16

Relevant period – 15 months to 31 March 2016

The rules for determining basis periods on a change of accounting date are complex. Significant examples of changes in accounting dates are:

- after the 3rd year of trading,
- with accounts of 18 months or less, and
- not straddling a tax year.

Test your understanding answers

Test your understanding 1

Jane

1 The correct answer is B.

Explanation

1 November 2013 (the date of commencement of trade) falls in the 2013/14 tax year.

2 The correct answer is C.

Explanation

The taxable profits in the first tax year are always the actual profits arising in the tax year.

Therefore the taxable profits are:

5 months ended 5 April 2014 (5/6 × £12,000)	£10,000

3 The correct answer is B.

Explanation

As the accounting period ending in the second tax year (2014/15) is less than 12 months long, the taxable period will be the first 12 months of trade.

Therefore the taxable profits are:

	£
6 months ended 30 April 2014	12,000
6 months ended 31 October 2014 (6/12 × £27,000)	13,500
	25,500

4 The correct answer is C.

Explanation

In the third tax year of trade (2015/16) the taxable trading profits are the profits for the 12 months ending on the accounting date falling in the tax year.

Therefore the taxable profits are the profits for the year ended 30 April 2015.

5 The correct answer is £23,500.

Explanation

There are two periods which are taxed twice.

Therefore the overlap profits are:

	£
5 months ended 5 April 2014 (5/6 × £12,000)	10,000
6 months ended 31 October 2014 (6/12 × £27,000)	13,500
	23,500

6 The correct answer is D.

Test your understanding 2

Robert and Jack

(a) Robert

Year of assessment	**Basis period**	**Assessment** £
2014/15	1 May 2014 – 5 April 2015	
	£20,250 + (£29,700 × 6/12)	35,100
2015/16	Year ending 30 September 2015	29,700
2016/17	Year ending 30 September 2016	36,450
2017/18	Year ending 30 September 2017	28,350

Overlap profits are:

1 Oct 2014 – 5 April 2015 (£29,700 × 6/12) £14,850

(b) Jack

Year of assessment	Basis period	Assessment £
2013/14	1 January 2014 – 5 April 2014	
	(£37,800 × 3/16)	7,087
2014/15	Year ending 5 April 2015	
	(£37,800 × 12/16)	28,350
2015/16	Year ending 30 April 2015	
	(£37,800 × 12/16)	28,350
2016/17	Year ending 30 April 2016	26,325
2017/18	Year ending 30 April 2017	29,350

Overlap profits are:

1 May 2014 – 5 April 2015 (£37,800 × 11/16) £25,987

Test your understanding 3

Adam, Ben and Catrina

The correct answer is D.

Explanation

The partnership continues despite Adam's resignation. Only Adam has to consider the closing rules to calculate his trading income assessments for 2016/17 (i.e. his final year).

The remaining partners continue to be assessed on a current year basis.

Test your understanding 4

Xavier

The correct answer is C.

Explanation

C is the correct answer because Xavier commenced trading in 2015/16, the assessment for which is calculated as the profits between 1 January 2016 and 5 April 2016.

There is no set of accounts ending in the second tax year, 2016/17, and therefore Xavier will be taxed on the basis of profits arising between 6 April 2016 and 5 April 2017.

Test your understanding 5

Mario

The correct answer is B.

Explanation

The statement is false because there are no accounts ending in 2016/17 and therefore Mario will be assessed on the basis of profits arising between 6 April 2016 and 5 April 2017.

Test your understanding 6

Rupert

The correct answer is B.

Explanation

Assessable trading profits:

Year of assessment	Basis period	Assessment £
2015/16	Actual basis – 1 July 2015 to 5 April 2016 9/22 × £33,000	13,500
2016/17	Actual basis – 6 April 2016 to 5 April 2017 12/22 × £33,000	18,000
2017/18	12 months to 30 April 2017 12/22 × £33,000	18,000

There are overlap profits for the period 1 May 2016 to 5 April 2017 of £16,500 (£33,000 × 11/22).

Test your understanding 7

Katrina

The correct answer is C.

Explanation

Assessable trading profits

Year of assessment	Basis period	Assessment £
2015/16	Year ended 30 June 2015	30,000
2016/17	1 July 2015 – 28 February 2017 (£27,000 + £20,000 – £12,000)	35,000

Test your understanding 8

James

Year of assessment	Basis period		Assessment
			£
2012/13	1 January 2013 to 5 April 2013	(£75,600 × 3/16)	14,175
2013/14	Actual basis (6 April 2013 to 5 April 2014)	(£75,600 × 12/16)	56,700
2014/15	12 months to 30 April 2014	(£75,600 × 12/16)	56,700
2015/16	Year ended 30 April 2015		52,650
2016/17	Year ended 30 April 2016		56,900
Overlap	1 May 2013 to 5 April 2014 (£75,600 × 11/16)		51,975

Test your understanding 9

Avril

Year of assessment	Basis period	Assessment
		£
2013/14	(1 Jan 2014 – 5 Apr 2014) (3 months) £80,000 × 3/6	40,000
2014/15	Accounting period is less than 12 months therefore use first 12 months	
	Period ended 30 Jun 2014 (6 months)	80,000
	Year ended 30 Jun 2015 (£100,000 × 6/12)	50,000
		130,000
2015/16	Current year basis to 30 Jun 2015	100,000
2016/17	Current year basis to 30 Jun 2016	110,000
Overlap	(1 Jan 2014 – 5 Apr 2014) £40,000 Plus (1 Jul 2014 – 31 Dec 2014) £50,000	90,000

Test your understanding 10

Benny

Year of assessment	**Basis period**	**Assessment** £
2014/15	(1 Jul 2014 – 5 Apr 2015) (9 months)	
	Period ended 31 Dec 2014 (6 months)	14,000
	Year ended 31 Dec 2015 (3 months) (£36,000 × 3/12)	9,000
		23,000
2015/16	Current year basis to 31 Dec 2015	36,000
2016/17	Current year basis to 31 Dec 2016	28,000
Overlap	(1 Jan 2015 – 5 Apr 2015) (£36,000 × 3/12)	9,000

Test your understanding 11

Elle

(a) Cessation on 31 May 2017

Year of assessment	**Basis period**	**Assessment** £
2015/16	Current year basis to 31 May 2015	22,000
2016/17	Current year basis to 31 May 2016	26,000
2017/18	Current year basis to 31 May 2017	27,000
	Less: Overlap profits	(5,000)
		22,000

(b) Cessation on 31 January 2017

Year of assessment	Basis period	Assessment £
2015/16	Current year basis to 31 May 2015	22,000
2016/17	Year to 31 May 2016	26,000
	Plus: Period to 31 Jan 2017 (cessation)	22,500
	Less: Overlap profits	(5,000)
		43,500

Test your understanding 12

Bernadette

Year of assessment	Basis period	Assessment £
2013/14	(1 October 2013 – 5 April 2014) ($^6/_{12}$ × £21,280)	10,640
2014/15	Year ended 30 September 2014	21,280
2015/16	Year ended 30 September 2015	24,688
2016/17	Year ended 30 September 2016	28,816
2017/18	Year ended 30 September 2017	30,304
	Plus period to cessation on 28 February 2018	16,792
	Less: Overlap profits (W)	(10,640)
		36,456

Working:

Overlap profits (1 Oct 2013 to 5 April 2014) (£21,280 × 6/12) = £10,640

Test your understanding 13

Bay

Year of assessment	**Basis period**	**Assessment**
		£
2012/13	1 January 2013 – 5 April 2013	
	(3/12 × £15,144) (W)	3,786
2013/14	Year ended 31 December 2013	15,144
2014/15	Year ended 31 December 2014	13,961
2015/16	Year ended 31 December 2015	13,618
2016/17	10 months to 31 October 2016	16,714
	Less: Overlap relief (W)	(3,786)
		12,928

Workings:

Overlap profits (1 Jan 2013 to 5 April 2013) (3/12 × £15,144) = £3,786

Adjusted profits after capital allowances

	Trading profit	**Capital allowances**	
	£	£	£
Year to 31 December 2013	19,487	(4,343)	15,144
Year to 31 December 2014	17,840	(3,879)	13,961
Year to 31 December 2015	16,928	(3,310)	13,618
10 months to 31 October 2016	18,040	(1,326)	16,714

Test your understanding 14

Ranjit

Year of assessment	Basis period	Assessment
		£
2014/15	1 Nov 2014 – 5 Apr 2015 (5 months of the 11 month period to 30 Sep 2015) (£2,306 × 5/11)	1,048
2015/16	Accounting period less than 12 months so: First 12 months	
	11 months to 30 Sep 2015 plus	2,306
	1 month to 31 Oct 2015 (£3,845 × 1/12)	320
		2,626
2016/17	Year ended 30 Sep 2016	3,845
2017/18	Year ended 30 Sep 2017	9,137

Overlap profits = (£1,048 + £320) = £1,368

Workings: Adjusted trading profits after capital allowances

	Trading profit	Capital allowances	
	£	£	£
Period ending 30 Sep 2015	6,106	(3,800)	2,306
Year ended 30 Sep 2016	8,845	(5,000)	3,845
Year ended 30 Sep 2017	19,087	(9,950)	9,137

Test your understanding 15

Violet

The tax year of change is the tax year in which accounts are prepared to the new accounting date (i.e. 2016/17).

As the new accounting date is later in the tax year, the basis period is the period ending with the new accounting date.

Tax year	Basis period	Taxable income
		£
2015/16	Year to 30 September 2015	15,600
2016/17	Period not yet assessed ending on the new accounting date	
	17-month period to 28 February 2017	42,500
	Less: overlap profits (£7,200 × 5/6)	(6,000)
		36,500

Note: In 2016/17 the period of account not yet assessed and ending with the new accounting date is 17 months. As no assessment can exceed 12 months, Peter is allowed to offset 5 months of his overlap profits.

The remaining month of overlap profits is carried forward as normal and is available for relief, either on a further change in accounting date or on the cessation of trade.

Test your understanding 16

Period of assessment

1	False	This is not true in the opening and closing years.
2	True	The taxable trade profits of 2015/16 will be those of the period to 5 April 2016, and for 2016/17 will be those of the year to 5 April 2017, and so on. There are no overlap periods.
3	False	The opening year rules apply to individuals joining a partnership as if they had commenced a new trade.

Test your understanding 17

John and Edward

The correct answer is A.

Explanation

A is the correct answer because profits are allocated to Joe in his first year of assessment as follows:

	John	Edward	Joe
	£	£	£
1 Apr 2016 – 31 Dec 2016			
(£60,000 × 9/12) – split evenly	22,500	22,500	
1 Jan 2017 – 31 Mar 2017			
(£60,000 × 3/12) – split 3:2:1	7,500	5,000	2,500
	30,000	27,500	2,500

Test your understanding 18

Richard and Brenda

The correct answer is B.

Explanation

This is the fourth year of trading for Richard and Brenda, so they are assessed on the normal current year basis.

It is the second year for Michael. The accounts ending in 2016/17 are for the 9 month period from the date he joined the partnership (1 October 2015) to 30 June 2016. As this period is less than 12 months his assessment is based on his first 12 months of trading.

The basis period for Michael will be:

2016/17 1 Oct 2015 – 30 Sep 2016 (1st 12 months)

The profits assessable on Michael will be:

(9/12 × £50,000/3) + (3/12 × £60,000/3) = £17,500

Trading losses for individuals

Introduction

Just like companies, individuals can also make trading losses. This chapter discusses how a loss is calculated and how it can be relieved.

ASSESSMENT CRITERIA

Assess and calculate available loss relief (4.1)

Advise on the best use of a trading loss for sole traders, partnerships and limited companies (4.2)

CONTENTS

1 Identification of a trading loss

A trading loss is calculated in exactly the same way as a trading profit.

In other words, the accounting profit (or loss) is adjusted for tax purposes, and capital allowances are taken into account.

The adjusted loss is then identified with the tax year in which it arose. This is shown in the examples below.

Example

A trader has a net accounting profit of £9,000 for the year ended 31 December 2016 which includes £3,000 of disallowable expenses. Capital allowances of £14,000 are available.

Calculate the taxable trade profits assessed in 2016/17 and the trading loss available for relief.

Solution

Year ended 31 December 2016	£
Net profit	9,000
Add: Disallowable expenses	3,000
	12,000
Less: Capital allowances	(14,000)
Adjusted loss	(2,000)

In this situation when a loss has arisen, the 2016/17 trading profits assessment is determined as £Nil and there is a (£2,000) trading loss available for relief.

Example

A trader has a net accounting loss of £9,000 for the year ended 31 December 2016 which includes £3,000 of disallowable expenses. Capital allowances of £14,000 are available.

Calculate the taxable trade profits assessed in 2016/17 and the trading loss available for relief.

Solution

	£
Accounting loss	(9,000)
Add: Disallowable expenses	3,000
	(6,000)
Less: Capital allowances	(14,000)
Adjusted loss	(20,000)

The assessment for 2016/17 is £Nil.

The trading loss available is £20,000.

It is easy to identify the wrong amount of loss available by not paying sufficient attention to the arithmetic.

Capital allowances, which normally reduce a profit, will increase a loss.

2 Ongoing businesses

2.1 Options available

There are two main ways of relieving a trading loss in an ongoing business:

- relief against total income of the current and/or the preceding tax year
- relief against future trading profits only.

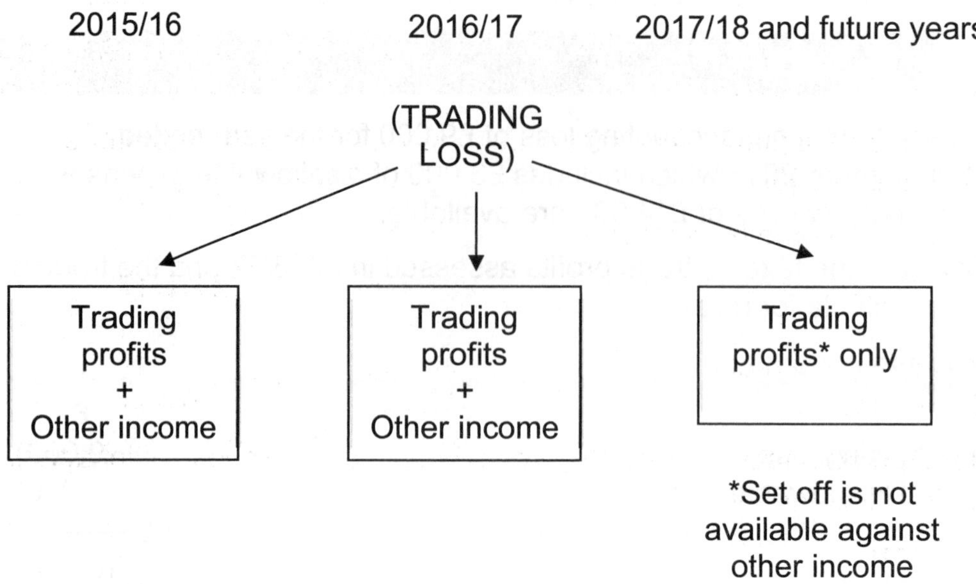

2.2 Set off of trading loss against total income

This relief allows the trading loss to be set **against total income** of:

(i) the **tax year of the loss**, and/or

(ii) the **preceding tax year**.

A claim can be made to obtain relief in either year in isolation, or in both years, in either order.

When applying the loss relief it cannot be restricted to preserve the personal allowance. The personal allowance is deducted from income after loss relief has been deducted.

The personal allowance for 2016/17 is £11,000. This means that if a trader has total income of £11,000 or less, it is not worth claiming loss relief against total income for that year as the income will be covered by the personal allowance.

Any excess loss over and above total income is available for relief by carrying forward.

The AAT reference material set out in section 8 below has the rules for this type of claim and factors to consider when considering which claim to make.

Example

Beryl has a trading loss in her accounting year ended 30 September 2016 of £18,000.

Her other income is as follows:

	2015/16	**2016/17**
	£	£
Taxable trade profits	14,000	Nil
Other income	2,000	6,000

State the alternative claims Beryl could make to obtain loss relief against her total income.

Solution

The loss for the year ended 30 September 2016 is identified with the tax year 2016/17 as the trading year ends in the tax year 2016/17.

As a result the taxable trade profits for 2016/17 are £Nil.

The loss could be offset against her total income in that year (2016/17) and/or the previous tax year (2015/16) as follows:

- set off £6,000 in 2016/17 and relieve the balance of £12,000 in 2015/16, or
- set off £6,000 in 2016/17 and make no claim for 2015/16, or
- set off £16,000 in 2015/16 and relieve the balance of £2,000 in 2016/17, or
- set off £16,000 in 2015/16 and make no claim for 2016/17.

It is important to identify all of the available options before deciding the course of action you will take.

2.3 Future relief for trading losses

The individual taxpayer does not *have* to claim relief for the loss against total income as described in section 2.2. If no such claim is made, all of the loss will be carried forward for relief in the future.

Alternatively a claim may have been made for loss relief against total income, but as it can only be used in the same tax year as the loss and/or the previous year, there may be an amount of trading loss still unrelieved after this relief. This remaining amount will be available to carry forward.

Whatever the reason, any trading loss *not* relieved in the same or previous tax year is automatically carried forward.

The trading loss carried forward must be relieved against the **first available** taxable **trading profits** from the **same trade**.

The set off cannot be restricted. If there are sufficient losses, future taxable trade profits will be reduced to £Nil.

Trading losses carried forward cannot be set against other sources of income.

Test your understanding 1

Sole trader losses

Which one of the following statements is correct with regard to a sole trader's losses?

A A loss can only be relieved against trading profits made in the same tax year

B A loss can be relieved in the preceding tax year, but only after a claim for relief has been made in the current tax year

C A carried forward loss must be relieved against profits from the same trade in future years

D A loss can be relieved against total income arising in future years

Example

Derek has been trading for some time preparing accounts to 31 July.

His recent adjusted trading results are as follows:

		£
Year ended 31 July 2014	Profit	18,000
Year ended 31 July 2015	Loss	43,200
Year ended 31 July 2016	Profit	13,000
Year ended 31 July 2017	Profit	15,000

Derek's other income in each year is £12,000.

Show Derek's net income after loss relief for all tax years affected by the above results assuming:

(a) no claim is made against total income for the trading loss

(b) full claims are made to obtain relief against total income as early as possible.

Solution

(a) If no claim is made against total income

The trading loss of 2015/16 is carried forward against future trading profits.

	2014/15	2015/16	2016/17	2017/18
	£	£	£	£
Taxable trade profits	18,000	Nil	13,000	15,000
Less: Loss relief b/f			(13,000)	(15,000)
	18,000	Nil	Nil	Nil
Other income	12,000	12,000	12,000	12,000
Net income after reliefs	30,000	12,000	12,000	12,000

Loss memorandum

	£
Year ended 31 July 2015 – Loss	43,200
Less: Utilised – 2016/17	(13,000)
– 2017/18	(15,000)
Loss left to carry forward to 2018/19	15,200

(b) Full claims made against total income

Claims against total income can only be made for 2014/15 and/or 2015/16, and any balance is carried forward for relief against future trading profits.

	2014/15	2015/16	2016/17	2017/18
	£	£	£	£
Taxable trade profits	18,000	Nil	13,000	15,000
Less: Loss relief b/f			(1,200)	–
			11,800	15,000
Other income	12,000	12,000	12,000	12,000
	30,000	12,000	23,800	27,000
Less: Loss relief				
– current year		(12,000)		
– preceding year	(30,000)			
Net income after reliefs	Nil	Nil	23,800	27,000

Loss memorandum

		£
Year ended 31 July 2015 – Loss		43,200
Less: Relief against total income	– 2014/15	(30,000)
	– 2015/16	(12,000)
		1,200
Less: Utilised in 2016/17		(1,200)
Loss left to carry forward		Nil

Test your understanding 2

Caroline

Caroline has been in business as a gourmet caterer since 1 July 2013.

She prepares accounts for calendar years and her adjusted trading results were as follows:

	£
Six months ended 31 December 2013	4,900
Year ended 31 December 2014	10,500
Year ended 31 December 2015	(45,000)
Year ended 31 December 2016	350

Caroline also receives a salary of £12,000 per annum from part-time secretarial work.

She has also received interest as follows:

2014/15 £220
2015/16 £8,715
2016/17 £8,700

Required:

Calculate Caroline's net income after reliefs (but before the personal allowance) for the years 2014/15 to 2016/17 inclusive, assuming reliefs for losses are claimed as early as possible.

3 New businesses and closing years

When an individual sets up a business or ceases to trade, the rules for trading loss relief are different.

However, only ongoing trading loss relief will be examined in your assessment.

4 Trading losses set against chargeable gains

If a trader still has loss remaining after offset against their total income for the year, they may treat the loss like a capital loss and set it off against chargeable gains of the same tax year. The claim can also be made for the previous tax year. Chargeable gains are dealt with in Chapter 18.

5 Partnership losses

5.1 Reliefs available to partners

Partners are allocated losses in the same way as profits. Each partner is then entitled to decide independently on how to use their individual share of the loss.

An ongoing partner could use their loss against total income in the current and/or preceding tax year or carry the loss forward against trading profits.

A new partner joining a partnership or an existing partner ceasing to be involved in the partnership has other loss relief opportunities available, however these are not examinable.

Test your understanding 3

Read the following statements and state whether they are true or false.

1 A sole trader can restrict the amount of loss relief claimed against total income in the current year so that the personal allowance is not lost.

2 Kate has been trading for many years. A trading loss for the year to 31 December 2016 can be relieved by set off against total income of 2015/16 and/or 2016/17 (in any order). Any balance unrelieved can be carried forward and set against future trading profits of the same trade.

3 If a partnership makes a loss, all partners must claim loss relief in the same way.

Test your understanding

Test your understanding 4

Belinda

Belinda has been trading for many years and incurred a tax adjusted trading loss for the period ended 31 December 2016.

Which one of the following statements is correct with regard to the use of the trading loss?

A The trading loss may be carried forward and set against trading income for 2016/17 arising from the same trade

B The trading loss can be set against total income for 2016/17, but only after the loss is set against total income for 2015/16

C The trading loss can be set against total income for 2015/16, irrespective of whether the loss has been set against total income for 2016/17

D The trading loss can be set against total income for 2015/16, but only after the loss is set against total income for 2016/17

Test your understanding 5

Bourbon

Bourbon has been trading as a self-employed biscuit maker for many years. His taxable trade profits or losses are given below.

		£
Year to 31 March 2016	Profit	12,200
Year to 31 March 2017	Loss	(24,050)
Year to 31 March 2018	Profit	12,750

Details of Bourbon's other income is as follows:

	2015/16	**2016/17**	**2017/18**
	£	£	£
Building society received	7,250	15,650	5,250

Required:

Set out the options available to an established continuing trade for relief of the loss and, together with calculations, advise Bourbon as to the best method of obtaining loss relief.

7 Summary

The loss reliefs available to an ongoing business are summarised below.

- Relief against total income – current and/or preceding tax year.
- Carry forward against future profits of the same trade.
- Relief against gains – current and/or preceding tax year provided a claim is made against income of the same tax year first.

8 AAT reference material

Trading losses for sole traders and partners

- A loss is computed in the same way as a profit, making the same adjustments to the net profit as per the accounts and deducting capital allowances.

Set off of trading loss against total income

- Set off loss against total income of the preceding tax year and/or the tax year of loss, e.g. loss in 2016/17 set off against total income in 2015/16 and/or 2016/17.
- Cannot restrict loss to preserve use of personal allowance so personal allowance may be wasted.
- For 2016/17 loss claim needed by 31 January 2019.

Carry forward of trading losses

- If any loss remains unrelieved after current year and carry back claim has been made, or no such claims are made, then carry forward the loss against first available profits of the same trade.

Choice of loss relief – consider the following:

- Utilise loss in the tax year in which income is taxed at a higher rate.
- Possible wastage of personal allowance.
- Review the projected future profits to ensure the loss can be utilised.
- If cash flow is important, a loss carry back claim may result in a tax refund being paid to the company.

Test your understanding answers

Test your understanding 1

Sole trader losses

The correct answer is C.

Explanation

Once a loss has been carried forward it must be set against future profits of the same trade. It cannot be set against total income in the future.

The taxpayer can choose whether to offset a trading loss against total income in the current tax year and/or the preceding year. It is not necessary to make these claims in any particular order.

Test your understanding 2

Caroline

Income tax computations

	2014/15	2015/16	2016/17
	£	£	£
Taxable trade profits	10,500	Nil	350
Less: Loss relief b/f	–	–	(350)[(3)]
	10,500	Nil	Nil
Employment income	12,000	12,000	12,000
Interest	220	8,715	8,700
Total income	22,720	20,715	20,700
Less: Loss relief			
– preceding year	(22,720)[(1)]		
– current year		(20,715)[(2)]	
Net income after reliefs	Nil	Nil	20,700

Notes:

1 Relief against total income can be in any order.

2 The question says offset the loss as early as possible, therefore the claim is made against 2014/15 first, then 2015/16.

3 The remaining loss is then carried forward to 2016/17 and set against the first available trading profits.

Loss memorandum

		£
Loss in 2015/16 – year ended 31 December 2015		45,000
Less: Claim 2014/15 (preceding year)	(1)	(22,720)
		22,280
Less: Claim 2015/16 (year of loss)	(2)	(20,715)
		1,565
Less: Carry forward claim 2016/17	(3)	(350)
Loss carried forward		1,215

Test your understanding 3

1 False Loss relief claims cannot be restricted to preserve the personal allowance.

2 True

3 False Each partner can choose independently what loss relief to claim.

Test your understanding 4

Belinda

The correct answer is C.

Explanation

The trading loss can be carried forward and set against future trading profits, but the loss is incurred in 2016/17 and will therefore be available to carry forward to 2017/18, not 2016/17.

The trading loss can be set against total income of 2016/17 and/or 2015/16. There is no need for the claim for 2016/17 to be made before that of 2015/16 or vice versa.

Test your understanding 5

Bourbon

(a) Alternative means of loss relief

(i) Carry forward for set off against the next available taxable trading income from the same trade until the loss is fully relieved.

(ii) Claim against the total income of:
- the tax year of loss; and/or
- the preceding tax year.

(b) Advice on relief

From the following computations it can be seen that the best method of obtaining relief is for Bourbon to claim relief against total income for 2015/16 to obtain relief as early as possible.

A claim against total income should also be made in 2016/17 for the balance of the loss, as there will still be enough income remaining after the loss claim to use up the personal allowance of £11,000.

	2015/16	2016/17	2017/18
	£	£	£
Trading profits	12,200	Nil	12,750
Less: Loss relief b/f	–	–	–
	12,200	Nil	12,750
Interest	7,250	15,650	5,250
	19,450	15,650	18,000
Less: Loss relief			
– Current year		(4,600)	
– Carry back	(19,450)		
Net income after reliefs	Nil	11,050	18,000

Payment and administration – individuals

Introduction

This chapter covers tax returns and amendments, the payment of tax and compliance checks for individuals.

ASSESSMENT CRITERIA
Tax return filing deadlines (3.1)
Payment rules for sole traders and partnerships: amounts and dates (3.1)
Penalties for late filing of tax returns and failing to notify chargeability (3.2)
Late payment interest and surcharges (3.2)
The enquiry window and penalties for incorrect returns (3.2)
What records need to be maintained by a business, how long these records need to be maintained and the penalties for failing to keep these records (4.3)

CONTENTS

1 Introduction to the self-assessment return

1.1 The self-assessment return

Certain individuals are required to complete a return for every tax year.

Amongst other things the return covers trading income and capital gains and, in some cases, a calculation of the tax payable.

The key details to grasp concerning the return are the filing dates.

The taxpayer has the choice of filing a paper return or filing electronically online. The date by which a return must be filed depends on the method used.

All completed and signed paper returns must be filed by:

- 31 October following the end of the tax year.

All online electronic returns must be filed by:

- 31 January following the end of the tax year.

The relevant dates for a 2016/17 return are therefore 31 October 2017 for a paper return and 31 January 2018 for an electronic return.

HMRC normally issue an individual with a notice to complete a tax return in April/May following the end of the tax year.

However, where HMRC issue a notice to complete a tax return late, the taxpayer has until the later of the filing dates mentioned above and 3 months after the notice is issued in which to file their return.

An individual who receives a notice to file a 2016/17 tax return from HMRC on 15 August 2017 therefore has until 15 November 2017 to file a paper return or until 31 January 2018 to file the return electronically.

31 January following the end of the tax year is known as the ‘filing date’, regardless of whether the return is filed on paper or electronically. This must be distinguished from the date on which the return is filed/submitted to HMRC (known as the ‘actual’ filing date).

The return consists of an eight page summary form with six supplementary pages for self-employed individuals.

In the assessment you will only be required to complete page 2 of the self-employment supplementary pages and/or page 6 of the partnership return.

Where a notice to file a tax return is not issued, an individual is required to notify HMRC by **5 October** following the tax year where there is chargeable income (i.e. new sources of income) or gains arising.

Notification is not required where there are no assessable gains or where the income is either covered by allowances or the full tax liability has been deducted at source.

Failure to notify may result in a penalty. The penalty is calculated in broadly the same way as penalties for incorrect returns (see below) and is a maximum of 100% of the tax outstanding.

The taxpayer is permitted to correct or 'repair' his self-assessment return within 12 months of the filing date (i.e.by 31 January 2019 for a 2016/17 return). HMRC can correct 'obvious errors' and anything else which they believe to be incorrect by reference to the information they hold in the period of nine months from actual filing.

Where an assessment is excessive due to an error or mistake in a return, the taxpayer can claim overpayment relief. The claim must be made within four years of the end of the tax year concerned. Note that this claim is currently referred to by the old terminology of an 'error or mistake claim' in the AAT reference material.

Note that many of the details about dates, time limits and penalties are contained in the AAT reference material set out below in section 8. You should refer to this throughout this chapter.

1.2 Records

An individual must retain certain records to support the completed tax return, to assist with providing evidence to support information given to HMRC.

Self-employed people (i.e. sole traders and partners in a partnership) must keep records for five years after the filing date (i.e. until 31 January 2023 for 2016/17 information).

Examples of records to be kept include the following:

- accounts
- supporting documentation such as receipts and invoices
- Dividend vouchers.

Failure to keep records can lead to a penalty of up to £3,000.

1.3 Penalties for late filing

Failure to submit a return by 31 January following a tax year will result in a penalty.

The system operates as follows:

• Immediate penalty	£100
• Delay of more than three months	an additional £10 per day (maximum 90 days = £900)
• Delay of more than six months	an additional 5% of tax due
• Delay of more than 12 months, the penalties above, plus:	
No deliberate withholding of information	5% of tax due
Deliberate withholding of information	70% of tax due
Deliberate withholding of information with concealment	100% of tax due

The penalties based on the tax due are each subject to a minimum of £300.

A penalty will not be charged if the taxpayer has a reasonable excuse for the late filing, for example a serious illness. A lack of knowledge of the tax system is not a reasonable excuse.

Test your understanding 1

Bob

Bob understands that he has responsibilities under the self-assessment system and is required to meet a number of deadlines. In particular he needs confirmation of the deadlines for the following actions.

1 Notifying HMRC that he started receiving rent for the first time on 1 January 2017.

2 Filing a paper return for 2016/17.

3 Filing his 2016/17 return electronically.

4 Amending his 2016/17 tax return.

Match each of Bob's responsibilities with the correct deadline:

A 5 October 2017

B 31 January 2018

C 31 October 2017

D 31 January 2019

2 Payment of income tax and capital gains tax

2.1 The instalment system

As well as submitting a tax return certain individuals will also need to make payments of tax.

Self-employed individuals are required to pay their tax liability in instalments.

The instalment system operates as follows:

- 31 January in the tax year: first payment on account (POA).
- 31 July *following* the tax year: second payment on account (POA).
- 31 January *following* the tax year: final payment

For example, for 2016/17 the following dates are relevant:

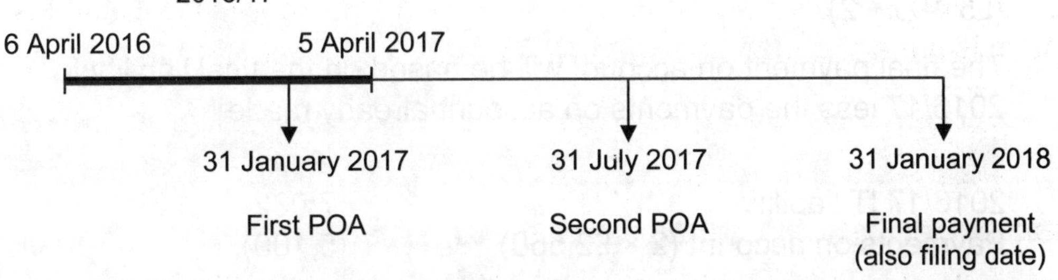

The payments on account are estimated, in that they are based on the previous year's income tax and class 4 national insurance contributions (NICs) payable. Note that the tax payable figure used in the payments on account calculation is net of any tax deducted under PAYE.

The taxpayer can claim to make reduced payments on account where this year's income tax payable is expected to be less than that of last year. The taxpayer will be charged a penalty if the claim to make reduced payments on account was made either fraudulently or negligently.

In the assessment a detailed understanding of the payments on account system is expected, including when payments are due and how to pay them.

Example

Roderic is self-employed. His only source of income is from his trade. The income tax payable for 2015/16 was £5,100.

His income tax payable for 2016/17 based on his taxable trade profits for the year ended 31 July 2016 is £7,032.

Ignoring NICs, state Roderic's payments in respect of his 2016/17 income tax liability.

Solution

Step 1: Determine the relevant dates

31 January 2017	–	first payment on account
31 July 2017	–	second payment on account
31 January 2018	–	final payment

Step 2: Determine the amounts due

- The amounts due for the 'payments on account' are based on an equal division of the previous year's tax payable, hence £2,550 (£5,100 ÷ 2).
- The final payment on account will be based on the final liability for 2016/17 less the payments on account already made.

	£
2016/17 IT liability	7,032
Payments on account (2 × £2,550)	(5,100)
Final payment	1,932

Step 3: Prepare a final summary

	£
31 January 2017	2,550
31 July 2017	2,550
31 January 2018	1,932

The amount due on 31 January following the end of the tax year consists of the final payment on account for the year just ended and the first payment on account for the new tax year

In Roderic's case this means that on 31 January 2018 he will start the instalment option all over again, by making the first payment on account of his 2017/18 liability based on 2016/17 tax payable.

Hence his 31 January 2018 payment is £5,448 ((£7,032 × ½) + £1,932).

The class 4 national insurance contributions payable by a self-employed person are also paid by the instalment system (see Chapter 14).

Test your understanding 2

Kazuo

Kazuo is required to pay tax in instalments.

For 2015/16, his income tax liability was £18,700, of which £2,000 was collected via PAYE. He estimates that his income tax payable for 2016/17 will be £22,000.

What is the amount of the first payment on account that Kazuo should make on 31 January 2017 in respect of his income tax liability for 2016/17?

Ignore national insurance.

A £8,350

B £9,350

C £10,000

D £11,000

2.2 No requirement for payments on account

Payments on account are not required in the following circumstances:

- The income tax and class 4 NICs payable for the previous tax year by self-assessment is less than £1,000, or
- More than 80% of the income tax liability for the previous tax year was met through tax deducted at source.

2.3 Class 2 NICs

Class 2 NICs (see Chapter 14) are payable on 31 January following the end of the tax year, together with the final payment of income tax. They are not subject to payments on account.

2.4 Capital gains tax

The capital gains tax due for a tax year (see Chapter 18) is payable on 31 January following the end of the tax year, together with the final payment of income tax.

CGT is therefore paid in one instalment on 31 January following the tax year regardless of whether there was a CGT liability for the previous year.

The CGT liability is not taken into account when determining the payments on account for income tax.

Payments on account of capital gains tax are never required.

Test your understanding 3

Required:

(a) State the latest date by which the taxpayer should submit the 2016/17 tax return if:

- (i) he wishes to file his return online; or
- (ii) he wishes to file a paper return.

(b) State:

- (i) the normal dates of payment of income tax and class 4 NICs for a sole trader in respect of the tax year 2016/17; and
- (ii) how the amounts of these payments are calculated.

(c) State:

- (i) the penalties that can be charged where a tax return is submitted within six months after the due date; and
- (ii) the penalties that can be charged where a tax return is submitted more than six months late.

2.5 How to pay

There are a number of ways to pay your tax liability.

HMRC recommends that you make your payments electronically using one of the methods described below.

Electronic payments are generally more efficient and secure, provided you give HMRC an accurate reference number.

Electronic payment methods

- Internet or telephone banking.
- Direct debit.
- Payment by debit or credit card over the Internet: (BillPay).
- Bank Giro.
- By cheque at the Post Office (this is regarded by HMRC as an electronic payment).

Payment by post

HMRC highly recommends using one of the other electronic methods set out above, however, it is also possible to pay by post with a cheque and an HMRC payslip.

If the taxpayer does not have a payslip they must provide their name, address, telephone number, self-assessment reference, the due date for the tax payment and confirm the amount of tax they are paying.

2.6 Recovery of overpaid tax

A taxpayer who believes that they have paid too much income tax or capital gains tax can submit a claim in order to have the excess tax repaid. The claim must be submitted within 4 years of the end of the relevant tax year.

3 Interest and penalties on payments of tax

3.1 Interest

Taxpayers that fail to make payments, whether payments on account (POA) or final payments, by the due date will be charged interest.

Interest is not perceived as being a penalty but merely as commercial compensation for late payment. It is not a deductible expense when computing taxable income.

Interest is charged from the day the tax is due until the day it is paid.

In addition to the interest charge there is also a penalty where tax is paid late.

An individual who receives a tax repayment may receive interest in respect of the amount repaid. This interest income is not taxable.

The tax treatment of interest on underpayments/overpayments of corporation tax paid by or to companies is different from that for individuals and is covered in Chapter 7.

Example

Rodney was due to make the following payments of tax for 2016/17.

		Actual date of payment
31 January 2017	£2,100	28 February 2017
31 July 2017	£2,100	31 August 2017
31 January 2018	£1,000	31 March 2018

For what periods will interest be charged?

Solution

On first POA	31 January 2017 – 28 February 2017	1 month
On second POA	31 July 2017 – 31 August 2017	1 month
On final payment	31 January 2018 – 31 March 2018	2 months

3.2 Penalty for late payment of tax

A penalty will be charged where there is income tax or capital gains tax outstanding after the day on which the final payment of tax is due (31 January after the end of the tax year). This penalty is in addition to any interest that is charged.

- More than 30 days late — 5% of tax overdue
- More than six months late — further 5% of tax overdue
- More than 12 months late — further 5% of tax overdue

A late payment penalty may be mitigated (i.e. reduced) where the taxpayer can provide a reasonable excuse, for example a serious illness.

Insufficiency of funds or lack of knowledge of self-assessment are not reasonable excuses.

Example

Star submitted the final payment in respect of his 2015/16 self-assessment return on 31 August 2017.

What penalties will be charged in respect of the late payment of the tax?

Solution

The final payment in respect of the 2015/16 self-assessment return was due on 31 January 2017. The payment is more than six months but less than 12 months late.

Because the return is more than six months late there will be a total penalty of 10% of the tax outstanding, i.e. 5% for being 30 days late and an additional 5% for being 6 months late.

(Note that Star will also be charged interest on the late paid tax from 31 January 2017 to 31 August 2017. However, the question only asked for the penalties.)

4 HM Revenue and Customs' compliance checks

4.1 Introduction

HMRC have the right to enquire into an individual's tax return (similar to the system on corporation tax returns) under their compliance check powers. This may be a random check or because they have reason to believe that income or expenses have been misstated in the tax return.

They must make their compliance check (enquiry) within 12 months of the date the return was filed.

4.2 Compliance check (enquiry) procedure

Once the compliance check notice is given, an Officer can request relevant documents and written particulars. If the individual fails to do so, a penalty of £300, plus up to £60 a day, may be imposed.

At the end of the compliance check a completion notice is issued stating the outcome of the enquiry, for example, no amendment made or business profits increased by a particular amount.

The taxpayer has 30 days from completion to ask for their case to be reviewed.

4.3 Discovery assessments

Although HMRC usually only have 12 months from the date a return is filed to open a compliance check (enquiry), they can replace a self-assessment at a later date by making a discovery assessment.

A discovery assessment can be made where tax has been lost perhaps because of insufficient information in the tax return.

The taxpayer can appeal to the Tax Tribunal against a discovery assessment.

4.4 Appeals procedure

The taxpayer can request an informal review of a disputed decision.

Alternatively, a formal appeal may be made to the Tax Tribunal.

Appeals from the Tax Tribunal on a point of law (but not on a point of fact) may be made to the Court of Appeal and from there to the Supreme Court.

The Tax Tribunal is independent of HMRC.

5 Penalties for incorrect returns

The common penalty regime described in Chapter 9 applies to income tax returns as well as corporation tax returns.

The penalties are the same for individuals in that a penalty will be charged where an inaccurate return is submitted to HMRC or where the individual fails to notify HMRC where an under assessment of tax is made by them.

Example

State the maximum and minimum penalties that may be levied on each of the following individuals who have submitted incorrect tax returns.

Lars Deliberately understated his tax liability and attempted to conceal the incorrect information that he had provided. HMRC have identified the understatement and Lars is helping them with their enquiries.

Sven Accidentally provided an incorrect figure even though he checked his tax return carefully. He realised his mistake a few days later and notified HMRC.

Jo Completed his tax return too quickly and made a number of errors. The day after he had submitted the tax return he decided to check it thoroughly and immediately provided HMRC with the information necessary to identify the errors.

Solution

Penalties for incorrect tax returns are a percentage of the under declared tax.

Lars The maximum percentage for a deliberate understatement with concealment is 100%. The minimum percentage for prompted disclosure of information (where the taxpayer provides information in response to HMRC identifying the error) in respect of deliberate understatement with concealment is 50%.

Sven No penalty is charged where a taxpayer has been careful and has made a genuine mistake.

Jo The maximum percentage for failing to take reasonable care is 30%. The minimum percentage for unprompted disclosure is nil.

Test your understanding 4

1 James commenced his own business in February 2017.

If he does not receive a notice to complete a tax return for 2016/17, by what date should he notify HMRC that he is chargeable to tax for 2016/17?

2 Isabel made her second payment on account of tax for 2016/17 on 15 September 2017.

What are the consequences?

3 Mike filed his 2016/17 tax return on 18 January 2018.

What is the latest date for HMRC to open a compliance check (enquiry)?

6 Test your understanding

Test your understanding 5

Payments on account

State the appropriate dates in respect of the following payments.

1 First instalment for tax year – 2016/17

2 Second instalment for tax year – 2016/17

3 Final instalment for tax year – 2016/17

4 Payment date for capital gains tax for tax year – 2016/17

Test your understanding 6

Income tax self-assessment

Read the following statements and state whether they are true or false.

1 An individual must retain their tax records for 2016/17 until 5 April 2022.

2 If an individual is two months late in submitting their tax return for 2016/17, they will receive a penalty of £100.

3 Penalties for errors made by individuals in their tax return vary from 30% to 100%.

4 Late payment penalties can be imposed on balancing payments made late.

Test your understanding 7

Income tax self-assessment

Clark is a new client who has come to you for information about the self-assessment system.

Explain to Clark:

(a) The latest date by which income tax returns for the year 2016/17 should be submitted to HM Revenue and Customs (HMRC).

(b) The date by which Clark should notify HMRC that he has received income in the year 2016/17 which is liable to income tax where no notice to complete an income tax return has been issued.

(c) The potential penalties for the late submission of income tax returns and when they apply.

(d) The penalty for the submission of an incorrect income tax return.

(e) The penalty for failing to maintain or retain adequate records to back up an income tax return.

7 Summary

This chapter covers a core topic – self-assessment.

Traders have to self-assess their tax liability and pay any tax due because they receive trading income gross, i.e. without deduction of tax at source.

Payment dates

31 January 2017

- Balance of income tax and class 4 NICs payable for 2015/16.
- CGT liability for 2015/16.
- First POA for 2016/17 (based on previous year's liability).

31 July 2017

- Second POA for 2016/17.

31 January 2018

- Balance of income tax and class 4 NICs payable for 2016/17.
- CGT liability for 2016/17.
- First POA for 2017/18 (based on liability for 2016/17).

Filing returns (2016/17 return)

Paper return – 31 October 2017

Electronic return – 31 January 2018 (the 'filing date')

Main penalties

Late filing – an immediate £100 penalty with further penalties if the return is more than three, six or 12 months late.

Incorrect returns – same as Corporation tax (see Chapter 7)

Tax unpaid 30 days after 31 January – 5% penalty with further 5% penalties if the tax remains outstanding after 6 and 12 months.

If no compliance check (enquiry) notice issued by the anniversary of the date the return is filed, the taxpayer can assume it is 'final'.

However, if HMRC are able to show they had insufficient information supplied in the tax return, they can make a 'discovery' assessment.

8 AAT reference material

Payment and administration – sole traders and partners

The return must be filed by:

- 31 October following the end of the tax year if filing a paper return.
- 31 January following the end of the tax year if filing online.

Penalties for late filing and payment

Late filing	Late payment	Penalty
Miss filing deadline		£100
	30 days late	5% of tax due or £300, if greater
3 months late		Daily penalty £10 per day for up to 90 days (max £900)
6 months late		5% of tax due or £300, if greater
	6 months late	5% of tax outstanding at that date
12 months late		5% or £300 if greater
	12 months late	5% of tax outstanding at that date
12 months and information deliberately withheld		Based on behaviour: • deliberate and concealed withholding – 100% of tax due, or £300 if greater. • deliberate but not concealed – 70% of tax due, or £300 if greater. Reductions of up to half of the above %'s apply for cooperation with investigation.

Disclosure and errors

- Taxpayer must notify HMRC by 5 October following end of the tax year if a tax return is needed.
- Taxpayer can amend a tax return within 12 months of filing date or make an error or mistake claim within 3 years of the filing date.

Payments on account (POA)

- Due 31 January (in tax year) and 31 July (after tax year end). Each instalment is 50% of the previous year's tax and Class 4 National Insurance contribution (NIC) liability.
- Balancing payment made 31 January after tax year end.
- No POA due if last year's tax and Class 4 NIC liability less than £1,000 or greater than 80% if last year's liability was deducted at source.
- Can reduce POA if this year's liability expected to be less than last year's. Penalties will be charged if a deliberate incorrect claim is made.
- Capital gains tax (CGT) liability is paid 31 January following the tax year end. No POA needed for CGT.

Interest on tax paid late/overpaid tax

- Interest charged daily on late payment.

Enquiries and other penalties

- HMRC must notify individual of enquiry within 12 months of submission of return.
- Basis of enquiry – random or HMRC believe income/expenses misstated.
- Penalty for failure to produce enquiry documents = £300 + £60 per day.
- Penalty for failure to keep proper records is up to £3,000. Records must be kept for 5 years after the filing date for the relevant tax year.
- Penalties for incorrect returns are:

Type of behaviour	**Maximum**	**Unprompted (minimum)**	**Prompted (minimum)**
Genuine mistake: despite taking reasonable care	0%	0%	0%
Careless error and inaccuracy is due to failure to take reasonable care	30%	0%	15%
Deliberate error but not concealed	70%	20%	35%
Deliberate error and concealed	100%	30%	50%

Test your understanding answers

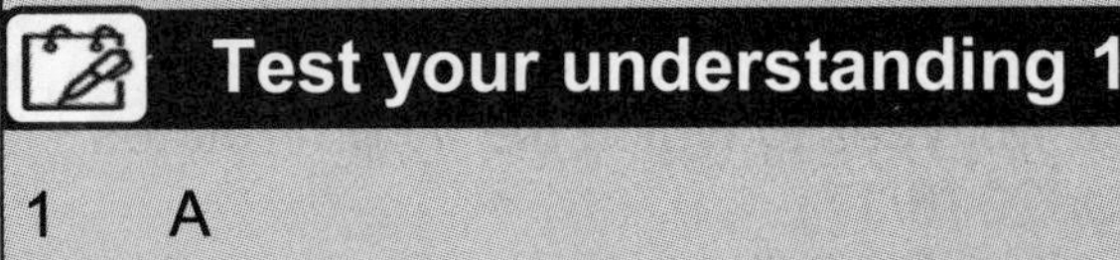

Test your understanding 1

1 A

2 C

3 B

4 D

Test your understanding 2

Kazuo

The correct answer is A.

Explanation

The payment on account is calculated as follows:

	£
2015/16 income tax liability	18,700
Less: PAYE	(2,000)
Income tax payable under self-assessment	16,700
First payment on account for 2016/17 (£16,700 ÷ 2)	8,350

Test your understanding 3

Self-assessment

(a) (i) 31 January following the tax year to which the return relates (i.e. 31 January 2018 for 2016/17).

(ii) 31 October following the tax year to which the return relates (i.e. 31 October 2017 for 2016/17).

(b) (i) (1) 31 January in the tax year (i.e. 31 January 2017).

(2) 31 July following the tax year (i.e. 31 July 2017).

(3) 31 January following the tax year (i.e. 31 January 2018).

(ii) Payments 1 and 2 are equal amounts each amounting to half the income tax and class 4 NIC payable in respect of the preceding tax year.

Payment 3 is the balancing figure (i.e. it is the amount of the final income tax and class 4 NIC liability for the year, less any tax deducted at source, less payments 1 and 2).

(c) (i) There will be an immediate penalty of £100.

A further penalty of £10 per day for a maximum of 90 days can be charged once the return is more than three months late.

(ii) As well as the penalties listed above, there will be a further penalty of 5% of the tax due (minimum £300) once the return is more than six months late.

Once the return is more than 12 months late there will be a further penalty equal to a percentage of the tax due (minimum £300). The percentage is determined by the reason for the delay.

No deliberate withholding of information	5%
Deliberate withholding	70%
Deliberate withholding with concealment	100%

Test your understanding 4

1 James must notify HMRC by 5 October 2017.

2 Isabel will be charged interest from the due date of 31 July 2017 until 15 September 2017, the day of payment.

3 The latest date for opening a compliance check (enquiry) is 18 January 2019; one year after Mike filed the return.

Test your understanding 5

Payments on account

1 31 January 2017

2 31 July 2017

3 31 January 2018

4 31 January 2018

Test your understanding 6

Period of assessment

1	False	The records must be retained until 31 January 2023.
2	True	
3	False	The penalties start at 0% for a genuine mistake.
4	True	

Test your understanding 7

Income tax self-assessment

(a) The date by which a return must be filed depends on the filing method used.

A paper return must be filed by 31 October 2017 for the tax year 2016/17 (i.e. 31 October following the end of the tax year).

An electronic return must be filed by 31 January 2018 for the tax year 2016/17 (i.e. 31 January following the end of the tax year).

(b) Notification is due by 5 October 2017 if a new source arises in 2016/17 and a tax notice to complete a tax return has not been issued.

(c) If a tax return is submitted late, a £100 fixed penalty is charged.

If it is still outstanding after 3 months, a further £10 per day can be charged for a maximum of 90 days.

If it is still outstanding after 6 months, a further penalty equal to 5% of the tax due is charged.

If the return is still outstanding after 12 months, a penalty of up to 100% of the tax outstanding is charged.

(d) The penalty for submitting an incorrect tax return is a percentage of the revenue lost.

The percentage ranges from 0% (where the taxpayer has simply made a mistake) to 100% (where the taxpayer has deliberately understated the return and concealed the error).

(e) The penalty for failing to maintain adequate records is up to £3,000.

National insurance contributions payable by self-employed individuals

Introduction

A self-employed individual has his/her own national insurance contributions to pay, but may also have to pay contributions as an employer.

ASSESSMENT CRITERIA
Determine who is liable to pay NI contributions (1.5)
Calculate NI contributions (1.5)

CONTENTS

1 Contributions as an employer

1.1 Class 1 secondary and class 1A contributions

A sole trader or partnership may employ staff.

As an employer, they may be liable to class 1 secondary and class 1A contributions in relation to the remuneration paid to their employees.

However, calculations of these contributions are outside the syllabus for business tax.

2 Contributions as a sole trader

2.1 Class 4 NICs

A self-employed person, whether operating as a sole trader or as a partner, pays two types of national insurance contributions:

- class 2 and
- class 4.

Class 4 NICs are calculated by applying a fixed percentage (currently 9%) to the amount by which the taxpayer's 'profits' (or share of 'profits', where the taxpayer is a member of a partnership) exceed a lower limit (£8,060 for 2016/17).

Example

If Nicholas has 'profits' of £12,775 for 2016/17, he will be liable to pay class 4 NICs calculated as follows:

	£
'Profits'	12,775
Less: Lower limit	(8,060)
Excess	4,715
Class 4 NICs (9% × £4,715)	424.35

The 9% rate only applies up to an upper limit of profits (£43,000 for 2016/17).

Where a taxpayer's 'profits' exceed the upper limit, the excess profit is liable to class 4 NICs at 2%.

For example, if a taxpayer has taxable trading profits of £50,000 for 2016/17 he is liable to class 4 NICs of £3,284.60 calculated as follows:

	£
(£43,000 – £8,060) × 9%	3,144.60
(£50,000 – £43,000) × 2%	140.00
	3,284.60

Note that where a taxpayer's 'profits' do not exceed the lower limit (i.e. £8,060 for 2016/17); there is no liability to class 4 NICs.

2.2 Profits

The 'profits' to be used in the calculation of the taxpayer's liability to class 4 NICs are:

	£
Taxable trade profits	X
Less: Trading losses brought forward	(X)
Profits for class 4 NICs	X

2.3 Payments of class 4 NICs

Class 4 NICs are payable under self-assessment at the same time as the related income tax liability (i.e. two payments on account and a balancing payment).

Interest will be charged on late payments.

A taxpayer does not have to pay class 4 NICs if they are:

- of State Pension age or over at the beginning of the tax year
- aged under 16 at the beginning of the tax year.

State Pension age is currently 65 for men and is gradually being increased for women from 60 to 65. You would be told in an assessment if a woman had reached State Pension age.

2.4 Class 2 NICs

In addition to class 4 NICs, a trader is also liable for class 2 NICs which are payable at a fixed rate of £2.80 per week. The liability relates to the individual trader, such that it does not increase where an individual has more than one trade.

There is no liability if the 'profits' are below the small profits threshold of £5,965.

'Profits' for class 2 NIC purposes are the same as for class 4 purposes (i.e. tax adjusted trading profits less losses brought forward).

Class 2 NICs are payable under the self-assessment system. They are reported on the tax return and payable on 31 January following the end of the tax year (i.e. 31 January 2018 for 2016/17). There are no payments on account for class 2 NICs.

A taxpayer does not have to pay class 2 NICs in respect of any week in which they are:

- aged under 16; or
- of State Pension age or over.

State Pension age is currently 65 for men and is gradually being increased for women from 60 to 65. You would be told in an assessment if a woman had reached State Pension age.

Note that the AAT reference material set out in section 6 below includes some details on Class 2 and 4 NIC.

3 Effect of partnerships

3.1 Each partner is treated as a separate sole trader

Each partner must pay:

- their own class 2 contributions; and
- their own class 4 contributions.

Both class 2 and class 4 contributions are based on his share of profits, as assessed to income tax for the tax year.

Test your understanding 1

1 A taxpayer has self-employed income of £80,000 for the tax year 2016/17. The amount of his income which will be chargeable to class 4 NICs at 2% is £

2 A taxpayer has self-employed income of £30,000. The amount of class 4 NICs payable would be £

3 Anne has tax adjusted trading profits for 2016/17 of £6,600.

Her accounts show a net profit of £6,000 for the year to 31 March 2017.

- What class 4 NICs are due? £
- What class 2 NICs are due? £

4 Which one of the following statements is correct?

A Self-employed taxpayers pay either class 2 or class 4 NICs, but not both

B Every self-employed taxpayer must pay class 2 NICs, regardless of the level of their profits

C Class 4 NICs are based on the amount of income a taxpayer withdraws from the business

D In a partnership, each partner is responsible for their own NICs

4 Test your understanding

Test your understanding 2

Naomi

Naomi, aged 45, has been self-employed for many years.

Required:

State the national insurance contributions payable by Naomi for 2016/17, assuming her taxable trade profits are:

(a) £6,000

(b) £24,500

(c) £44,500

Test your understanding 3

Adrian

Adrian's tax liability for 2015/16 was as follows:

	£
Income tax liability	9,400
Less: PAYE	(2,100)
Income tax payable	7,300
Class 2 NICs	146
Class 4 NICs	700
CGT	5,000
	13,146

What will each of the payments on account be for 2016/17?

A £6,573

B £4,073

C £4,000

D £3,650

5 Summary

Sole traders and partners may have to pay the following contributions:

- class 2, and
- class 4.

6 AAT reference material

National Insurance contributions

- Self-employed individuals pay Class 2 and Class 4 contributions.

  Class 4 contributions are at 9% on profits between the lower and upper limits, then 2% on profits above the upper limit.
- Percentages and limits are provided in the Taxation Tables.

Test your understanding answers

Test your understanding 1

1 £37,000 (£80,000 – £43,000)

2 £1,974.60 (£30,000 – £8,060) × 9%

3 Anne's NICs for 2016/17 are:

- class 4 – £Nil, taxable profits less than £8,060
- class 2 – £145.60 (£2.80 per week for 52 weeks), as taxable profits exceed £5,965.

4 The correct answer is D.

Explanation

Taxpayers are required to pay class 2 NICs if their taxable profits for the tax year exceed £5,965 and class 4 NICs if their taxable profits exceed £8,060, so they can be liable to both classes 2 and 4.

Class 4 NICs are based on the taxable trading profits, **not** the amount of income a taxpayer withdraws from the business.

Test your understanding 2

Naomi

Naomi must pay class 2 NICs of £2.80 per week. In all cases her taxable profits exceed the small earnings limit of £5,965.

She is liable to pay class 4 NICs as follows:

		£
(a)	Profits do not exceed lower limit, no class 4 NIC	Nil
(b)	Class 4 NICs (£24,500 – £8,060) × 9%	1,479.60
(c)	Class 4 NICs (£43,000 – £8,060) × 9% + (£44,500 – £43,000) × 2%	3,174.60

Test your understanding 3

Adrian

The correct answer is C.

Explanation

The relevant amount for income tax is £7,300
The relevant amount for class 4 NIC is £700

Payments on account will be due for 2016/17 as follows:

	£
31 January 2017 (£7,300 + £700 = £8,000 × ½)	4,000
31 July 2017	4,000

No payments on account of class 2 NICs or capital gains tax are required.

Introduction to chargeable gains

Introduction

Both individuals and companies pay tax on chargeable gains.

Individuals pay capital gains tax on their chargeable gains.

Companies include chargeable gains in their taxable total profits and therefore pay corporation tax on them.

This chapter helps identify when chargeable gains arise.

ASSESSMENT CRITERIA

Apply the rules relating to chargeable persons, disposals and assets (5.1)

CONTENTS

1 Principle of a chargeable gain

1.1 The three essential elements

In order for a chargeable gain to be calculated there are three essential requirements.

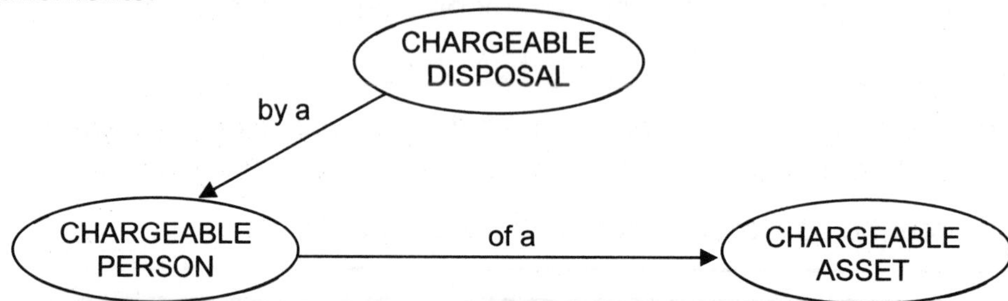

2 Chargeable disposal

2.1 Main types of disposal

A chargeable disposal includes:

- a sale of an asset (whole or part of an asset)
- a gift of an asset
- an exchange of an asset
- the loss or destruction of an asset.

Where a gift is made the sale proceeds are deemed to be the asset's market value.

Where an asset is lost or destroyed the sale proceeds are likely to be nil or insurance proceeds.

2.2 Exempt disposals

The following occasions are exempt disposals and so no CGT computation is required:

- the sale is a trading disposal (badges of trade – Chapter 9)
- on the death of an individual
- on a gift to a charity.

In the assessment it will be obvious whether the disposal is of:

- stock/inventory, therefore dealt with as trading income; or
- a capital item (for example land), therefore calculate a gain.

3 Chargeable person

3.1 Types of person

Chargeable gains will be calculated on disposals by:

- Individuals
- Partners in partnership } – pay capital gains tax
- Companies – pay corporation tax on chargeable gains (see Chapter 5 pro forma)

4 Chargeable asset

4.1 Exempt assets

All assets are chargeable unless they are on the specific list of exempt assets. The main types of exempt asset are listed below.

Exempt assets in the list below need to be learned so that you can identify them in a question.

- Motor vehicles, including vintage and veteran cars.
- Cash (i.e. legal tender in the UK).
- Any form of loan stock (i.e. qualifying corporate bonds, loan notes, debentures, gilt edged securities, Treasury stock, Exchequer stock).
- Wasting chattels:
  - a chattel is property that is tangible and moveable
  - 'wasting' means that it has a life of less than or equal to 50 years.

  The most common examples of wasting chattels that you will encounter in an assessment are:

  - all animals (racehorses, greyhounds etc.), boats and caravans.
- Non-wasting chattels, which have both sale proceeds and cost of £6,000 or less.

  The most common examples of non-wasting chattels are works of art, jewellery and antique furniture.

Test your understanding 1

Chargeable disposals

For each of the following transactions, state whether it is a chargeable or an exempt disposal for the purpose of capital gains.

1 Bill gave his trading premises to his daughter Beatrice.

2 ABC Ltd is a building company. It built a small development of five houses and sold them.

3 DEF Ltd, a manufacturing company, sold a racehorse for £10,000.

4 DEF Ltd also sold a portrait for £10,000 which had been hanging in the boardroom.

5 Test your understanding

Test your understanding 2

Chargeable disposals

For each of the following transactions, state whether it is a chargeable or an exempt disposal for the purpose of capital gains.

1 Sale of a motor car that was purchased for £12,000 and sold for £13,000 and used for business purposes throughout the period of ownership.

2 Sale of a half share in a racehorse that was purchased for £12,000 and sold for £17,000.

3 Gift of a painting which was purchased for £5,000 and sold for £8,500.

4 Sale of land that was purchased for £2,900 and sold for £5,800.

6 Summary

The requirements for a chargeable gain to be calculated are:

- a chargeable disposal; by
- a chargeable person; of
- a chargeable asset.

Test your understanding answers

Test your understanding 1

1	Chargeable	Even though Bill receives no actual payment for the property, a gift of a capital item is still a chargeable disposal.
2	Exempt	As ABC Ltd is a building company, the proceeds will be dealt with as trading income.
3	Exempt	A racehorse is a wasting chattel (i.e. life of 50 years or less).
4	Chargeable	The painting is a non-wasting chattel which was sold for more than £6,000. It is not a wasting chattel as it will have a life of more than 50 years.

Test your understanding 2

1	Exempt	Motor cars are exempt regardless of the use of the asset, cost or sale proceeds.
2	Exempt	A racehorse is a wasting chattel.
3	Chargeable	The painting is a non-wasting chattel that was bought for less than £6,000 but sold for more than £6,000. It would only be exempt if it had also been sold for less than £6,000.
4	Chargeable	The land, although bought and sold for less than £6,000, is not moveable property and therefore not a chattel.

Gains and losses for companies

Introduction

A company pays corporation tax on its chargeable gains.

A calculation of gains may be required in your assessment.

This chapter sets out the pro forma for calculating a chargeable gain, and explains the separate entries required in the computation.

ASSESSMENT CRITERIA

Apply the rules relating to disposals and assets (5.2)

Calculate the computation of chargeable gains and allowable losses (5.2)

CONTENTS

1 Pro forma computation

1.1 The pro forma computation (for corporation tax)

Gains and losses are calculated for chargeable accounting periods.

Once you have calculated all the individual chargeable gains and allowable capital losses for an accounting period, summarise them as follows:

	£
Chargeable gain (1)	X
Chargeable gain (2)	X
Allowable loss (3)	(X)
Net chargeable gains/(losses) for the current year	X
Less: Capital losses brought forward	(X)
Net chargeable gains	X

The net chargeable gains are then put into the computation of taxable total profits and the corporation tax liability is calculated in the normal way.

If there is an overall capital loss, it is carried forward and set against future chargeable gains. It cannot be relieved against other income.

Example

Alpha Ltd made three disposals in its year ended 31 March 2017, giving the following results:

Asset	Gain/(loss)
	£
1	20,000
2	5,000
3	(8,000)

Calculate the net chargeable gains shown on the corporation tax computation.

Solution

Included within taxable total profits will be net chargeable gains of £17,000 (£20,000 + £5,000 – £8,000).

If the loss on asset 3 had been £28,000, the corporation tax computation would show net chargeable gains of nil.

A net loss of £3,000 (£20,000 + £5,000 – £28,000) would then be carried forward to offset against the next available net chargeable gains.

Test your understanding 1

Bubbles Ltd

Bubbles Ltd disposed of two assets during its accounting period to 31 March 2017, realising a chargeable gain of £13,000 and an allowable loss of £4,000.

It had allowable capital losses brought forward of £2,000.

How much will be included in taxable total profits for the year to 31 March 2017?

The remainder of this chapter considers how to calculate the gains and losses on each chargeable disposal made by a company.

2 The chargeable gain computation

2.1 The standard pro forma

The following pro forma should be used:

	Notes	£
Gross sale proceeds	1	X
Less: Selling costs	2	(X)
Net sale proceeds (NSP)		X
Less: Allowable cost	3	(X)
Unindexed gain	4	X
Less: Indexation allowance (IA) = Cost × 0.XXX	5	(X)
Chargeable gain		X

Notes to the pro forma

1 The sale proceeds are usually given in the question.

However, where a disposal is not a sale at arm's length (e.g. a gift) then *market value* will be substituted for sale proceeds in the computation.

2 The selling costs incurred on the disposal of an asset are an allowable deduction.

Examples of such allowable costs include valuation fees, advertising costs, legal fees, auctioneer's fees.

3 The purchase price of an asset is the main allowable cost, but this will also include any incidental purchase expenses, including legal fees, stamp duty, etc.

4 The gain after deducting the costs above is known as an unindexed gain.

5 An indexation allowance (IA) may then be available to reduce that gain.

The indexation allowance is intended to give relief for inflation and is based upon the movement in the retail prices index (RPI).

2.2 The indexation allowance (IA)

The IA is relief for inflation covering the period since the asset was purchased up to the date of disposal.

The indexation allowance runs:

- from the month of the purchase (i.e. when the cost was incurred)
- to the month of disposal.

It is computed by multiplying the acquisition cost by an indexation factor.

The formula for calculating the indexation factor is:

$$\frac{\text{RPI for month of disposal} - \text{RPI for month of acquisition}}{\text{RPI for month of acquisition}}$$

This produces a decimal figure which must be rounded to three decimal places.

In the assessment you will be given the indexation factor or the amount of the indexation allowance.

Example

Eli Ltd sells a chargeable asset on 31 March 2017 for £24,600 after deducting auctioneer's fees of £400. The asset was acquired on 1 May 2004 for £10,000.

Calculate the chargeable gain. Assume that the indexation factor for May 2004 to March 2017 is 0.426.

Solution

	£
Gross sales proceeds (March 2017)	25,000
Less: Selling costs	(400)
Net sale proceeds	24,600
Less: Allowable cost (May 2004)	(10,000)
Unindexed gain	14,600
Less: Indexation allowance (£10,000 × 0.426)	(4,260)
Chargeable gain	10,340

Be careful to ensure that you index the allowable cost and not the unindexed gain – a very easy mistake to make!

Note also that the indexation allowance:

- cannot be used to turn a gain into a loss
- is not available where there is an unindexed loss.

Example

JNN Ltd is considering selling a field at auction in August 2016. It acquired the field in August 1992 for £10,000 and the sale proceeds are likely to be one of three results.

(a) £25,000

(b) £12,000

(c) £8,000

Calculate the chargeable gain or loss under each of these alternatives.

Assume the indexation factor from August 1992 to August 2016 is 0.894.

Solution

	(a)	(b)	(c)
	£	£	£
Sale proceeds	25,000	12,000	8,000
Less: Cost	(10,000)	(10,000)	(10,000)
Unindexed gain or (loss)	15,000	2,000	(2,000)
Less: Indexation allowance			
(0.894 × £10,000) = £8,940	(8,940)	(2,000)*	Nil**
Chargeable gain/(allowable loss)	6,060	Nil	(2,000)

Notes:

* Restricted, because indexation cannot create a loss.

** No indexation because indexation cannot increase a loss.

Test your understanding 2

JHN Ltd

JHN Ltd made the following disposals in the year ended 31 March 2017.

1 On 9 June 2016 it sold a machine for £15,000. The machine was bought in October 1998 for £8,000.

2 On 5 September 2016 it sold a building which had been purchased for £27,500 in November 1999. Sale proceeds were £26,500.

3 On 1 March 2017 it sold a car, a Trabant, which was bought in February 1993 for £3,000. By the time of the sale, it had become a collector's item and JHN Ltd managed to obtain proceeds of £9,000, out of which it paid £450 in auctioneer's fees.

4 On 3 March 2017 it sold a collection of military memorabilia for £19,000. The collection had cost £7,000 in March 1993.

5 Also on 3 March 2017, it sold some land which was purchased in April 1992 for £15,000. The land was sold for £25,000.

Required:

Calculate the chargeable gain on each of the above transactions and the net chargeable gains for the year ended 31 March 2017.

You should use the following indexation factors.

April 1992 – March 2017	0.916
Feb 1993 – March 2017	0.916
March 1993 – March 2017	0.909
Oct 1998 – June 2016	0.595
Nov 1999 – Sept 2016	0.581

Approach to the question

It is important that the chargeable gain or allowable loss on each transaction is *separately* computed.

Finally, prepare a summary adding gains and losses together to arrive at one overall net chargeable gains figure.

Note that details of the pro forma computation and treatment of indexation allowance is included in the AAT reference material set out in section 6 below.

3 Special rules

3.1 Changes to the calculation of the gain

There are a number of special situations that will give rise to slight changes in the calculation of the gains. They are:

- Enhancement expenditure (see section 3.2 below)
- Part disposals (see section 3.3 below)
- Non-wasting chattels (see section 3.4 below).

3.2 Enhancement expenditure

The main allowable cost in computing an unindexed gain is the purchase cost (including incidental acquisition costs).

Any additional capital expenditure incurred at a later date on the asset is also an allowable cost. This normally takes the form of improvement (i.e. enhancement) expenditure.

As the additional expenditure is incurred later than the original expenditure, there will be an impact on the calculation of the indexation allowance.

Indexation allowance can only be calculated from the actual date of expenditure; therefore, where there is cost plus enhancement expenditure, *two* indexation allowance calculations will be required.

Example

RMY Ltd bought a shop in November 1996 for £13,200. The company spent £3,800 on improvements in May 1999. The shop was sold for £49,000 in October 2016.

The indexed rise from November 1996 to October 2016 is 0.715 and from May 1999 to October 2016 is 0.594.

Calculate the chargeable gain on the sale of the shop.

Solution

	£
Sale proceeds (October 2016)	49,000
Less: Cost (November 1996)	(13,200)
Enhancement (May 1999)	(3,800)
Unindexed gain	32,000
Less: Indexation allowance	
Cost £13,200 × 0.715	(9,438)
Enhancement £3,800 × 0.594	(2,257)
Chargeable gain	20,305

Test your understanding 3

Linda Ltd

On 15 February 2017, Linda Ltd sold a factory building for £420,000.

The factory had been purchased on 14 October 2003 for £194,000, and was extended at a cost of £58,000 during March 2005.

During May 2007, the roof of the factory was repaired at a cost of £12,000 following damage in a fire.

Linda Ltd had incurred legal fees of £3,600 in connection with the original purchase of the factory, and £6,200 in connection with the disposal.

What is the chargeable gain on the disposal?

A £30,066

B £45,522

C £68,490

D £158,200

You should use the following indexation factors, where relevant.

October 2003 – February 2017	0.454
March 2005 – February 2017	0.396
May 2007 – February 2017	0.288

3.3 Part disposal

A disposal can be of all or part of an asset. It could for example apply to a disposal of part of a plot of land.

When only part of an asset is sold, we know how much the proceeds are, but we cannot immediately determine what the cost was of that part of the asset.

The allowable cost of the part disposed of is calculated using the following formula:

$$\text{Allowable cost of the part disposed of} = \text{Cost of whole asset} \times \frac{A}{A+B}$$

Where A = gross sale proceeds of part disposed of (i.e. before deducting selling costs).

B = market value of the remaining part (will be given in assessment).

Example

John Ltd bought a piece of land in January 2000 for £5,000.

In March 2017 the company sold part of the land for £4,500. At the same time the remaining part was valued at £20,500.

The indexation factor from January 2000 to March 2017 is 0.596.

Calculate the chargeable gain arising on the part disposal of land.

Solution

	£
Sale proceeds	4,500
Less: Allowable cost (£5,000 × $\frac{£4,500}{£4,500+£20,500}$)	(900)
Unindexed gain	3,600
Less: Indexation allowance (0.596 × £900)	(536)
Chargeable gain	3,064

Test your understanding 4

Smith Ltd

Smith Ltd sold three acres out of a 12 acre plot of land on 14 December 2016 for £15,000. The whole plot had been purchased for £4,500 on 15 June 2012. On 14 December 2016 the unsold acres had an agreed market value of £25,000.

What is the chargeable gain?

You should use an indexation factor of 0.095.

3.4 Non-wasting chattels

In the previous chapter we noted that wasting chattels (i.e. expected life of no more than 50 years) are exempt (e.g. animals, boats, caravans).

Special rules apply to non-wasting chattels (e.g. furniture, works of art, jewellery, antique furniture).

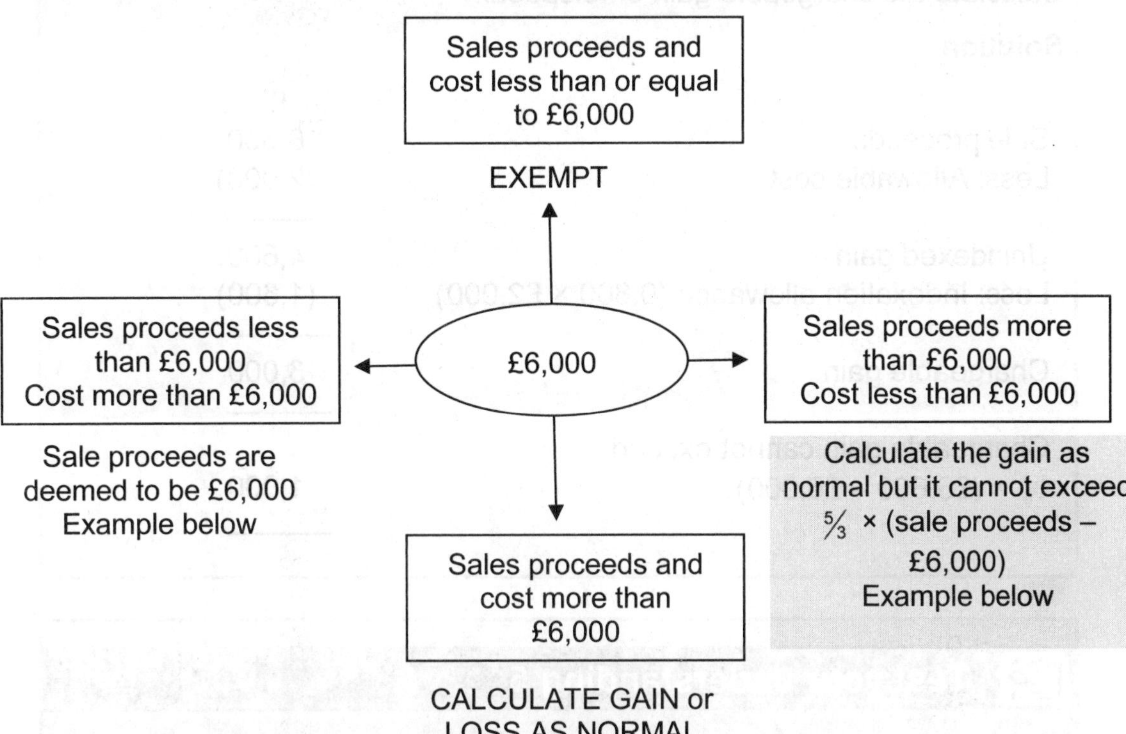
Sales proceeds and cost less than or equal to £6,000
EXEMPT
£6,000
Sales proceeds less than £6,000 Cost more than £6,000
Sale proceeds are deemed to be £6,000 Example below
Sales proceeds more than £6,000 Cost less than £6,000
Calculate the gain as normal but it cannot exceed 5/3 × (sale proceeds – £6,000) Example below
Sales proceeds and cost more than £6,000
CALCULATE GAIN or LOSS AS NORMAL

Example

Harry Ltd sold an antique table for £5,000 in January 2017. It had originally purchased the table in August 2005 for £8,000.

Calculate the chargeable gain or allowable loss on disposal.

Solution

	£
Sale proceeds (deemed)	6,000
Less: Allowable cost	(8,000)
Unindexed loss	(2,000)
Less: Indexation allowance (restricted as it cannot increase a loss)	Nil
Allowable loss	(2,000)

Example

Kevin Ltd sold a painting for £6,600 that it originally purchased for £2,000. The indexation factor is 0.800.

Calculate the chargeable gain on disposal.

Solution

	£
Sale proceeds	6,600
Less: Allowable cost	(2,000)
Unindexed gain	4,600
Less: Indexation allowance (0.800 × £2,000)	(1,600)
Chargeable gain	3,000
Chargeable gain cannot exceed:	
$\frac{5}{3}$ × (£6,600 – £6,000)	1,000

Test your understanding 5

Chattel disposals

1 ABC Ltd sold a non-wasting chattel for £6,500 realising a gain of £2,000.

What is the chargeable gain?

2 DEF Ltd sold a non-wasting chattel for £4,000. It had originally cost £7,500.

How much of the loss is allowable?

3 GHI Ltd sold a painting for £14,000 in March 2017. The painting had been acquired for £5,000 in November 2008. The indexation factor from November 2008 to March 2017 was 0.231.

Complete the following computation.

	£
Proceeds	
Less: Cost	
Less: Indexation allowance	
Gain	
Chargeable gain cannot exceed:	
Chargeable gain	

4 Test your understanding

Test your understanding 6

RBQ Ltd

RBQ Ltd made the following disposals in the year ended 31 March 2017.

(1) On 11 August 2016, it sold a shop for £15,000. The shop was bought in May 2003 for £8,000.

(2) On 16 October 2016, it sold a painting which had been purchased for £30,000 in November 2000. Sale proceeds were £25,000.

(3) On 1 February 2017, it sold a car, a VW Beetle, which was bought in February 1997 for £2,000.

By the time of the sale, it had become a collector's item and RBQ Ltd managed to obtain proceeds of £10,000.

(4) On 3 January 2017, it sold a piece of land for £29,000. It had cost £6,000 in May 2001.

Required:

Calculate the total net chargeable gains on the above transactions in the year ended 31 March 2017.

You should use the following indexation factors, where relevant:

February 1997 – February 2017	0.713
November 2000 – October 2016	0.533
May 2001 – January 2017	0.522
May 2003 – August 2016	0.450

Test your understanding 7

Jackson Ltd

During the year to 30 September 2016, Jackson Ltd had the following capital transactions:

(a) In October 2015 it sold land for £27,000. It bought the land in February 1998 for £14,000.

(b) It also sold a factory unit in December 2015 for £100,000. Out of that the company had to pay legal fees of £1,200. It had originally bought the factory unit in March 1997 for £10,500, extended it in April 2001 for £3,000 and extended it again in June 2004 for £4,600.

(c) In March 2016, Jackson Ltd sold a racehorse for £22,000. It had purchased the horse for £4,000 on 1 December 2009.

Required:

Calculate the chargeable gain on each of the above transactions in the year ended 30 September 2016.

Use the following indexation factors, where relevant:

March 1997 – December 2015	0.677
February 1998 – October 2015	0.619
April 2001 – December 2015	0.505
June 2004 – December 2015	0.395
December 2009 – March 2016	0.193

Test your understanding 8

Alphabet Ltd

1 Alphabet Ltd sold an antique table for £7,500 realising an indexed gain of £3,000. What will be the chargeable gain?

2 Delta Ltd sold a painting for £3,000. It had originally cost £8,500.

How much of the loss is allowable?

3 Golf Ltd sold an antique desk for £17,000 in January 2017. The desk had been acquired for £4,000 in September 2009. The indexation factor from September 2009 to January 2017 was 0.231.

Complete the following computation.

	£
Proceeds	
Less: Cost	
Less: Indexation allowance	
Gain	
Chargeable gain cannot exceed	
Chargeable gain	

5 Summary

There is a pro forma computation for the calculation of gains and losses on individual asset disposals.

The gains and losses of the accounting period are netted off to give the net chargeable gains to include in the company's corporation tax computation.

Companies receive an indexation allowance. Original and improvement costs are indexed from the month the cost is incurred to the month of disposal.

Special rules exist for the treatment of improvement costs, part disposals (using the formula A/A+B), and for chattels.

6 AAT reference material

Calculation of gains and losses for companies

Pro forma computation

	£	£
Consideration received		X
Less Incidental costs of sale		(X)
Net sale proceeds		NSP
Less Allowable expenditure		
Acquisition cost + incidental costs of acquisition	X	
Indexation allowance [indexation factor × expenditure]	X	
Enhancement expenditure	X	
Indexation allowance	X	
		(Cost)
Chargeable gain		Gain

- Indexation allowance is not available where there is an unindexed loss; nor can it turn an unindexed gain into an indexed loss.
- Note that companies do not get an annual exempt amount.
- Losses relieved in order – current year first followed by losses brought forward.

Only relief available to companies is rollover relief:

- Rollover relief is a deferral relief – see [Chargeable gains – reliefs available to individuals] for main rollover relief rules.
- Key differences applying for companies:
  - Indexation is given on disposal of the original asset.
  - Goodwill is not a qualifying asset for companies.
  - Gain deferred is the indexed gain.
  - On disposal of the replacement asset, indexation is calculated on the 'base cost' not actual cost.

(Note rollover relief is covered in Chapter 20 of this study text).

Test your understanding answers

Test your understanding 1

Bubbles Ltd

The amount to include in taxable total profits will be £7,000 (£13,000 – £4,000 – £2,000 b/f).

Test your understanding 2

JHN Ltd

Chargeable gains

	£
Machine (W1)	2,240
Building (W2)	(1,000)
Car – exempt	Nil
Memorabilia (W3)	5,637
Land (W4)	Nil
Net chargeable gains	6,877

Workings:

(W1) Machine

	£
Proceeds	15,000
Less: Cost	(8,000)
Unindexed gain	7,000
Less: Indexation allowance (£8,000 × 0.595)	(4,760)
Chargeable gain	2,240

(W2) Building

	£
Proceeds	26,500
Less: Cost	(27,500)
Allowable loss	(1,000)

No indexation is available to increase the loss.

(W3) Memorabilia

	£
Proceeds	19,000
Less: Cost	(7,000)
Unindexed gain	12,000
Less: Indexation allowance (£7,000 × 0.909)	(6,363)
Chargeable gain	5,637

(W4) Land

	£
Proceeds	25,000
Less: Cost	(15,000)
Unindexed gain	10,000
Less: Indexation allowance (£15,000 × 0.916) (restricted)	(10,000)
	Nil

The IA is restricted because indexation cannot create an allowable loss.

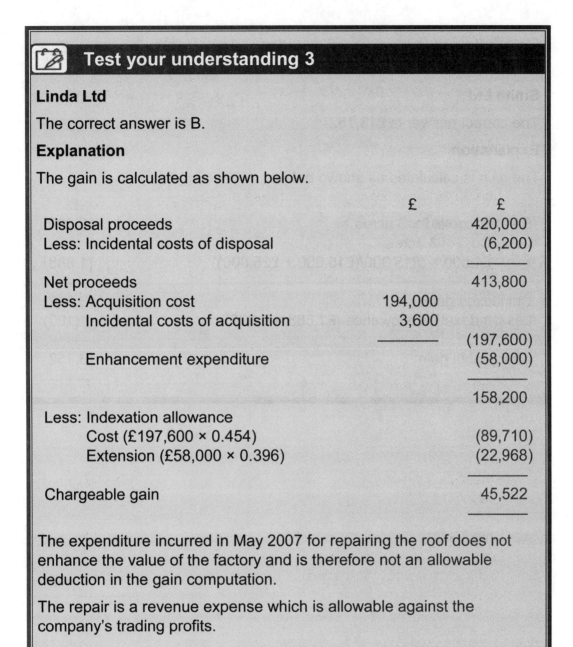

Test your understanding 3

Linda Ltd

The correct answer is B.

Explanation

The gain is calculated as shown below.

	£	£
Disposal proceeds		420,000
Less: Incidental costs of disposal		(6,200)
Net proceeds		413,800
Less: Acquisition cost	194,000	
Incidental costs of acquisition	3,600	
		(197,600)
Enhancement expenditure		(58,000)
		158,200
Less: Indexation allowance		
Cost (£197,600 × 0.454)		(89,710)
Extension (£58,000 × 0.396)		(22,968)
Chargeable gain		45,522

The expenditure incurred in May 2007 for repairing the roof does not enhance the value of the factory and is therefore not an allowable deduction in the gain computation.

The repair is a revenue expense which is allowable against the company's trading profits.

Test your understanding 4

Smith Ltd

The correct answer is £13,152.

Explanation

The gain is calculated as shown below.

	£
Sale proceeds for 3 acres	15,000
Less: Cost of 3 acres	
£4,500 × (£15,000/(£15,000 + £25,000))	(1,688)
Unindexed gain	13,312
Less: Indexation allowance (£1,688 × 0.095)	(160)
Chargeable gain	13,152

Test your understanding 5

Chattel disposals

ABC Ltd

The chargeable gain cannot exceed:

5/3 × (£6,500 – £6,000) = £833.

Therefore the chargeable gain will be restricted to £833.

DEF Ltd

The allowable loss will be restricted to (£6,000 – £7,500) = £1,500.

GHI Ltd

	£
Proceeds	14,000
Less: Cost	(5,000)
	9,000
Less: Indexation allowance (£5,000 × 0.231)	(1,155)
Gain	7,845
Chargeable gain cannot exceed: (5/3 × (£14,000 – £6,000)	13,333
Chargeable gain	7,845

Test your understanding 6

RBQ Ltd

	£
Shop (W1)	3,400
Painting (W2)	(5,000)
Car – exempt	Nil
Land (W3)	19,868
Total net chargeable gains	18,268

Workings:

(W1) Shop

	£
Proceeds	15,000
Less: Cost	(8,000)
Unindexed gain	7,000
Less: Indexation allowance (£8,000 × 0.450)	(3,600)
Chargeable gain	3,400

(W2) Painting

	£
Proceeds	25,000
Less: Cost	(30,000)
Allowable loss	(5,000)

No indexation is available to increase the cost

(W3) Land

	£
Proceeds	29,000
Less: Cost	(6,000)
Unindexed gain	23,000
Less: Indexation allowance (£6,000 × 0.522)	(3,132)
Chargeable gain	19,868

Test your understanding 7

Jackson Ltd

		£	£
(a)	**Land**		
	Sales proceeds	27,000	
	Less: Cost	(14,000)	
	Unindexed gain	13,000	
	Less: Indexation allowance (£14,000 × 0.619)	(8,666)	
	Chargeable gain		4,334
(b)	**Factory**	£	
	Sale proceeds	100,000	
	Less: Legal fees	(1,200)	
		98,800	
	Less: Cost (March 1997)	(10,500)	
	Extension (April 2001)	(3,000)	
	Extension (June 2004)	(4,600)	
	Unindexed gain	80,700	
	Less: Indexation allowance		
	Cost (£10,500 × 0.677)	(7,109)	
	Extension (£3,000 × 0.505)	(1,515)	
	Extension (£4,600 × 0.395)	(1,817)	
	Chargeable gain		70,259
(c)	**Racehorse** – exempt asset (wasting chattel)		Nil

Test your understanding 8

Chattel disposals

Alphabet Ltd

The gain will be restricted to 5/3 × (£7,500 – £6,000) = £2,500.

Delta Ltd

The allowable loss will be restricted to (£6,000 – £8,500) = £2,500.

Golf Ltd

	£
Proceeds	17,000
Less: Cost	(4,000)
	13,000
Less: Indexation allowance (£4,000 × 0.231)	(924)
Gain	12,076
Chargeable gain cannot exceed: 5/3 × (£17,000 – £6,000)	18,333
Chargeable gain	12,076

Shares and securities – disposals by companies

Introduction

A company may hold another company's shares as an investment. Special rules apply to the calculation of chargeable gains on the disposal of shares.

ASSESSMENT CRITERIA

Apply the rules relating to the disposal of shares (5.2)

CONTENTS

1 The matching rules

1.1 Disposal of shares and securities

What distinguishes a share disposal from other asset disposals is the need for matching rules.

Before considering what these matching rules are, it helps to understand why we need them.

1.2 Principle of matching rules

Suppose that a company makes the following purchases of shares in another company, A plc:

1 September 1995	800 shares for	£2,000
3 February 1998	300 shares for	£1,000
1 July 2004	500 shares for	£1,000

On 1 November 2016, 400 of these shares are sold – but which 400?

- It could be the 300 acquired in 1998 and 100 acquired in 1995.
- It could be 400 out of the 500 acquired in 2004.
- It could be based on 400 out of the total 1,600 with costs being averaged.

We need matching rules so that we can establish *which* shares have been sold, and consequently what allowable costs and indexation allowances can be deducted from the sale proceeds.

The matching rules dictate the order in which the shares disposed of are matched with purchases.

1.3 The matching rules for companies

Shares of the same type in the same company (for example Lionel Ltd ordinary shares) are matched as follows:

(1) first, with shares bought on the same day; then

(2) second, with shares bought in the previous nine days (on a first in first out basis); then

(3) third, with shares in the 'share pool' (sometimes referred to as the s104 pool or the FA1985 pool).

The matching rules are given in the AAT reference material set out in section 6 below.

The 'share pool' is considered in detail below. For companies, shares are pooled together from 10 days after purchase.

Note that the matching rules for individuals are different and are covered in Chapter 19.

Example

Minnie Ltd has sold 3,000 shares in Mickey plc for £15,000 on 2 February 2017. The shares in Mickey plc were purchased as follows:

Date	Number	Cost
		£
1 July 1997	1,000	2,000
1 September 2007	1,000	2,500
27 January 2017	500	1,200
2 February 2017	1,500	6,000

Explain which shares Minnie Ltd is deemed to have sold.

Solution

Using the matching rules, the 3,000 shares sold are as follows:

		Number
2 February 2017 (same day purchase)		1,500
27 January 2017 (in previous 9 days)		500
		2,000
Share pool: All other shares were purchased more than 9 days ago, therefore must be in the pool.		
1 July 1997	1,000	
1 September 2007	1,000	
Total number of shares in pool	2,000	
Out of the pool (1,000 out of 2,000)		1,000
Shares disposed of		3,000

Note: When dealing with the pool we do not identify which 1,000 shares are sold.

1.4 Calculation of gains on same day and previous 9 day purchases

If a disposal is matched with the first two rules (i.e. matching against a same day purchase or purchases in the previous 9 days), there will be no indexation allowance available.

Hence, the gain is calculated as:

	£
Sale proceeds	X
Less: Allowable cost	(X)
Chargeable gain	X

Example

For Minnie Ltd in the previous example, calculate the gains on the shares purchased:

(1) on the same day; and

(2) in the previous 9 days.

Solution

Step 1: Calculate the gain on the same day purchase (1,500 shares)

3,000 shares are sold for £15,000.

	£
Sale proceeds (1,500/3,000 × £15,000)	7,500
Less: Allowable cost	(6,000)
Chargeable gain	1,500

Step 2: Calculate the gain on the previous 9 days purchase (500 shares)

	£
Sale proceeds (500/3,000 × £15,000)	2,500
Less: Allowable cost	(1,200)
Chargeable gain	1,300

1.5 The operation of a share pool

Any purchases from 1 April 1982 are 'pooled' in the 'share pool'.

Purchases before 1 April 1982 are not in the syllabus.

Indexation will apply to the pool from the date of acquisition to the date of disposal.

To enable the correct indexation to be calculated, a separate working is needed to identify the amount available. The working is also used to find the average cost of a partial disposal.

The pool is initially set up with three columns as follows:

	Number	Cost	Indexed cost
		£	£
Purchases (say) June 1991	1,000	2,000	2,000

Then every time there is an 'operative event' (an event involving cash – i.e. a sale or a purchase), two steps must be performed.

Step 1: An indexation update.

In the indexed cost column, add in indexation from the last operative event until this one.

This is calculated by multiplying the balance in the indexed cost column by the increase in the RPI since the last operative event.

Step 2: Deal with the operative event.

- for a purchase add in the new shares. The cost must be added in to both the cost and indexed cost columns.
- for a sale eliminate some shares. The amounts to be deducted from the cost and indexed cost columns are calculated in proportion to the number of shares being removed from the pool.

The following working should be produced:

Pro forma for the share pool

	Number	**Cost**	**Indexed cost**
		£	£
Purchase	X	X	X
Index to next event			X
Record next event (e.g. purchase)	X	X	X
	X	X	X
Index to next event			X
	X	X	X
Record next event (e.g. sale)	(X)	(X) (W1)	(X) (W2)
Pool carried forward	X	X	X

Note: For the 'indexed rises' the indexation factor is **not** rounded in practice. This is the only situation where a non-rounded factor is ever used.

However, in the assessment you will always to be given a rounded indexation factor, therefore use the factor given.

Workings:

(W1) Total cost × (number of shares sold/number of shares in pool)

(W2) Total indexed cost × (number of shares sold/number of shares in pool)

The purpose of the share pool working is to find:

- the average pool cost of shares disposed of = working 1 (W1)
- the *indexation* of shares disposed of = (working 2 – working 1).

The gain on the shares is then calculated as normal:

	£
Sale proceeds	X
Less: Cost (W1)	(X)
Unindexed gain	X
Less: Indexation allowance (W2 – W1)	(X)
Chargeable gain	X

The indexation factor is **always** applied to the total on the indexed cost column **(not** cost).

A partial disposal from a share pool uses straight line apportionment of cost and indexation.

In your assessment you will be provided with a grid to enter your calculations (section 3).

Note that a basic pro forma is given in the AAT reference material set out in section 6 below.

Example

For Minnie Ltd in the previous example, calculate the gain on the disposal from the share pool.

The indexation factors to use are as follows:

July 1997 – September 2007	0.321
September 2007 – February 2017	0.276

Solution

Step 1: Calculate cost and indexed cost from the share pool.

	Number	Cost	Indexed cost
		£	£
July 1997 purchase	1,000	2,000	2,000
Index to next event (July 1997 to September 2007) Indexed cost × 0.321 (£2,000 × 0.321)			642
September 2006 purchase	1,000	2,500	2,500
	2,000	4,500	5,142
Index to next event (September 2007 to February 2017) (£5,142 × 0.276)			1,419
	2,000	4,500	6,561
February 2017 sale (half)	(1,000)	(2,250)	(3,281)
Pool carried forward	1,000	2,250	3,280

Step 2: Calculate the gain on share pool shares.

	£
Sale proceeds (1,000/3,000 × £15,000)	5,000
Less: Allowable cost	(2,250)
Unindexed gain	2,750
Less: Indexation allowance (£3,281 – £2,250)	(1,031)
Chargeable gain	1,719

Step 3: Calculate total chargeable gains on the disposal of all 3,000 shares in Minnie Ltd

The total chargeable gains
= (£1,500 + £1,300 + £1,719) = £4,519

Test your understanding 1

FDC Ltd

FDC Ltd has purchased shares in DCC Ltd. The share pool information of the shares in DCC Ltd is given below.

		Cost
		£
1 June 1993	4,000 shares for	8,000
30 July 2002	1,800 shares for	9,750

FDC Ltd disposed of 2,000 of its shares in DCC Ltd for £20,571 in March 2017.

The indexation factors to use are as follows:

June 1993 – July 2002	0.248
July 2002 – March 2017	0.512

Required:

Calculate the chargeable gain on the share pool shares.

2 Bonus issues and rights issues

2.1 Principle of bonus issues and rights issues

A bonus issue is the distribution of free shares to shareholders based on existing shareholdings.

A rights issue involves shareholders paying for new shares, usually at a rate below market price and in proportions based on existing shareholdings.

Matching

In both cases, therefore, the shareholder is making a new acquisition of shares. However, for *matching* purposes, such acquisitions arise out of the original holdings.

Bonus and rights issues therefore attach to the original shareholdings for the purposes of the identification rules.

Example

Alma Ltd acquired shares in S plc, a quoted company, as follows.

- 2,000 shares acquired in June 1994 for £11,500.
- In October 1995 there was a 1 for 2 bonus issue.
- In December 2001 there was a 1 for 4 rights issue at £3 per share.

Alma Ltd sold 2,600 shares in December 2016 for £30,000.

Calculate the number of shares in the share pool.

Solution

	Number
June 1994 purchase	2,000
October 1995 bonus issue (1 for 2)	
½ × 2,000	1,000
	3,000
December 2001 rights issue (1 for 4)	
¼ × 3,000	750
	3,750
December 2016 sale	(2,600)
Balance in pool c/f	1,150

2.2 Bonus issue

A bonus issue is the issue of free shares (i.e. no cost is involved). As there is no expenditure involved it is not an operative event and therefore no indexation is calculated before recording the event.

Simply add the number of bonus issue shares received to the pool.

When the next event occurs (a sale, purchase or rights issue), index from the operative event prior to the bonus issue.

Example

For Alma Ltd in the previous example, set up the share pool and deal with events up to and including the bonus issue.

Solution

Share pool	**Number**	**Cost**	**Indexed cost**
		£	£
Purchase June 1994	2,000	11,500	11,500
Bonus issue October 1995 (1 for 2) ½ × 2,000	1,000	Nil	Nil
	3,000	11,500	11,500

Note: We have NOT indexed the pool before recording the bonus issue (as no cost is involved).

Therefore, next time there is an operative event we will index from June 1994 (the last operative event involving cost).

2.3 Rights issue

A rights issue involves a payment for new shares. Accordingly, it is treated simply as a purchase of shares (usually at a price below the market rate).

Hence, it should be treated in the same way as a purchase in the share pool:

- index up to the rights issue; then
- add in the number and cost of new shares.

Example

For Alma Ltd in the previous example, you are required to calculate the gain on disposal.

Assume that the indexed rise from June 1994 to December 2001 is 0.198 and from December 2001 to December 2016 is 0.527.

Solution

Share pool	**Number**	**Cost**	**Indexed cost**
		£	£
Purchase June 1994	2,000	11,500	11,500
Bonus issue October 1995 (1 for 2)	1,000	Nil	Nil
	3,000	11,500	11,500
Indexed rise to December 2001 (£11,500 × 0.198)			2,277
	3,000	11,500	13,777
Rights issue (1 for 4) at £3	750	2,250	2,250
	3,750	13,750	16,027
Indexed rise to December 2015 (£16,027 × 0.527)			8,446
	3,750	13,750	24,473
Disposal December 2016	(2,600)		
Allocate costs (2,600/3,750) × £13,750/£24,473		(9,533)	(16,968)
Balance c/f	1,150	4,217	7,505

Computation of gain – share pool

	£
Proceeds	30,000
Less: Cost	(9,533)
Unindexed gain	20,467
Less: Indexation (£16,968 – £9,533)	(7,435)
Chargeable gain	13,032

Note that the indexed cost is updated prior to the rights issue, because there is a purchase which involves additional cost.

Following the disposal there are 1,150 shares in the pool with a cost of £4,217 and an indexed cost of £7,505. This will be used as the starting point when dealing with the next operative event.

In the assessment you may be given details of brought forward amounts, rather than the complete history of the share pool.

Test your understanding 2

Scarlet Ltd

On 20 September 2016, Scarlet Ltd sold 1,500 ordinary shares in Red plc for £4,725. The company's previous transactions were as follows.

Balance on the share pool at 5 May 2004 is 2,500 shares with a qualifying cost of £3,900 and an indexed cost of £4,385.

Transactions from 5 May 2004 were as follows:

4 April 2005	Took up 1 for 2 bonus issue
19 January 2006	Took up 1 for 3 rights issue at 140p per share

The indexed rise from May 2004 to January 2006 is 0.037 and from January 2006 to September 2016 is 0.362.

Required:

Calculate Scarlet Ltd's chargeable gain on the disposal on 20 September 2016.

3 Approach to assessment questions

In the assessment you will normally be asked to calculate a gain on shares. If so, this question will be manually marked. Hence it is important that you enter your answer into the table supplied correctly and show your workings.

In the specimen assessment a table is supplied with up to 5 columns. The first one or two columns are for description and narrative whilst the other columns are for numerical entry.

This should allow you to enter your answer in the same layout as used throughout this chapter although with a little less detail. For example, you do not need to include lines marking totals and subtotals.

 **Example**

JTD Ltd bought 1,000 shares in VPZ plc for £4.40 each in December 2006.

In July 2014 it received a 1 for 5 rights issue at £4.80 each.

In May 2016 it sold 400 shares for £35,000.

The indexed rise from December 2006 to July 2014 is 0.263 and from July 2014 to May 2016 is 0.023.

What is the chargeable gain? Your answer should clearly show the balance of shares carried forward. Show all workings.

Solution

Pool	Number	Cost (£)	Indexed cost (£)
12.06 Purchase	1,000	4,400	4,400
Index to July 2014			
(£4,400 × 0.263)			1,157
			5,557
July 2014 Rights issue			
1,000/5 × £4.80	200	960	960
			6,517
Index to May 2016			
(£6,517 × 0.023)			150
	1,200	5,360	6,667
May 2016 Sale			
(400/1,200) ×	(400)		
£5,360 / £6,667		(1,787)	(2,222)
Balance c/f	800	3,573	4,445
		£	
Proceeds		35,000	
Less cost (pool)		(1,787)	
		33,213	
Indexation			
(£2,222 – £1,787)		(435)	
Gain		32,778	

4 Test your understanding

Test your understanding 3

Share disposals for companies

Read the following statements and state whether they are true or false.

1 The matching rules for a company are as follows:
   - first with same day acquisitions; then
   - acquisitions within the previous nine days; then
   - finally with the share pool.

2 You must apply an indexed rise when there is a bonus issue.

3 For identification purposes rights issues are treated as separate acquisitions.

4 You must apply an indexed rise when there is a rights issue.

Test your understanding 4

Jerry Ltd

Jerry Ltd sold ordinary 25p shares in Blue plc as follows:

	Number of shares	Proceeds
September 1999	2,000	£9,000
March 2017	2,000	£14,500

At 1 July 1995, Jerry Ltd had 4,100 shares in the share pool, with an indexed cost of £10,744 and a cost of £8,200.

Purchases were made as follows:

	Number of shares	Cost
January 2001	200	£450

Required:

Compute the gains arising on all of the above transactions in quoted securities.

Use the following indexation factors as appropriate:

July 1995 – September 1999	0.115
September 1999 – January 2001	0.029
January 2001 – March 2017	0.554

Test your understanding 5

Purple Ltd

On 8 August 2016, Purple Ltd sold 5,000 ordinary shares in Indigo plc for £15,000. The company's previous transactions were as follows.

Balance on share pool at 9 June 1998, 3,000 shares with a qualifying cost of £4,000 and an indexed cost of £5,010.

Transactions from 9 June 1998 were as follows:

12 August 2003	Took up 1 for 3 bonus issue
7 May 2008	Took up 1 for 2 rights issue at 150p per share
4 August 2016	500 shares purchased for £1,410

The indexed rise from June 1998 to May 2008 is 0.316 and from May 2008 to August 2016 is 0.223.

Required:

Calculate Purple Ltd's chargeable gain on the disposal on 8 August 2016.

Test your understanding 6

Chrome Ltd

Chrome Ltd sold all of its ordinary shares in Copper plc for £17,760 on 1 October 2016.

Chrome Ltd acquired its shares in Copper plc as follows:

10 May 2007	Purchased 3,200 shares for £9,600
9 June 2011	Took up 1 for 4 rights issue at 260p per share
20 January 2013	Purchased 2,100 shares for £4,400

Indexation factors were:

May 2007 to June 2011	0.141
June 2011 to January 2013	0.045
January 2013 to October 2016	0.074

Required:

Calculate Chrome Ltd's chargeable gain on the disposal on 1 October 2016.

5 Summary

When disposing of shares we apply matching rules to identify which shares have been disposed of.

These rules are needed so that we can deduct the appropriate acquisition costs from the disposal proceeds.

The matching rules for companies generally match disposals with shares held in the share pool.

Bonus and rights issues attach themselves to the original shareholdings.

6 AAT reference material

Shares and securities – disposals by companies

The identification rules – a disposal of shares is matched:

- firstly, with same-day transactions
- secondly, with transactions in the previous 9 days (FIFO). No indexation allowance is available
- thirdly, with shares from the 1985 pool (shares bought from 1 April 1982 onwards).

1985 pool – pro forma working	**No.**	**Cost** £	**Indexed cost** £	
Purchase	X	X	X	
Index to next operative event			X	
			X	
Operative event (purchase)	X	X	X	
	X	X	X	
Index to next operative event			X	
			X	
Operative event (sale)	(X)	(X)	(X)	A
Pool carried forward	X	X	X	

Operative event = purchase, sale, rights issue. Bonus issue is not an operative event.

Computation

	£
Proceeds	X
Less indexed cost (A from pool)	(X)
Indexed gain	X

Test your understanding answers

Test your understanding 1

FDC Ltd

Share pool working	**Note**	**Number**	**Cost**	**Indexed cost**
			£	£
Purchase 1 June 1993	1	4,000	8,000	8,000
Indexed rise to July 2002	2			
£8,000 × 0.248				1,984
Purchase – July 2002		1,800	9,750	9,750
		5,800	17,750	19,734
Indexed rise to March 2017				
£19,734 × 0.512				10,104
		5,800	17,750	29,838
Sale of 2,000 shares	3	(2,000)		
$\frac{2,000}{5,800}$ × £17,750/£29,838			(6,121)	(10,289)
Carried forward		3,800	11,629	19,549

Notes:

(1) Any entry in the cost column must also be made in the indexed cost column.

(2) Indexation must be added before the purchase in July 2002 is added to the pool.

(3) Use apportionment to allocate cost and indexed cost.

Gain on share pool shares

	£
Sale proceeds	20,571
Less: Cost	(6,121)
Unindexed gain	14,450
Less: Indexation allowance (£10,289 – £6,121)	(4,168)
Chargeable gain	10,282

Note: If the proceeds exceed the indexed cost then it is an acceptable short cut to just deduct the indexed cost from the proceeds in calculating the gain on the pool shares.

Test your understanding 2

Scarlet Ltd

Share pool	**Number**	**Cost**	**Indexed cost**
		£	£
Balance at 5 May 2004	2,500	3,900	4,385
4 April 2004 Bonus issue (1 for 2)	1,250	–	–
	3,750	3,900	4,385
Indexed rise to January 2006 £4,385 × 0.037			162
19 January 2006			4,547
Rights issue (1 for 3) × 140p	1,250	1,750	1,750
	5,000	5,650	6,297
Indexed rise to September 2016 £6,297 × 0.362			2,280
	5,000	5,650	8,577
Cost of sale $\frac{1,500}{5,000}$ × £5,650/£8,577	(1,500)	(1,695)	(2,573)
Pool balance c/f	3,500	3,955	6,004

Gain on the disposal of shares

	£
Proceeds	4,725
Less: Cost	(1,695)
Unindexed gain	3,030
Less: Indexation allowance (£2,573 – £1,695)	(878)
Chargeable gain	2,152

Test your understanding 3

Share disposals for companies

1	True	
2	False	You do not apply an indexed rise as you do not need to add or deduct anything to or from the cost column.
3	False	The rights shares relate to the underlying shares.
4	True	

Test your understanding 4

Jerry Ltd

	£
Disposal – September 1999	
Proceeds	9,000
Less: Cost (W)	(4,000)
Unindexed gain	5,000
Less: Indexation (£5,844 – £4,000)	(1,844)
Chargeable gain	3,156
Disposal – March 2017	
Proceeds	14,500
Less: Cost (W)	(4,043)
Unindexed gain	10,457
Less: Indexation (£9,140 – £4,043)	(5,097)
Chargeable gain	5,360

Share pool working

	Number of shares	Unindexed cost	Indexed cost
		£	£
1 July 1995 Balance	4,100	8,200	10,744
September 1999			
(i) Indexed rise (0.115 × £10,744)			1,236
			11,980
(ii) Disposal			
(2,000/4,100) × £8,200 and £11,980	(2,000)	(4,000)	(5,844)
	2,100	4,200	6,136
January 2001			
(i) Indexed rise (0.029 × £6,136)			178
(ii) Acquisition	200	450	450
	2,300	4,650	6,764
March 2017			
(i) Indexed rise (0.554 × £6,764)			3,747
			10,511
(ii) Disposal			
(2,000/2,300) × £4,650 and £10,511	(2,000)	(4,043)	(9,140)
	300	607	1,371

Test your understanding 5

Purple Ltd

Disposal – 8 August 2016

(Sale of 500 shares purchased in previous 9 days)

	£
Sale proceeds (500/5,000 × £15,000)	1,500
Less: Cost	(1,410)
Unindexed gain	90
Less: Indexation allowance	Nil
Chargeable gain	90

Disposal – 8 August 2016 (Sale of 4,500 shares from the pool)

	£
Sale proceeds (£15,000 – £1,500)	13,500
Less: Cost	(5,250)
Unindexed gain	8,250
Less: Indexation allowance (£8,799 – £5,250)	(3,549)
Chargeable gain	4,701

Total gains (£90 + £4,701) = £4,791

Note that no indexation allowance is given for disposals matched with shares purchased on the same day or the previous 9 days.

Share pool working

	Number	**Cost**	**Indexed cost**
		£	£
Balance at 9 June 1998	3,000	4,000	5,010
12 August 2003 Bonus issue (1 for 3)	1,000	Nil	Nil
	4,000	4,000	5,010
Indexed rise to May 2008 (£5,010 × 0.316)			1,583
7 May 2007 Rights issue (1 for 2 × 150p)	2,000	3,000	3,000
	6,000	7,000	9,593
Indexed rise to August 2016 (£9,593 × 0.223)			2,139
			11,732
8 August 2016 Sale $\frac{4,500}{6,000}$ × £7,000/£11,732	(4,500)	(5,250)	(8,799)
Pool c/f	1,500	1,750	2,933

Test your understanding 6

Chrome Ltd

	£
Disposal – October 2016	
Proceeds	17,760
Less: Cost (W)	(16,080)
Unindexed gain	1,680
Less: Indexation (£19,355 – £16,080)	
Restricted, indexation allowance cannot create a loss	(1,680)
Chargeable gain	Nil

Share pool working

	Number of shares	Unindexed cost	Indexed cost
		£	£
May 2007			
(i) Acquisition	3,200	9,600	9,600
June 2011			
(i) Indexed rise (0.141 × £9,600)			1,354
(ii) Rights issue (3,200/4 × £2.60)	800	2,080	2,080
	4,000	11,680	13,034
January 2013			
(i) Indexed rise (0.045 × £13,034)			587
(ii) Acquisition	2,100	4,400	4,400
	6,100	16,080	18,021
October 2016			
(i) Indexed rise (0.074 × £18,021)			1,334
			19,355
(ii) Disposal	(6,100)	(16,080)	(19,355)
	Nil	Nil	Nil

Gains and losses for individuals

Introduction

An individual (including a sole trader or a partner) pays capital gains tax on his chargeable gains.

This chapter compares and contrasts the rules for capital gains for individuals with those for companies.

ASSESSMENT CRITERIA

Calculate chargeable gains and allowable losses (5.1)

Apply the rules relating to the disposal of chattels and wasting assets (5.1)

Apply current reliefs and allowances (5.1)

Apply capital gains tax rates (5.1)

CONTENTS

1 Individual v company – similarities

1.1 Calculation of individual gains and losses

The standard pro forma used to calculate a gain or loss on disposal of an asset is essentially the same as for companies except that individuals are not entitled to an indexation allowance.

	£
Gross sale proceeds	X
Less: Selling costs	(X)
Net sale proceeds (NSP)	X
Less: Allowable cost	(X)
Capital gain	X

1.2 Special rules

The special rules discussed in Chapter 16 also apply for individuals, namely:

- enhancement expenditure
- part disposals
- non-wasting chattels.

Note that the AAT reference material set out in section 5 below has details of these special computational rules.

Test your understanding 1

Which of the following transactions carried out by an individual may give rise to a chargeable gain?

Select yes or no for each disposal.

1	Sale of shares	yes / no
2	Sale of a motor car	yes / no
3	Gift of a holiday home	yes / no
4	Sale of an antique table (cost £4,000) for £5,000	yes / no
5	Gift of an antique wardrobe (cost £4,000) when it was valued at £15,000	yes / no

2 Individual v company – differences

2.1 Capital gains tax

Individuals pay capital gains tax on their taxable gains for the tax year (e.g. 2016/17).

Individuals are entitled to an annual exempt amount for each tax year (£11,100 in 2016/17).

The annual exempt amount is deducted from the total net chargeable gains of the year to give the taxable gains.

	£
Capital gains	X
Less: Capital losses	(X)
Net chargeable gains	X
Less: Annual exempt amount	(11,100)
Taxable gains	X

If an individual has trading losses for the tax year they can claim to set them against their income, but if any loss remains then a claim can be made to treat the trade loss like a capital loss of the same tax year.

Note that this does not work the other way round. Capital losses cannot be offset against income.

Capital gains tax is then calculated on the taxable gains.

2.2 The annual exempt amount and brought forward losses

Brought forward capital losses are not allocated against gains where this would lead to wastage of the annual exempt amount.

The loss relief is restricted to preserve the annual exempt amount.

This rule does not apply to current tax year capital losses, which must be set off against current year gains and cannot be restricted to preserve the annual exempt amount.

The offset of current year losses may therefore result in wastage of the annual exempt amount.

Note that the AAT reference material set out in section 5 below covers the treatment of current year and brought forward capital losses.

Example

Mica has the following capital gains and losses for the two years ended 5 April 2017.

	2015/16	**2016/17**
	£	£
Gains	12,500	13,300
Losses	(14,000)	(2,000)

What gains (if any) are chargeable after considering all reliefs and exemptions?

Solution

	2015/16	**2016/17**
	£	£
Current gains	12,500	13,300
Current losses	(12,500)	(2,000)
Brought forward losses*		(200)
	Nil	11,100
Less: Annual exempt amount	Wasted	(11,100)
Taxable gain	Nil	Nil
Loss carried forward		
(£14,000 – £12,500)	1,500	
(£1,500 – £200)		1,300

*Utilised to reduce gains to annual exempt amount.

Test your understanding 2

Read the following statements and state whether they are true or false.

1 Capital losses are deducted before the annual exempt amount.

2 Excess capital losses can be offset against taxable income.

3 Excess trading losses can be offset against capital gains.

4 Any available capital losses must always be relieved in full.

5 Capital gains are taxed at 40% for higher rate taxpayers.

Test your understanding 3

Manuel made chargeable gains and allowable losses for 2016/17 as set out below:

Gain of £60,000

Gain of £12,000

Capital loss of £4,000

Calculate Manuel's taxable gains for 2016/17.

A £56,900

B £60,900

C £68,000

D £72,000

2.3 Calculating the tax payable

Taxable gains are treated as an additional amount of income in order to determine the rates of CGT. However, the gains must not be included in the income tax computation.

Where the taxable gains fall within any remaining basic rate band (after income has been taxed) they are taxed at 10%. For 2016/17 the basic rate band is £32,000.

The balance of the taxable gains is taxed at 20%.

Taxable gains arising in respect of the disposal of a residential property are taxed at 18% and 28% rather than 10% and 20%. Capital losses and the annual exempt amount should therefore be deducted from gains on residential property in priority to gains on other assets.

Example

Carl sold three assets in 2016/17 and made chargeable gains of £9,400 in respect of a painting, £21,700 in respect of a residential property and a capital loss of £2,500.

Carl has capital losses brought forward as at 6 April 2016 of £3,300.

Carl's taxable income for the year, after deducting the personal allowance, is £30,215.

What is Carl's CGT liability for 2016/17?

Solution

	Painting	Property	Total
	£	£	£
Chargeable gains for the year	9,400	21,700	31,100
Less: Current year capital losses	–	(2,500)	(2,500)
Net chargeable gains for the year	9,400	19,200	28,600
Less: Capital losses brought forward	–	(3,300)	(3,300)
Net chargeable gains	9,400	15,900	25,300
Less: Annual exempt amount	–	(11,100)	(11,100)
Taxable gains	9,400	4,800	14,200
CGT			
Property:			
£1,785 (£32,000 – £30,215) × 18%		321.30	321.30
£3,015 (£4,800 – £1,785) × 28%		844.20	844.20
Painting			
£9,400 × 20%	1,880.00		1,880.00
Capital gains tax liability			3,045.50

Test your understanding 4

Bert made chargeable gains of £13,300 and capital losses of £5,000 in 2016/17. He had losses brought forward of £3,000.

How much capital loss will be carried forward to 2017/18?

2.4 Connected persons

Where a disposal is between connected persons:

(i) sale proceeds are deemed to be market value (any actual sale proceeds are ignored); and

(ii) if a loss arises on a disposal to a connected person it can only be offset against a gain made on a disposal to the **same** connected person.

Connected persons are mainly relatives and their spouses/civil partners or relatives of your spouse/civil partner.

Note that connected persons are covered in the AAT reference material set out in section 5 below.

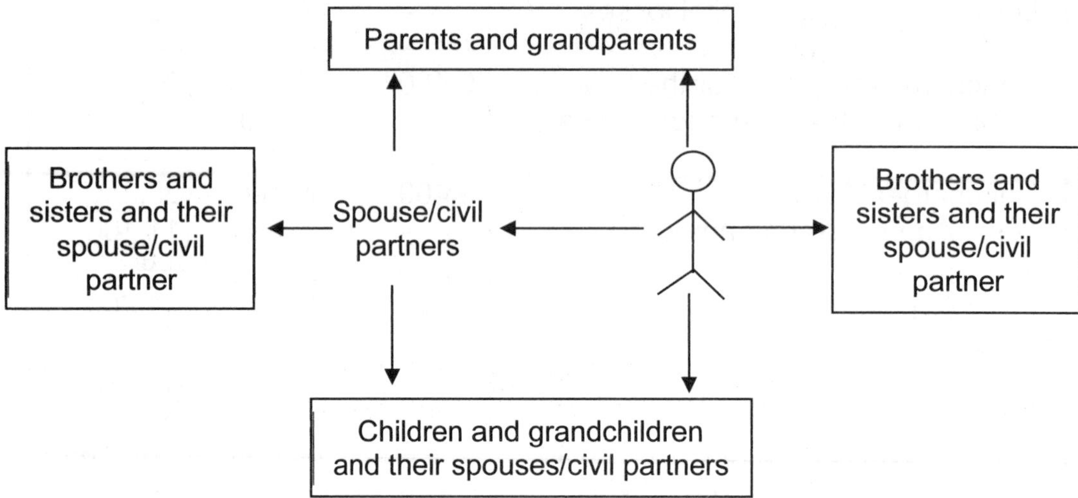

An individual is also connected with a company they control and a partner is connected with their other business partners.

Whilst an individual is connected to their spouse, transactions between spouses are not made at market value but on the basis that no gain or loss arises.

Transfers between civil partners also take place on a no gain/no loss basis.

This gives an opportunity for tax saving as assets can be transferred to the spouse or civil partner with unused annual exempt amount or available capital losses.

Test your understanding 5

Fred sold a painting to his wife on 1 March 2017 for £10,000. The market value of the painting at that date was £20,000.

Fred had purchased the painting in June 2007 for £22,000.

A loss arises on the disposal which can only be offset against gains arising on future disposals to his wife.

True or False?

3 Test your understanding

Test your understanding 6

1 Mary made a capital loss of £4,000 in 2015/16. In 2016/17 she made a chargeable gain of £12,400 and a capital loss of £3,000.

How much capital loss is carried forward at the end of 2016/17?

A £Nil

B £4,000

C £5,700

D £7,000

2 What would your answer be if Mary had only made the chargeable gain of £12,400 in 2016/17 and not the capital loss?

A £Nil

B £1,300

C £2,700

D £4,000

Test your understanding 7

Misha sold two assets (not residential property) in 2016/17 and made two chargeable gains of £17,000 and £11,400. Her taxable income for the year, after deducting the personal allowance, is £21,900.

What is Misha's capital gains tax liability for 2016/17?

Test your understanding 8

John

John made the following disposals in the tax year 2016/17. John is a higher rate taxpayer for the purposes of income tax.

(1) On 20 June 2016 he sold a holiday cottage, a residential property, for £73,600. The cottage was bought in October 2003 for £29,000.

(2) On 12 August 2016 he sold an investment property. It had been purchased for £30,000 in November 2000. Sale proceeds were £26,000.

(3) On 31 March 2017 he sold 2 acres out of a 10 acre plot of land that he had acquired in June 2009 for £50,000. He sold the 2 acres for £60,000.

In March 2017 the remaining 8 acres were worth £250,000.

Required:

Calculate John's capital gains tax liability for 2016/17.

4 Summary

The main differences between calculating gains for individuals and those for companies are:

- individuals are not entitled to the indexation allowance
- individuals are entitled to an annual exempt amount which is deducted from chargeable gains in arriving at taxable gains
- individuals pay capital gains tax on the taxable gains arising from assets which are not residential property in a tax year at 10% and 20% depending on the level of their taxable income and gains
- individuals pay capital gains tax at 18% and 28% on gains arising from residential property. Capital losses and the annual exempt amount should therefore be deducted from gains on residential property in priority to gains on other assets.

5 AAT reference material

Introduction to chargeable gains

- Individual pays Capital Gains Tax (CGT) on net chargeable gains in a tax year.
- For companies, chargeable gains are included as income in calculating total profits.
- Individuals receive an annual exempt amount from CGT – for 2016/17 this is £11,100.
- Gains/losses arise when a chargeable person makes a chargeable disposal of a chargeable asset.
- Chargeable person – individual or company.
- Chargeable disposal – sale, gift or loss/destruction of the whole or part of an asset.

  Exempt disposals – on death and gifts to approved charities.
- Chargeable asset – all assets unless exempt. Exempt assets are motor cars and some chattels.

Calculation of capital gains tax

Net chargeable gains – total gains in the tax year after netting off any current year or brought forward losses and the annual exempt amount.

Annual exempt amount (AE)

- For individuals only.
- AE cannot be carried forward or carried back.
- Current year losses must be netted off against current year gains before AE. This means AE can be wasted.
- Brought forward capital losses are set off against current year gains after AE so AE is not wasted.

Calculation of gains and losses for individuals

Pro forma computation

		£	£
Consideration received			X
Less	Incidental costs of sale		(X)
Net sale proceeds			NSP
Less Allowable expenditure			
	– Acquisition cost	X	
	– Incidental costs of acquisition	X	
	– Enhancement expenditure	X	
			(Cost)
Gain/(Loss)			X/(X)

- Consideration received is usually sales proceeds, but market value will be used instead of actual consideration where the transaction is a gift or between connected persons.
- An individual is connected with their spouse, lineal relatives (and their spouses) and spouse's relatives (and their spouses).
- Husband and wife/civil partner transfers – nil gain nil loss. Tax planning opportunity.

Part disposals – the cost allocated to the disposal = Cost × (A/(A+B))

A = consideration received on part disposal

B = market value of the remainder of the asset

Chattels – tangible moveable object. Two types:

- Wasting – expected life of 50 years or less (e.g. racehorse or boat). CGT exempt.

  Non-wasting – expected life greater than 50 years (e.g. antiques or jewellery).

CGT, £6,000 rule

Buy **Sell**	**£6,000 or less**	**More than £6,000**
Less than £6,000	Exempt	Allowable loss but proceeds are deemed = £6,000
More than £6,000	Normal calculation of the gain, then compare with 5/3(gross proceeds – £6,000) – Take the lower gain	Chargeable in full

Test your understanding answers

Test your understanding 1

1	Yes	A chargeable disposal of a chargeable asset by a chargeable person.
2	No	A motor car is not a chargeable asset.
3	Yes	Gifts are chargeable disposals.
4	No	A chattel sold at a gain where the proceeds are less than £6,000 is exempt.
5	Yes	The proceeds (i.e. the value) exceed £6,000.

Test your understanding 2

1	True	
2	False	Capital losses cannot be set against anything except gains.
3	True	Once trade losses have been set against total income for the tax year, they can be treated like a capital loss of the year and deducted from capital gains.
4	False	Current year losses must be relieved in full but brought forward losses are only utilised to the extent that they reduce net gains to the level of the annual exempt amount.
5	False	Higher rate taxpayers pay 20% capital gains tax.

Test your understanding 3

The correct answer is A.

Explanation

Taxable gains are defined as net chargeable gains after the deduction of the annual exempt amount, as follows:

	£
Total chargeable gains (£60,000 + £12,000)	72,000
Less: Capital loss	(4,000)
Net chargeable gains	68,000
Less: Annual exempt amount	(11,100)
Taxable gain	56,900

Test your understanding 4

Bert

The correct answer is £3,000.

Explanation

Bert's net gains for 2016/17 are £8,300.

The capital losses brought forward of £3,000 will be carried forward to 2017/18 as the net gains for 2016/17 are less than the annual exempt amount of £11,100.

Test your understanding 5

False – The transaction is between husband and wife and therefore takes place on a no gain/no loss basis.

Test your understanding 6

Mary

1 The correct answer is B.

2 The correct answer is C.

Explanation

1 Net chargeable gains for 2016/17 are £9,400 (£12,400 – £3,000). As this is less than the annual exempt amount, the loss brought forward of £4,000 is carried forward to 2017/18.

2 If Mary had only made the chargeable gain of £12,400 in 2016/17, losses brought forward of £1,300 would have been offset to reduce the gain to the level of the annual exempt amount. The balance of the capital losses of £2,700 (£4,000 – £1,300) would have been carried forward.

Test your understanding 7

Misha

The correct answer is £2,450.00.

	£
Chargeable gains (£17,000 + £11,400)	28,400
Less: Annual exempt amount	(11,100)
Taxable gains	17,300
£10,100 (£32,000 – £21,900) × 10%	1,010.00
£7,200 (£17,300 – £10,100) × 20%	1,440.00
Capital gains tax liability	2,450.00

Test your understanding 8

John

	£	£
Cottage		
Proceeds	73,600	
Less: Cost	(29,000)	
		44,600
Investment property		
Proceeds	26,000	
Less: Cost	(30,000)	
		(4,000)
Land		
Proceeds	60,000	
Less: Cost		
$£50{,}000 \times \frac{60{,}000}{60{,}000 + 250{,}000}$	(9,677)	
		50,323
Net chargeable gains		90,923
Less: Annual exempt amount		(11,100)
Taxable gains		79,823
CGT		
Cottage £29,500 (£44,600 – £4,000 – £11,100) × 28%		8,260.00
Land £50,323 × 20%		10,064.60
Capital gains tax liability		18,324.60

Shares and securities – disposals by individuals

Introduction

As part of the assessment you may be required to calculate the gain on a disposal of shares by an individual.

As for companies, there are special rules applying to share disposals as it is necessary to determine which particular shares have been sold.

ASSESSMENT CRITERIA

Apply the rules relating to the disposal of shares (5.1)

CONTENTS

1 The matching rules

As for companies, matching rules are required so that, if only some of the shares are sold we know which they are in order to identify their cost.

However, the matching rules for individuals are different to those for companies.

In relation to *individuals,* we match shares disposed of in the following order:

- first, with shares acquired on the same day as the disposal
- second, with shares acquired within the *following* 30 days (using the earliest acquisition first, i.e. on a FIFO basis)
- third, with the share pool (sometimes referred to as the s104 pool or the FA1985 pool).

  This pool of shares brings together the shares bought by the individual since 6 April 1982 to the date before the day of disposal.

Note that the matching rules for individuals are covered in the AAT reference material set out in section 8 below.

Example

Frederic had the following transactions in the shares of DEF plc, a quoted company.

1 June 1994	Bought	4,000 shares for	£8,000
30 July 2001	Bought	1,800 shares for	£9,750
20 May 2009	Bought	1,000 shares for	£8,500
15 March 2017	Sold	3,500 shares for	£36,000
20 March 2017	Bought	400 shares for	£3,900

You are required to match the shares sold with the relevant acquisitions.

Solution

		Number	Number
Shares sold			3,500
(1)	Shares acquired on same day		Nil
(2)	Shares acquired in following 30 days		(400)
			3,100
(3)	Share pool		
	1 June 1994	4,000	
	30 July 2001	1,800	
	20 May 2009	1,000	
		6,800	
	The disposal from the pool is therefore 3,100 out of 6,800		(3,100)
			Nil

Test your understanding 1

Petra sold 200 shares in Red plc on 13 December 2016. She had acquired her shares in the company as follows:

	Number of shares
1 January 2007	650
14 February 2008	250
5 January 2017	50

In accordance with the share matching/identification rules the 200 shares sold by Petra are correctly identified as follows:

A The 50 shares acquired on 5 January 2017 and then 150 of the remaining 900 shares in the pool

B The 50 shares acquired on 5 January 2017 and then 150 of the shares acquired on 14 February 2008

C 200 of the shares acquired on 1 January 2007

D 200 shares in the share pool which includes all 950 shares acquired

Once the correct acquisition is identified, then the computation of the gains can be carried out. This is looked at in detail over the next few sections.

2 Same day and next 30 days

2.1 Calculation of the gain

The calculation of the gain on disposal is straightforward.

	£
Sale proceeds or market value	X
Less: Allowable cost	(X)
Chargeable gain	X

Example

Using the example details above (Frederic) calculate the gain on the sale of the shares acquired in the 30 days following the sale.

Solution

This consists of the sale of 400 shares.

Sale proceeds of £36,000 relates to 3,500 shares so must be apportioned. The proceeds relating to 400 shares will be:

$$\frac{400}{3,500} \times £36,000 = £4,114$$

	£
Sale proceeds	4,114
Less: Cost	(3,900)
Chargeable gain	214

The balance of the proceeds (£36,000 – £4,114) = £31,886 will be applied to shares sold from the share pool.

3 Share pool

3.1 Calculation of the pooled cost

The share pool consists of all shares of the same type in the same company purchased since 6 April 1982 (we do not need to consider those purchased before 6 April 1982).

The pool is used to calculate the cost of shares sold by reference to the average cost of all shares purchased.

The pool is set up with two columns; number (of shares) and cost.

Shares purchased are added to the pool and shares sold are deducted.

- For a purchase, add the number of shares acquired to the number column and the cost to the cost column.
- For a sale, deduct the number of shares sold from the number column and an appropriate proportion of the cost from the cost column.

Note that there is no indexed cost column for individuals, as individuals are not entitled to indexation.

Example

Using the example details above (Frederic), calculate the cost to be eliminated from the pool.

Solution

Share pool

		Number	*Cost*
			£
1 June 1994	purchase	4,000	8,000
30 July 2001	purchase	1,800	9,750
20 May 2009	purchase	1,000	8,500
		6,800	26,250
15 March 2017	disposal		
£26,250 × (3,100 / 6,800)		(3,100)	(11,967)
Pool balance c/f		3,700	14,283

3.2 Calculation of the gain on the share pool

The gain is calculated as normal:

	£
Sale proceeds	X
Less: Allowable cost	(X)
Chargeable gain	X

Example

Using the details from the example Frederic, what is the gain on the share pool disposals?

Solution

Sale proceeds are £31,886 (from Frederic example above).

	£
Sale proceeds	31,886
Less: Allowable cost (above)	(11,967)
Chargeable gain on share pool shares	19,919

Hence, the total chargeable gain on disposal of the 3,500 shares = (£214 + £19,919) = £20,133

Test your understanding 2

Ken has carried out the following transactions in shares in CYZ plc.

	Number	*Cost*
		£
Purchase (8 February 2000)	1,800	3,100
Purchase (12 September 2009)	1,200	4,400
Purchase (10 October 2016)	400	6,000
	Number	*Proceeds*
Sale (10 October 2016)	2,000	£33,000

What is the chargeable gain?

4 Bonus issues and rights issues

4.1 Principles of bonus issues and rights issues

A bonus issue is the distribution of free shares to existing shareholders based on existing shareholdings.

The number of shares acquired is added to the number column but there is no cost to add to the cost column.

A rights issue involves shareholders acquiring new shares in proportion to their existing shareholdings. The shares are not free but are usually priced at a rate below the market price.

The number of shares acquired is added to the number column and the cost to the cost column. Accordingly, a rights issue is no different from any other purchase of shares.

Note that the rules for share pools, including the treatment of bonus and rights issues, is included in the AAT reference material set out in section 8 below.

 **Example**

Alma acquired shares in S plc, a quoted company, as follows.

2,000 shares acquired in June 1995 for £11,500.

In October 2005 there was a 1 for 2 bonus issue.

In December 2007 there was a 1 for 4 rights issue at £3 per share.

Alma sold 1,350 shares in November 2016 for £30,000.

What is the chargeable gain?

Solution

	£
Sale proceeds	30,000
Less: Cost (W)	(4,950)
Chargeable gain	25,050

Working: Share pool

	Number	*Cost*
		£
June 1995 purchase	2,000	11,500
October 2005 bonus issue (1 for 2)		
No cost so simply add in new shares	1,000	–
	3,000	11,500
December 2007 rights issue		
(1 for 4) (£3 × 750)	750	2,250
	3,750	13,750
November 2016 disposal		
$\frac{1,350}{3,750}$ × £13,750	(1,350)	(4,950)
Pool carried forward	2,400	8,800

Test your understanding 3

Mr Jones

In October 2016 Mr Jones sold 3,000 shares in Smith plc for £36,000.

He had purchased 4,200 shares in June 1993 for £11,600. In August 2007 there was a 1 for 3 rights issue at £5.60 per share.

Required:

Calculate the chargeable gain on disposal.

5 Approach to assessment questions

In the assessment you will normally be asked to calculate a gain on shares. If so, this question will be manually marked. Hence it is important that you enter your answer correctly into the table supplied and show your workings.

In the specimen assessment a table is supplied. The first one or two columns can be used for description and narrative whilst the other columns are for numerical entry.

This should allow you to enter your answer in the same layout as used throughout this chapter although with a little less detail. You will not be able to type in lines to indicate totals and subtotals.

Example

Jason bought 1,000 shares in VZ plc for £4.20 each in December 2006.

In July 2015 he received a 1 for 5 rights issue at £6.52 each.

On 4 May 2016 he sold 400 shares for £45,000.

On 12 May 2016 he bought 100 shares for £10,000.

What is the chargeable gain? Your answer should clearly show the balance of shares carried forward. Show all workings.

Solution

100 shares		£	
(following 30 days)			
Proceeds	100/400 × £45,000	11,250	
Cost		(10,000)	
Gain		1,250	
300 shares – pool			
Proceeds	£45,000 – £11,250	33,750	
Less cost (pool)		(1,376)	
Gain		32,374	
Total gain		33,624	
Pool		*Number*	*Cost* (£)
12.06 Purchase		1,000	4,200
July 2015 Rights issue	1,000/5 × £6.52	200	1,304
		1,200	5,504
May 2016 Sale	300/1,200 ×	(300)	
	£5,504		(1,376)
Balance c/f		900	4,128

6 Test your understanding

Test your understanding 4

Ben bought 1,000 shares in XYZ plc on 1 May 2007 and a further 500 shares on 5 September 2016. He sold 750 shares on 25 August 2016.

Which shares are the shares sold identified with?

A 750 of the shares acquired on 1 May 2007

B 500 of the shares acquired on 1 May 2007 and 250 of the shares acquired on 5 September 2016

C The 500 shares acquired on 5 September 2016 and 250 of the remaining 1,000 shares in the pool

D 750 of the shares in the share pool which includes 1,500 shares acquired

Test your understanding 5

Tony bought 15,000 shares in Last Chance Ltd for £6 per share in August 2005. He received a bonus issue of 1 for 15 shares in January 2008.

In November 2016 Tony sold 9,000 shares for £14 per share.

Required:

Calculate the gain made on the sale of the shares and show the balance of shares and their value to carry forward.

All workings must be shown in your calculations.

Test your understanding 6

Conrad sold all of his 2,145 ordinary shares in Turnip plc on 19 November 2016 for net sale proceeds of £8,580.

His previous dealings in these shares were as follows:

July 2012 purchased 1,750 shares for £2,625

May 2013 purchased 200 shares for £640

June 2014 took up 1 for 10 rights issue at £3.40 per share

Required:

Calculate the gain made on the sale of the shares.

All workings must be shown in your calculations.

Test your understanding 7

David bought 2,000 shares in PQR plc for £4,000 on 6 October 2003 and a further 1,000 shares for £3,000 in March 2009.

PQR plc made a rights issue of 1 new share for every 5 held at £4 per share in February 2011. David sold 400 shares in September 2016 for £4,150.

What is the cost of the shares sold?

A £3,106

B £1,600

C £933

D £1,044

Test your understanding 8

Irving sold 1,500 ordinary shares in Corniche plc on 9 September 2016 for net sale proceeds of £5,550.

His previous dealings in these shares were as follows:

3 June 2011	purchased 4,800 shares for £15,360
11 April 2015	received a 1 for 4 bonus issue
4 October 2016	purchased 700 shares for £2,450

Required:

Calculate the gain on the sale of the shares on 9 September 2016.

All workings must be shown in your calculations.

7 Summary

Share disposals require special matching rules.

Shares sold by individuals are matched with:

- purchases on the same day
- purchases within the following 30 days
- share pool.

Bonus issues increase the number of shares held in the pool.

Rights issues affect both the number of shares held in the pool and the pool cost.

8 AAT reference material

Shares and securities – disposals by individuals

CGT on shares and securities

Disposal of shares and securities are subject to CGT except for listed government securities (gilt-edged securities or 'gilts'), qualifying corporate bonds (e.g. company loan notes/debentures) and shares held in an Individual Savings Account (ISA).

The identification rules

Used to determine which shares have been sold and so what acquisition cost can be deducted from the sale proceeds (e.g. match the disposal and acquisition).

Disposals are matched:

- Firstly, with acquisitions on the same day as the day of disposal.
- Secondly, with acquisitions made in the 30 days following the date of disposal (FIFO basis).
- Thirdly, with shares from the share pool.

The Share Pool

- The share pool contains all shares acquired prior to the disposal date.
- Each acquisition is not kept separately, but is 'pooled' together with other acquisitions and a running total kept of the number of shares and the cost of those shares.
- When a disposal from the pool is made, the appropriate number of shares are taken from the pool along with the average cost of those shares.
- The gain on disposal is then calculated.

Bonus issues and rights issues

- Bonus issue – no adjustment to cost needed.
- Rights issue – adjustment to cost needed.

Test your understanding answers

Test your understanding 1

Petra

The correct answer is A.

Explanation

A is the correct answer because the share identification rules match shares in the following priority.

1 Shares acquired on the same day as the disposal – not applicable here.

2 Shares acquired in the following 30 days – 50 shares acquired on 5 January 2017.

3 Shares in the share pool (all acquisitions up to date of disposal).

Test your understanding 2

Ken

10 October 2016 disposal of 2,000 shares identified with:

		£
(a)	Shares acquired on the same day	400
(b)	Shares from share pool	1,600
		2,000

Sale proceeds are £33,000 for 2,000 shares = £16.50 each

(a) 10 October 2016 acquisition

	£	£
Sale proceeds (400 × £16.50)	6,600	
Less: Cost	(6,000)	
Chargeable gain		600

(b) Share pool

	£	£
Sale proceeds (1,600 × £16.50)	26,400	
Less: Cost (W)	(4,000)	
Chargeable gain		22,400
Total chargeable gains		23,000

Workings: Share pool

	Number	*Cost* £
February 2000 purchase	1,800	3,100
September 2009 purchase	1,200	4,400
	3,000	7,500
October 2016 disposal	(1,600)	(4,000)
Pool balance c/f	1,400	3,500

Test your understanding 3

Mr Jones

	£
Sale proceeds	36,000
Less: Cost (W)	(10,414)
Chargeable gain	25,586

Workings: Share pool	*Number*	*Cost* £
June 1993 purchase	4,200	11,600
August 2007 rights issue (⅓ × 4,200) = 1,400 × £5.60	1,400	7,840
	5,600	19,440
October 2016 disposal $\frac{3,000}{5,600}$ × £19,440	(3,000)	(10,414)
Pool balance c/f	2,600	9,026

Test your understanding 4

Ben

The correct answer is C.

Explanation

C is the correct answer because the share identification rules match shares in the following priority.

1 Shares acquired on the same day as the disposal – not applicable here.

2 Shares acquired in the following 30 days – 500 shares acquired on 5 September 2016.

3 Shares in the share pool.

Test your understanding 5

Tony

	£
Sale proceeds (9,000 × £14)	126,000
Less: Cost (W)	(50,625)
Chargeable gain	75,375

Workings: Share pool

	Number	*Cost*
		£
August 2005 purchase (15,000 × £6)	15,000	90,000
January 2008 bonus issue	1,000	
	16,000	90,000
November 2016 disposal $\frac{9,000}{16,000}$ × £90,000	(9,000)	(50,625)
Pool balance c/f	7,000	39,375

Test your understanding 6

Conrad

	£
Proceeds	8,580
Less: Cost (W)	(3,928)
Chargeable gain	4,652

Working: Share pool

		Shares number	*Cost £*
July 2012	purchase	1,750	2,625
May 2013	purchase	200	640
		1,950	3,265
June 2014 (1 for 10)	rights issue @ £3.40	195	663
		2,145	3,928
Nov 2016	sale	(2,145)	(3,928)
		Nil	Nil

Test your understanding 7

David

The correct answer is D.

Explanation

Working: Share pool		*Shares number*	*Cost £*
October 2003	purchase	2,000	4,000
March 2009	purchase	1,000	3,000
		3,000	7,000
February 2011 (1 for 5)	rights issue @ £4.00	600	2,400
		3,600	9,400
September 2016	sale	(400)	(1,044)
		3,200	8,356

Test your understanding 8

Irving

September 2016 disposal of 1,500 shares identified with:

		£
(a)	Shares acquired in the next 30 days	700
(b)	Shares from share pool	800
		1,500

Net sale proceeds = £5,550 for 1,500 shares = £3.70 each

		£	£
(a)	**4 October 2016 acquisition**		
	Sale proceeds (700 × £3.70)	2,590	
	Less: Cost	(2,450)	
	Chargeable gain		140
(b)	**Share pool**		
	Sale proceeds (800 × £3.70)	2,960	
	Less: Cost (W)	(2,048)	
	Chargeable gain		912
	Total chargeable gains		1,052

Workings: Share pool

	Number	*Cost* £
June 2011 purchase	4,800	15,360
April 2015 bonus issue (4,800/4)	1,200	
	6,000	15,360
October 2016 disposal	(800)	(2,048)
Pool balance c/f	5,200	13,312

Chargeable gains – reliefs

Introduction

The sale of a substantial asset within a business, or the sale of a whole business, could give rise to a large gain. If all of the gain was subject to tax it would make it difficult for business assets to be sold if the owner could not afford the tax due.

Reliefs exist to reduce the tax payable or the gain in specific circumstances, including when a replacement asset is acquired or when an asset is given away.

ASSESSMENT CRITERIA

Apply current reliefs and allowances (5.1, 5.2)

Apply capital gains tax rates (5.1)

CONTENTS

1 Entrepreneurs' relief

Entrepreneurs' relief reduces the capital gains tax payable by an individual on qualifying business disposals; for example where an individual sells all or part of their unincorporated business.

1.1 The relief

The relief operates as follows:

- Gains on 'qualifying business disposals' of up to £10 million are taxed at a lower rate of 10%.
- Any qualifying gains above the £10 million limit are taxed at the normal rates of 10% and 20%.
- The limit is a lifetime limit that is diminished each time a claim for the relief is made.
- In order to maximise tax savings, allowable losses and the annual exempt amount should be deducted from gains on disposals of assets that do not qualify for entrepreneurs' relief wherever possible.
- The amount of qualifying gains that is taxed at 10% must be deducted from the remaining basic rate band when determining the rate of tax to be paid on non-qualifying gains (which will therefore usually be 20%).

The relief must be claimed within 12 months of the 31 January following the end of the tax year in which the disposal is made.

For 2016/17 disposals, the relief must be claimed by 31 January 2019.

The relief is not available to companies.

1.2 Qualifying business disposals

The relief applies to the disposal of:

- the whole or part of a business carried on by the individual either alone or in partnership
- assets of the individual's or partnership's trading business that has **now ceased**

- shares, provided:
  - the shares are in the individual's 'personal trading company', and
  - the individual is an employee of the company (part time or full time).

An individual's 'personal trading company' is one in which the individual:

- owns at least 5% of the ordinary shares
- which carry at least 5% of the voting rights.

Note in particular that:

- the disposal of an individual business asset used for the purposes of a continuing trade does not qualify. There must be a disposal of the whole or part of the trading business; the sale of an asset in isolation does not qualify.

With effect from 17 March 2016:

- the relief will be extended to external investors in unlisted trading companies, i.e. it will not be necessary to work for the company or own at least 5% of the shares.
- The new rules will apply to newly issued shares purchased on or after 17 March 2016 provided they are held continually for a minimum of three years from 6 April 2016.
- The three year holding period means that these new rules cannot apply until 2019/20 disposals at the earliest.

1.3 Qualifying ownership period

The asset(s) being disposed of must have been owned by the individual making the disposal in the 12 months prior to the disposal.

Where the disposal is of an asset of the individual's or partnership's trading business that has now ceased the individual must have owned the business for 12 months prior to the date of cessation and the disposal of the asset must also take place within three years of the cessation of trade.

Note that the AAT reference material set out in section 6 below includes details of the qualifying assets and ownership period.

1.4 Applying the relief

When a qualifying disposal is made:

- Calculate the qualifying gains arising on the disposal of the individual assets as normal.
- Add the individual gains arising on the qualifying disposals together.
- Deduct any capital losses and the annual exempt amount from gains that do **not** qualify for the relief.
- Deduct any remaining capital losses and/or annual exempt amount from the gains qualifying for the relief.
- The taxable qualifying gains are taxed at 10%.
- The non-qualifying gains are taxed at 10%/20% depending on the amount of basic rate band (currently £32,000) available.

Example

In July 2016, Katie sold her unincorporated trading business which she set up in 1996. The following gains arose on the disposal of the business:

	£
Factory	275,000
Goodwill	330,000
Warehouse	100,000

In August 2016 Katie also realised a gain of £20,000 on the sale of a painting.

Calculate the capital gains tax payable by Katie in respect of 2016/17.

Solution

	Qualifying gains	Non-qualifying gains
	£	£
Business:		
Factory	275,000	
Goodwill	330,000	
Warehouse	100,000	
Painting		20,000
Less: Annual exempt amount		(11,100)
Taxable gains	705,000	8,900

CGT payable:	
£705,000 × 10%	70,500.00
£8,900 × 20%	1,780.00
Capital gains tax payable	72,280.00

Note: The gain on the painting is taxed at 20% because the gains qualifying for entrepreneurs' relief are deemed to use up any basic rate band available.

Test your understanding 1

Oliver

In 2016/17 Oliver sold his unincorporated business and made a total gain on the assets used in the business of £600,000. He also made a gain of £9,400 on the sale of an antique table. Oliver has capital losses brought forward as at 6 April 2016 of £22,000.

How much of the gain on the sale of the business is taxed at 10%?

A £576,300

B £600,000

C £566,900

D £578,000

2 Rollover relief

2.1 Principle of rollover relief

Rollover relief allows a company to defer a chargeable gain, provided certain conditions are met.

This relief is also available for unincorporated businesses (sole traders and partnerships).

This is the only relief in this chapter which is available to both companies and unincorporated businesses.

In order to qualify for relief, the company, sole trader or partnership must reinvest the proceeds from the sale of a qualifying business asset into another qualifying business asset.

Any gain on the disposal of the first asset is then 'rolled over' (i.e. deferred) against the capital gains cost of the new asset.

Unlike entrepreneurs' relief, which *reduces* the tax paid, rollover relief simply *defers* the gain on the sale of the asset until the later disposal of the replacement asset. A typical situation can be depicted as follows.

A company sells a building and then buys a new bigger building.

		£
Building (1)	Sale proceeds	100,000
	Less: Cost and indexation allowance	(40,000)
	Indexed gain	60,000
	Less: Rollover relief	(60,000)
	Chargeable gain	Nil
Building (2)	Purchase price	150,000
	Less: 'Rolled over gain'	(60,000)
	Base cost	90,000

The gain on building (1) has been deferred against the base cost of building (2).

Provided that *at least* an amount equal to the proceeds received is reinvested, then *full* deferral applies.

On the sale of the second building, a higher gain will result as the building's allowable cost has been reduced by the rolled over gain from the first building. This higher gain represents both the gain on the second asset and the deferred gain from the first.

	If no rollover relief claimed on building (1)		**If rollover relief is claimed on building (1)**
	£		£
Sale of building (2)			
Sale proceeds, say	200,000	Sale proceeds	200,000
Less: Original cost	(150,000)	Less: Base cost	(90,000)
Unindexed gain	50,000	Unindexed gain	110,000

The benefit of rollover relief is that tax which would otherwise be payable now is deferred, possibly for many years.

There is a drawback however in that, for companies, the indexation allowance on the second gain is calculated on a lower base cost if rollover relief is claimed.

2.2 Conditions for relief

Now that we have considered the mechanics, it is necessary to look at the other conditions which apply.

There must be a disposal of and reinvestment in:

- a qualifying business asset
- within a qualifying time period.

Qualifying business assets

The assets must be used in a *trade*. Where they are only partly used in a trade then only the gain on the trade portion is eligible.

The main qualifying assets are:

- land and buildings (freehold and leasehold)
- fixed plant and machinery
- goodwill (for unincorporated business only, see below).

The following assets are **not** qualifying assets:

- shares in a company
- buildings rented out to tenants.

Note that the replacement asset does not have to be the same type as the asset sold. A company could sell a factory and reinvest in fixed plant and still claim the relief.

Qualifying time period

The qualifying period for reinvestment in the replacement asset is up to 12 months before the sale to within 36 months after the sale.

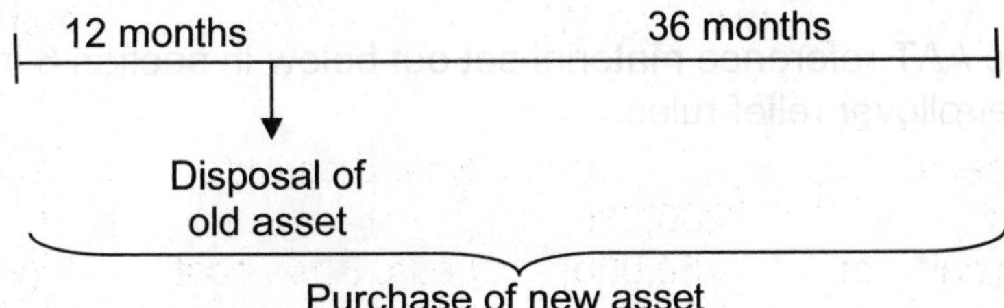

Goodwill

For a company, goodwill is not a chargeable asset so cannot be used as a qualifying replacement asset for rollover relief purposes.

However, goodwill is a qualifying asset for unincorporated businesses (sole traders and partnerships).

Claims

A claim for rollover relief must be made within four years from the later of the end of the tax year (individuals) or accounting period (companies) in which:

- the disposal takes place or
- the replacement asset is purchased.

Therefore, for a sole trader disposal and replacement in 2016/17, the election must be made by 5 April 2021.

For a company disposal and replacement in the year ended 31 December 2016, the election must be made by 31 December 2020.

Note that it is not possible to make a partial claim for rollover relief. If a claim is made then the whole of the eligible gain must be rolled over.

2.3 Partial reinvestment

Rollover relief may still be available even where only part of the proceeds is reinvested. However, it will be restricted, as there is some cash retained which is available to settle tax liabilities. This is logical as the main purpose of the relief is not to charge tax where cash has been reinvested in the business.

The amount which is chargeable now is the lower of:

- the proceeds not reinvested
- the chargeable gain.

This amount cannot be rolled over (i.e. cannot be deferred).

The following example will demonstrate where full relief is available, partial relief is available and no relief is available.

Note that the AAT reference material set out below in section 6 includes details of the rollover relief rules.

Example

AB Ltd sold an office block for £500,000 in December 2016. The office block had been acquired for £200,000 and was used throughout AB Ltd's ownership for trade purposes. The indexation allowance on the disposal was £213,100. A replacement office block was acquired in February 2017.

Assuming rollover relief is claimed where possible, calculate the gain assessable on AB Ltd and the base cost of the replacement office block if it cost:

(a) £610,000

(b) £448,000

(c) £345,000

Solution

Gain on sale of old office block.

	£
Proceeds	500,000
Less: Cost	(200,000)
Unindexed gain	300,000
Less: Indexation allowance	(213,100)
Chargeable gain before reliefs	86,900

(a) New asset cost £610,000

As all the proceeds have been reinvested, the full gain is rolled over and no gain is immediately chargeable.

	£
Chargeable gain before reliefs	86,900
Less: Rollover relief	(86,900)
Chargeable gain	Nil
Base cost of new asset	
Cost	610,000
Less: Gain rolled over	(86,900)
Base cost	523,100

Note that it is not possible to elect to rollover less than £86,900 i.e. a partial claim cannot be made.

(b) New asset cost £448,000

As not all of the proceeds have been reinvested, a gain arises when the old office block is sold as follows:

Gain chargeable now = lower of

(i)	Proceeds not reinvested (£500,000 – £448,000)	£52,000
(ii)	The whole of the chargeable gain	£86,900

	£
Chargeable gain before reliefs	86,900
Less: Rollover relief (£86,900 – £52,000)	(34,900)
Chargeable gain now	52,000

Base cost of new asset	
Cost	448,000
Less: Gain rolled over	(34,900)
Base cost	413,100

(c) New asset cost £345,000

As not all of the proceeds have been reinvested, a gain arises immediately

Gain chargeable now = lower of

(i)	Proceeds not reinvested (£500,000 – £345,000)	£155,000
(ii)	The whole of the chargeable gain	£86,900

	£
Chargeable gain before reliefs	86,900
Less: Rollover relief (balance)	(Nil)
Chargeable gain now	86,900

As the proceeds not reinvested exceed the gain, the full gain of £86,900 is chargeable and no rollover relief is available.

Base cost of new asset	£345,000

Test your understanding 2

Karim

Karim purchased a freehold building in September 1995 and sold it for £450,000 in May 2016, generating a chargeable gain before reliefs of £190,000. The asset qualifies as a business asset.

Karim purchased a new building in February 2016 for £415,000. This building is also a qualifying business asset.

Assuming a claim for rollover relief is made, what is the chargeable gain on the sale of the original building?

A £190,000

B £155,000

C £35,000

D £14,778

Test your understanding 3

Spares Ltd

An office building was sold by Spares Ltd on 30 April 2015. Spares Ltd has a year end of 31 December.

The dates during which the proceeds must be reinvested are:

From:

A 30 April 2014

B 30 April 2015

C 31 December 2014

D 31 December 2015

To:

A 30 April 2018

B 30 April 2019

C 31 December 2018

D 31 December 2019

3 Gift relief

3.1 Principle of gift relief

When a gift is made by an individual, the capital gains tax rules require any gain to be calculated as if the disposal had been a sale at full market value.

The legislation allows a claim to defer the gain where the asset is a qualifying 'business asset' as defined for 'gift relief' purposes.

The broad purpose of gift relief is to enable sole traders and shareholders of family companies to pass on their business or shares to the next generation. Note that this relief is not available for gifts by companies.

Gift relief works by 'deducting' the gain (often described as 'holding over' the gain) from the base cost to the donee (i.e. the person receiving the asset).

	Donor		**Donee**
	£		£
Market value	50,000	Deemed cost	50,000
Less: Cost	(10,000)		
	40,000		
Less: Gift relief	(40,000)	Less: Held over gain	(40,000)
Chargeable gain	Nil	CGT base cost	10,000

In effect, the donee 'takes over' the responsibility for the donor's gain until such time as he makes a disposal of the asset.

3.2 Conditions for relief

There are various conditions which must be considered before applying gift relief. We discuss them under the following headings:

- assets which qualify for the relief
- administration of the election.

Assets which qualify for the relief include the following:

- assets used in a trade by the donor or by his personal trading company
- shares and securities in an unquoted trading company (regardless of how many shares are owned)
- shares and securities in the donor's personal trading company (quoted or unquoted).

A 'personal company' is one in which the donor holds at least 5% of the voting rights.

Note that relief is therefore only available for quoted company shares if the donor holds at least a 5% interest in the company.

Administration of the election

Gift relief requires a joint election by the donor and the donee.

This must be made within four years of the end of the tax year in which the gift takes place. Therefore, for a gift in 2016/17, the election must be made by 5 April 2021.

It is not possible to specify the amount of the gain to holdover in a claim. All the gain qualifying is held over if a claim is made.

Note that the AAT reference material set out below in section 6 has some details about gift relief.

Example

Jones, aged 48, gave the factory that he used in his business to his son on 16 June 2016 when it was valued at £600,000. The factory cost him £150,000 on 16 October 2003.

Calculate the chargeable gain arising and show the base cost of the factory for Jones' son, assuming gift relief is claimed.

Solution

Step 1: Calculate the gain on the gift using market value

	£
Proceeds (use market value)	600,000
Less: Cost	(150,000)
Chargeable gain before reliefs	450,000

Step 2: Consider whether the gift relief conditions are satisfied

- Asset used in Jones' trade.
- Factory is a qualifying asset.

Step 3: Hold over the gain against the base cost of the factory

	£
Chargeable gain before reliefs	450,000
Less: Gift relief	(450,000)
Chargeable now	Nil

Base cost of factory for Jones' son.

Market value of factory	600,000
Less: Gain held over	(450,000)
Base cost	150,000

Test your understanding 4

Matt and Ella

Matt gave a business asset to Ella on 1 February 2017. The asset originally cost Matt £21,000. On 1 February 2017 the asset had a market value of £60,000. A joint election for gift relief is made.

Which one of the following statements is correct?

A Ella's deemed cost is £21,000

B Ella's deemed cost is £60,000

C Ella's deemed cost is £39,000

D Matt has a chargeable gain of £39,000

Test your understanding 5

Gift relief

Which one of the following statements is false?

A Gift relief is available on the gift of quoted shares or securities in a trading company provided the individual holds at least 5% of the voting rights in the company

B Gift relief is available on the gift of unquoted shares or securities in a trading company regardless of the number of shares held by the individual

C Gift relief is only available on the assets of a trade when the trade is disposed of as a whole or after it has ceased

D Gift relief is available on any assets used in a trade by the donor or by his personal trading company

4 Test your understanding

Test your understanding 6

Entrepreneurs' relief

Which of the following statements is correct?

A The maximum entrepreneurs' relief available is £10,000,000 per business disposal

B Entrepreneurs' relief is not available in respect of a gain on a sale of shares

C Where a gain qualifies for entrepreneurs' relief the relief is given automatically

D Gains qualifying for entrepreneurs' relief are taxed at 10% even if the vendor is a higher rate taxpayer

Test your understanding 7

Leon

Leon is a sole trader. He sold a factory in December 2016 which he had used in his business since 2006.

Leon can claim to rollover the gain on the factory against which of the following?

A The purchase of a commercial property in January 2017 which will be let to tenants

B The purchase of a shop in December 2016 which will be rented by his sister

C The purchase of a new factory in May 2016 which will be used in Leon's trade

D The purchase of a new forklift truck in December 2016 for use in Leon's trade

Test your understanding 8

Brian

Brian bought a factory for £600,000 in March 2008. In November 2016, it was sold for £900,000. In the same month another factory was bought for £825,000.

The amount of the gain that can be rolled over is:

A £Nil

B £75,000

C £225,000

D £300,000

Test your understanding 9

Taylor

Taylor disposed of his freehold factory on 18 July 1995 for £120,000, realising a gain of £30,000.

On 1 December 1995, he invested £115,000 of the proceeds in a warehouse for use in his business.

On 22 December 2016, he sold the warehouse for £320,000.

Required:

Compute the amount of Taylor's taxable gains which would be subject to capital gains tax as a result of the above transactions, showing the years in which they would be assessed.

Assume the annual exempt amount is £11,100 in all years.

Test your understanding 10

Jonald

On 5 June 2016 Jonald, aged 49, gifted his 80% shareholding in Jonald Limited (with a market value of £5 million) to his son Reg.

The resulting gain for the purposes of capital gains tax was £900,000.

Required:

Assuming gift relief is claimed, compute:

(a) the amount chargeable on Jonald in 2016/17

(b) Reg's base cost in respect of the shares gifted.

Test your understanding 11

DRV Ltd (1)

DRV Ltd prepares accounts to 31 March annually.

The company sold the freehold of a factory on 3 March 2017 for £325,000, having previously purchased it as a replacement freehold factory for £200,000 in October 1995.

The factory which it replaced was acquired in May 1991 for £65,000 and sold in December 1995 for £140,000.

Required:

Calculate the chargeable gains, assuming all available reliefs are claimed. The indexation factors are:

May 1991 – December 1995	0.129
October 1995 – March 2017	0.775

Test your understanding 12

DRV Ltd (2)

DRV Ltd prepares accounts to 31 March annually.

The company sold the freehold of a factory on 3 March 2017 for £325,000, having previously purchased it as a replacement freehold factory for £115,000 in October 1995.

The factory which it replaced was acquired in May 1991 for £65,000 and sold in December 1995 for £140,000.

Required:

Calculate the chargeable gains, assuming all available reliefs are claimed.

The indexation factors are:

May 1991 – December 1995	0.129
October 1995 – March 2017	0.775

Test your understanding 13

Columbus

Columbus sold one of his factories on 30 April 2016 for £900,000. The factory had been purchased in September 1991 for £300,000.

In March 2016, Columbus purchased another factory for £700,000 and claimed rollover relief on the gain on the factory sold in April 2016.

Required:

Calculate the chargeable gain on the sale of the first factory, the amount of any rollover relief available and the base cost of the second factory.

Test your understanding 14

Astute Ltd

Astute Ltd sold a factory on 15 February 2017 for £320,000. The factory was purchased on 24 October 2006 for £164,000, and was extended at a cost of £37,000 during March 2008.

Astute Ltd incurred legal fees of £3,600 in connection with the purchase of the factory, and legal fees of £6,200 in connection with the disposal.

Astute Ltd is considering the following alternative ways of reinvesting the proceeds from the sale of its factory.

(1) A freehold warehouse can be purchased for £340,000.

(2) A freehold factory building can be purchased for £300,000.

The reinvestment will take place during May 2017. All of the above buildings have been, or will be, used for business purposes.

Required:

(a) State the conditions that must be met in order that rollover relief can be claimed.

You are not expected to list the categories of asset that qualify for rollover relief.

(b) Before taking account of any available rollover relief, calculate Astute Ltd's chargeable gain in respect of the disposal of the factory.

(c) Advise Astute Ltd of the rollover relief that will be available in respect of EACH of the two alternative reinvestments.

Your answer should include details of the base cost of the replacement asset for each alternative.

Indexation factors are as follows:

October 2006 to February 2017	0.325
March 2008 to February 2017	0.252

Test your understanding 15

Roy and Colin

In September 2016 Roy gave his business premises to his son Colin.

At that time the premises had a market value of £500,000 and had been purchased by Roy in September 1990 for £100,000.

Roy and Colin made a joint claim for any capital gain to be held over.

Required:

Calculate the gain assessable on Roy for 2016/17, before deduction of the annual exempt amount, and the cost which will be available to Colin when computing the gain on a future disposal of the premises.

Test your understanding 16

Alan

On 1 August 2016 Alan sold the trade and assets of his business for £13,000,000.

The only assets of the business chargeable to capital gains tax were goodwill and a factory. The goodwill and the factory were acquired in June 2009 for £10,000 and £1,300,000 respectively.

The proceeds received on the sale of the business included £5,500,000 for goodwill and £6,000,000 for the factory.

Alan is a higher rate taxpayer and made no other disposals in 2016/17.

Required:

Calculate the capital gains tax payable by Alan for 2016/17 on the assumption that all beneficial claims are made.

Test your understanding 17

Herbert

In 2016/17 Herbert, a higher rate taxpayer, made the following disposals:

(1) On 1 July 2016 he sold his 25% shareholding in Osprey Ltd, a trading company for which he had worked for the last five years. Herbert acquired his shares in the company in May 2012 for £20,000. He sold the shares for £500,000.

(2) On 1 August 2016 he sold an antique table for £8,000, incurring selling costs of £900. He had acquired the table for £2,000 in May 2009.

(3) On 1 September 2016 he sold a painting for £20,000. He had acquired the painting for £22,000 in June 2008.

Required:

Calculate the capital gains tax payable by Herbert for 2016/17.

5 Summary

The reliefs available are as follows:

	For companies	For individuals
Entrepreneurs' relief		
– first £10 million of gains taxed at 10%	×	✓
Rollover relief		
– defer the gain against cost of the new asset	✓	✓
Gift relief		
– defer the gain by reducing the donee's cost	×	✓

6 AAT reference material

Chargeable gains – reliefs available to individuals

Replacement of business assets (Rollover) relief – when a qualifying business asset is sold at a gain, taxpayer can defer gain by reinvesting proceeds in a qualifying replacement asset.

- Deferred gain is deducted from the cost of the replacement asset so gain crystallises when the replacement asset is sold.
- Qualifying assets (original and replacement) – must be used in a trade by the vendor and be land and buildings, fixed plant and machinery or goodwill.
- Qualifying time period – replacement asset must be purchased between 1 year before and 3 years after the sale of the original asset.
- Partial reinvestment – only some of the sales proceeds reinvested then the gain taxable is the lower of the full gain and the proceeds not reinvested.

Gift relief (holdover relief) – donee takes over asset at donor's base cost i.e. the gain is given away along with the asset.

- Qualifying assets – trade assets of donor or shares in any unquoted trading company or personal trading company (individual owns at least 5% of company).

Entrepreneurs' relief – gain taxable at 10% capital gains tax rate.

- The £10 million limit is a lifetime limit which is reduced each time a claim for the relief is made.
- For 2016/17 claim must be made by 31 January 2019.

- Qualifying business disposals (assets must be owned for at least 12 months prior to sale).
  - The whole or part of a business carried on by the individual (alone or in partnership).
  - Assets of the individual's or partnership's trading business that has now ceased.
  - Shares in the individual's 'personal trading company'. Individual must have owned the shares and been an employee of the company for 12 months prior to sale.
- From 17 March 2016, newly issued shares in unlisted trading companies purchased on or after 17 March 2016 by external investors qualify for entrepreneurs' relief provided they are continually held for a minimum of 3 years from 6 April 2016.

Test your understanding answers

Test your understanding 1

Oliver

The correct answer is A.

Explanation

The gain is calculated as follows:

	£
Gain on disposal of business assets	600,000
Less: Capital losses (£22,000 – £9,400)	(12,600)
Annual exempt amount	(11,100)
Chargeable gain	576,300

The capital losses are offset against the gain on the sale of the antique table in preference to the gain on the sale of the business as this is more tax efficient.

Test your understanding 2

Karim

The correct answer is C.

Explanation

The gain on the sale of the original building can be rolled over against the cost of the new building as follows:

	£
Gain on sale of building	190,000
Less: Rollover relief	(155,000)
Chargeable gain = proceeds not reinvested (£450,000 − £415,000)	35,000

Test your understanding 3

Spares Ltd

The correct answers are both A.

Explanation

A business or company has from 12 months before the disposal to 3 years after the disposal to reinvest the proceeds.

Test your understanding 4

Matt and Ella

The correct answer is A.

Explanation

The gain is calculated as follows:

	£
Market value	60,000
Less: Cost	(21,000)
Chargeable gain before reliefs	39,000
Less: Gift relief	(39,000)
Chargeable gain	Nil

Base cost to Ella:

Deemed cost (MV)	60,000
Less: Gift relief	(39,000)
Base cost	21,000

Test your understanding 5

Gift relief

The correct answer is C.

Explanation

C is the correct answer because gift relief is available on:

- quoted shares or securities in a trading company provided the individual holds at least 5% of the voting rights in the company
- unquoted shares regardless of the number of shares held, and
- any assets used in a trade by the donor or by his personal trading company.

It is entrepreneurs' relief that is only available on the assets of a trade when the trade is disposed of as a whole or after it has ceased.

Test your understanding 6

Entrepreneurs' relief

The correct answer is D.

Explanation

The maximum entrepreneurs' relief is £10,000,000 per lifetime not per disposal.

Entrepreneurs' relief is available on the disposal of shares in the individual's personal trading company in which he is employed.

The relief must be claimed within 12 months of the 31 January following the end of the tax year in which the disposal occurs.

Test your understanding 7

Leon

The correct answer is C.

Explanation

C is the correct answer because rollover relief is available against qualifying assets purchased within 12 months before and 3 years after the sale of the original factory.

However, property let out to tenants does not qualify for rollover relief, nor does moveable (rather than fixed) plant and machinery (i.e. the forklift truck).

Test your understanding 8

Brian

The correct answer is C.

Explanation

The rollover relief is restricted because the proceeds have not been fully reinvested.

The chargeable gain now will be calculated as follows:

	£
Proceeds	900,000
Less: Cost	(600,000)
	300,000
Less: Rollover relief (balancing figure)	(225,000)
Chargeable gain (£900,000 – £825,000)	75,000

Test your understanding 9

Taylor

Disposal of freehold factory (18 July 1995)

£115,000 has been reinvested in a business asset (warehouse) within three years and therefore part of the gain may be rolled over.

The £5,000 (£120,000 – £115,000) proceeds not reinvested is taxed in 1995/96, but will be covered by the annual exempt amount.

The gain rolled over is £25,000 (£30,000 – £5,000).

Disposal of warehouse (22 December 2016)

	£	£
Proceeds		320,000
Less: Cost	115,000	
Gain rolled over	(25,000)	
Base cost of warehouse		(90,000)
Capital gain		230,000
Less: Annual exempt amount		(11,100)
Taxable gain in 2016/17		218,900

Test your understanding 10

Jonald

(a) Amount chargeable on Jonald in 2016/17

Gain eligible to be held over = £900,000

The gain assessable in 2016/17 is therefore £Nil.

(b) Reg's base cost for shares gifted

Market value at date of gift less gain held over
= (£5,000,000 – £900,000) = £4,100,000

Test your understanding 11

DRV Ltd (1)

Sale of original freehold factory (purchased May 1991)

	£
Sale proceeds (December 1995)	140,000
Less: Cost	(65,000)
Unindexed gain	75,000
Less: Indexation allowance (May 1991 – December 1995) (0.129 × £65,000)	(8,385)
Chargeable gain before relief	66,615
Less: Rollover relief upon purchase of replacement factory in October 1995	(66,615)
Chargeable gain – year ended 31 March 1996	Nil

Sale of replacement factory

	£	£
Sale proceeds (March 2017)		325,000
Cost (October 1995)	200,000	
Less: Rolled over gain	(66,615)	
		(133,385)
Unindexed gain		191,615
Less: Indexation allowance (October 1995 – March 2017) (0.775 × £133,385)		(103,373)
Chargeable gain (Note)		88,242

Note: DRV Ltd may be able to roll this gain over if it makes a further qualifying purchase in the qualifying time period.

Test your understanding 12

DRV Ltd (2)

Sale of original freehold factory (purchased May 1991)

	£
Sale proceeds (December 1995)	140,000
Less: Cost	(65,000)
Unindexed gain	75,000
Less: Indexation allowance	
(May 1991 – December 1995) (0.129 × £65,000)	(8,385)
Indexed gain (as above)	66,615
Less: Rollover relief (balancing figure)	(41,615)
Chargeable gain – year ended 31 March 1996 (Note)	25,000

Note: Not all of the sale proceeds are reinvested.

Therefore, the chargeable gain arising now is the sale proceeds not reinvested = £25,000 (£140,000 – £115,000).

Sale of replacement factory

	£	£
Sale proceeds (March 2017)		325,000
Cost	115,000	
Less: Rolled over gain	(41,615)	
		(73,385)
Unindexed gain		251,615
Less: Indexation allowance		
(October 1995 – March 2017) (0.775 × £73,385)		(56,873)
Chargeable gain		194,742

Test your understanding 13

Columbus

Disposal of first factory

	£
Proceeds	900,000
Less: Cost	(300,000)
Chargeable gain before reliefs	600,000
Gain taxable in 2016/17:	
Lower of	
(1) Sale proceeds not reinvested (£900,000 – £700,000)	200,000
(2) Chargeable gain before reliefs	600,000
Therefore a gain of £200,000 is taxable in 2016/17	
Rollover relief is therefore: (£600,000 – £200,000)	400,000

Base cost of second factory

	£
Cost of second factory	700,000
Less: Gain rolled over	(400,000)
Base cost	300,000

Test your understanding 14

Astute Ltd

(a) Conditions for rollover relief

(i) The reinvestment must be within the period starting 12 months before the disposal and ending 36 months after the date of disposal of the original asset.

(ii) The original asset and the replacement asset must be qualifying business assets used for a trading purpose by the taxpayer.

(iii) The replacement asset must be brought into use by the taxpayer for a trading purpose on acquisition.

(b) Disposal of the factory – 15 February 2017

	£
Proceeds (£320,000 – £6,200)	313,800
Less Cost (October 2006)	(164,000)
Legal fees of purchase	(3,600)
Extension (March 2008)	(37,000)
Unindexed gain	109,200
Less Indexation allowance	
On cost: (£164,000 + £3,600) × 0.325	(54,470)
On extension: (£37,000 × 0.252)	(9,324)
Chargeable gain	45,406

(c) Alternative reinvestments

(1) **Freehold warehouse costing £340,000**

As the full sale proceeds will have been reinvested, the company can claim to rollover the gain in full.

The base cost of the warehouse will be £294,594 (£340,000 – £45,406).

(2) **Freehold factory building costing £300,000**

As less than the full proceeds will have been reinvested, only part of the gain can be rolled over.

The proceeds not reinvested of £20,000 (£320,000 – £300,000) results in a gain of £20,000 remaining chargeable (see notes).

The balance of £25,406 (£45,406 – £20,000) is rolled over.

The base cost of the factory building becomes £274,594 (£300,000 – £25,406).

Note: HMRC allow the 'proceeds not reinvested' to be calculated as the difference between the **net** sale proceeds (i.e. after selling costs) and the purchase cost (including purchase expenses) of the replacement asset.

In (c) (2) this would mean only £13,800 (£313,800 – £300,000) of the gain remaining chargeable. However, you may not be expected to know this and would not be penalised either way.

Test your understanding 15

Roy and Colin

Roy

	£
Deemed disposal proceeds	500,000
Less: Cost	(100,000)
Chargeable gain before reliefs	400,000

If a joint claim for gift relief is made, there will be no chargeable gain arising on Roy in 2016/17.

Colin

The cost available to Colin when computing the gain on a future disposal of the building is (£500,000 – £400,000) = £100,000.

Test your understanding 16

Alan

	£	£
Goodwill		
Proceeds	5,500,000	
Less: Cost	(10,000)	
		5,490,000
Factory		
Proceeds	6,000,000	
Less: Cost	(1,300,000)	
		4,700,000
Total chargeable gains		10,190,000
Less: Annual exempt amount		(11,100)
		10,178,900

Qualifying gains (£10,000,000 × 10%)	1,000,000.00
Remaining gains (£178,900 × 20%)	35,780.00
Capital gains tax payable	1,035,780.00

Test your understanding 17

Herbert

	Not qualifying for ER	**Qualifying for ER**
	£	£
Shares		
Proceeds		500,000
Less: Cost		(20,000)
Chargeable gain		480,000
Table		
Proceeds	8,000	
Less: Selling costs	(900)	
Net proceeds	7,100	
Less: Cost	(2,000)	
Chargeable gain	5,100	
Chargeable gain restricted to 5/3 × (£8,000 – £6,000)	3,333	
Painting		
Proceeds	20,000	
Less: Cost	(22,000)	
Allowable loss	(2,000)	
Total net chargeable gains on non-qualifying assets (£3,333 – £2,000)	1,333	
Less: Annual exempt amount	(1,333)	(9,767)
Taxable gains	Nil	470,233
Capital gains tax payable (£470,233 × 10%)		47,023.30

Duties and responsibilities of a tax adviser

Introduction

A tax adviser must ensure that he has the best interests of his clients in mind at all times, whilst ensuring that he complies with his legal duties.

ASSESSMENT CRITERIA
The distinction between tax planning, tax avoidance and tax evasion (4.3)
AAT's ethical standards relating to tax advice and professional conduct in relation to taxation (4.3)

CONTENTS

1 Duties and responsibilities

1.1 AAT expectations

The AAT expects its members to:

- master skills and techniques through learning and maintain them through continuing professional development
- adopt an ethical approach to work as well as to their employers and clients
- acknowledge their professional duty to society as a whole
- maintain an objective outlook
- provide professional, high standards of service, conduct and performance at all times.

These expectations are discussed in greater depth in the 'Code of Professional Ethics' that can be found on the website (www.aat.org.uk).

A person advising either a company or an individual on taxation issues has duties and responsibilities towards both:

- his client, and
- HM Revenue and Customs.

An adviser owes the greatest duty to his or her client.

2 Confidentiality

2.1 Dealings with third parties

A tax adviser has an overriding duty of confidentiality towards his client. Under normal circumstances a client's tax affairs should not be discussed with third parties. This duty remains even after the adviser no longer works for the client.

The exceptions to this rule mentioned in the Guidelines are where:

- authority has been given by the client, or
- there is a legal, regulatory or professional duty to disclose (e.g. in the case of suspected money laundering).

2.2 Dealings with HM Revenue and Customs

The duty of confidentiality also relates to dealings with HMRC.

However, the tax adviser must ensure that, whilst acting in the client's best interests, he consults with HMRC staff in an open and constructive manner (see below).

3 Ethical issues

3.1 Dealing with problems

In spite of guidelines being available, there can be situations where the method of resolving an ethical issue is not straightforward.

In those situations additional advice should be sought from:

- a supervisor
- a professional body, or
- a legal adviser.

3.2 Tax avoidance and tax evasion

Tax avoidance is the use of legitimate means in order to reduce a tax liability. It is acceptable to advise a client on ways in which their tax liabilities may be reduced.

Tax evasion is unlawful. A taxpayer who dishonestly withholds or falsifies information in order to evade tax may be subject to criminal proceedings or suffer civil penalties.

3.3 Dealing with errors in clients' tax returns

Where a tax adviser realises that an error has been made in a client's or employer's tax return he must recommend that the client/employer informs HMRC.

If the client/employer refuses to do so, the member must not act for them in connection with that return or related matters.

Test your understanding 1

Which of the following statements is not correct?

A Accountants need to follow the rules of confidentiality even in a social environment.

B If money laundering is suspected, accountants are allowed to break the rules of confidentiality.

C Rules of confidentiality towards a client must be followed even after the business relationship has ended.

D Accountants must follow the rules of confidentiality irrespective of the situation.

Test your understanding 2

When an accountant is advising a client, to whom does he owe the greatest duty of care?

A HMRC

B The professional body to which the accountant belongs

C The client

D The public

4 Money laundering

4.1 What is money laundering?

Money laundering is the exchange of funds acquired through crime for funds that do not appear to be linked to crime.

The AAT and its members are required to comply with the money laundering laws and regulations.

4.2 Requirements under the laws and regulations

A tax adviser should check the identity of prospective clients via a review of appropriate documentation, for example, a passport.

A firm of accountants must appoint a money laundering officer.

Suspicion that a person is involved in money laundering should be reported to the money laundering officer who will determine whether it needs to be reported to the appropriate authorities.

5 Tax advice

5.1 Providing tax advice

When providing tax advice and preparing tax returns, a person should act in the best interests of his client.

However, he must ensure that his services are consistent with the law and are carried out competently.

At all times an adviser 'must not in any way impair integrity or objectivity'.

5.2 Providing information to HM Revenue and Customs/ other authorities

The 'Code of Professional Ethics' state that:

'A member should not be associated with any return or communication where there is reason to believe that it:

- contains a false or misleading statement
- contains statements or information furnished recklessly, or
- omits or obscures information required to be included and such omission or obscurity would be misleading.'

Test your understanding 3

1 All individuals must submit a tax return – TRUE or FALSE?

2 A member of the AAT working for a firm of accountants should report any suspicion that a person is involved in money laundering to the AAT.

6 Summary

A tax adviser has an overriding duty of confidentiality towards his client.

However, his responsibilities include openness in dealing with HMRC and reporting suspicion of money laundering.

7 AAT reference material

Duties and responsibilities of a tax adviser

- Maintain client confidentiality at all times.
- AAT members must adopt an ethical approach and maintain an objective outlook.
- Give timely and constructive advice to clients.
- Honest and professional conduct with HMRC.
- A tax advisor is liable to a £3,000 penalty if they assist in making an incorrect return.

Test your understanding answers

Test your understanding 1

The answer is **D**.

The duty of confidentiality can be overridden if the client gives authority or if there is a legal, regulatory or professional duty to disclose.

Test your understanding 2

The correct answer is **C**.

Test your understanding 3

1 **False** – Individuals only have to submit a tax return if the tax legislation requires them to do so. Some individuals are not required to submit a return because they are non-taxpayers or all of their tax liability is settled by deduction at source (e.g. PAYE).

2 **False** – a suspicion that a person is involved in money laundering should be reported to the firm's money laundering officer.

MOCK ASSESSMENT
AQ 2016

1 Mock Assessment Questions

This assessment contains 11 TASKS and you should attempt to complete every task.

Each task is independent. You will not need to refer to your answers to previous tasks.

Read every task carefully to make sure you understand what is required.

Where the date is relevant, it is given in the task data.

You may use minus signs or brackets to indicate negative numbers UNLESS task instructions say otherwise.

You must use a full stop to indicate a decimal point.

For example, write 100.57 NOT 100,57 or 100 57

You may use a comma to indicate a number in the thousands, but you don't have to.

For example, 10000 and 10,000 are both acceptable.

If rounding is required, normal mathematical rounding rules should be applied UNLESS task instructions say otherwise.

Task 1 (12 marks)

(a) **For each item, tick whether the following items are capital or revenue expenditure for tax purposes for a trading company.**

(4 marks)

	Capital	*Revenue*
Stationery		
Legal costs on purchase of a second hand building		
Repairs to the building to make it useable		
Computer software which will be replaced in two years		

(b) **Tick the appropriate box to show how the following items should be dealt with when calculating adjusted profit for a sole trader. All items have been charged or credited (as appropriate) in arriving at net profit of £190,000. (8 marks)**

	Increase net profit	*Decrease net profit*	*No adjustment needed*
Staff salaries			
Profit on the sale of a capital asset			
Decrease in general bad debt provision			
Legal fees for an unsuccessful appeal against a business rating assessment			
Costs of installing new machinery			
Food hampers given to staff as Christmas gifts			
Boxes of chocolates given to customers who spent over £250			
Leasing costs for car for sales person. The car has CO_2 emissions of 120 g/km			

Task 2 (14 marks)

Armin is a sole trader who has prepared annual accounts to 31 January in the past. He decides to change his year end and prepares accounts for the period to 31 March 2017. His capital allowance information is as follows:

	£
Tax written down value at 1 February 2016	
General pool	74,000
Armin's car	8,200

Armin's car originally cost £14,000, has CO_2 emissions of 120 g/km and 60% business use.

During the year ended 31 March 2017, Armin makes the following additions and disposals.

Additions:

1 April 2016	Car for employee – CO_2 emissions 72 g/km (private use 40%)	12,000
1 June 2016	Plant and machinery	37,000
15 March 2016	New car for Armin – CO_2 emissions 170 g/km and 60% business use	22,000

Disposals:

13 March 2016	Armin's old car	10,000

Using the following grid, calculate the total capital allowances and show the balances to carry forward to the next accounting period.

(14 marks)

Task 3 (12 marks)

(a) Wasim ceased to trade on 31 January 2017. His previous tax adjusted trading profits were as follows:

	£
Year ended 30 September 2014	70,000
Year ended 30 September 2015	81,000
Year ended 30 September 2016	56,000
Period ended 31 January 2017	13,000

His overlap profits from the commencement of his business were £8,000. Wasim has calculated that if this amount was inflated to today's value it would be £11,200.

Calculate the taxable profits and state the tax year and basis period for the last three tax years of trading. **(6 marks)**

Tax year	*Basis period*	*Profit* £

(b) David, George and Nick are in partnership sharing profits equally. On 1 August 2016 they changed their profit sharing arrangements so that David received a salary of £24,000. The balance of profits was to be shared 2:3:1 for David, George and Nick.

For the year ended 31 March 2017, their tax adjusted trading profit was £180,000.

Show the division of profit between the partners. **(6 marks)**

	Total	*David*	*George*	*Nick*
	£	£	£	£
Period to				
Salary				
Balance				
Period to				
Salary				
Balance				
Total				

Task 4 (12 marks)

(a) Sirtis Ltd has prepared accounts for the 15 months to 30 June 2017.

(i) **How will this period be split for tax purposes? (1 mark)**

A 3 months to 30 June 2016: Year ended 30 June 2017

B 9 months to 31 December 2016: 6 months to 30 June 2017

C 10 months to 31 January 2017: 5 months to 30 June 2017

D 12 months to 31 March 2017: 3 months to 30 June 2017

(ii) The tax adjusted trading profit before capital allowances is £450,000.

How will this be split between the two periods? (2 marks)

(iii) Sirtis Ltd has a tax written down value of £70,000 on their capital allowances pool at the beginning of the 15 month period. There are no additions or disposals during the 15 month period.

What are the capital allowances for each period? (3 marks)

(iv) Sirtis Ltd does not pay tax by instalments.

State the due dates for payment of the corporation tax for the period ended 30 June 2017. (2 marks)

First period	
Second period	

(v) Riker Ltd's tax liability for the year ended 31 December 2016 is £112,000. They filed their corporation tax return and paid their tax liability on 1 August 2018.

They have always filed their returns on time in previous years.

What is the maximum late filing penalty that they can be charged? (2 marks)

(b) XYZ plc owns the 80% of the ordinary share capital of PQR Ltd, 20% of the ordinary share capital of DEF Ltd and 10% of the ordinary share capital of STU Ltd.

XYZ plc has taxable total profits of £420,000 for the eight months ended 30 September 2016. It received dividends of £35,000 from PQR Ltd and £12,000 from DEF Ltd.

Complete the following for XYZ plc for the eight months ended 30 September 2016: **(2 marks)**

	£
Augmented profits	
Limit for determining the date on which the corporation tax liability is due	

Task 5 (4 marks)

Your answers for parts (a) and (b) should be to the nearest penny. If your answer is zero enter 0.

(a) A 40 year old taxpayer has taxable business profits of £60,000 for 2016/17.

How much class 4 NIC is due on these profits? **(2 marks)**

£

(b) A 67 year old taxpayer receives the State Pension and also has taxable business profits of £8,000 for 2016/17.

How much class 2 NIC is due for 2016/17? **(1 mark)**

£

(c) **Which one of the following statements is correct?** **(1 mark)**

A Class 2 NIC is paid monthly.

B Joseph is a sole trader who will reach State Pension age on 7 April 2016. He has taxable business profits of £35,000 for 2016/17 but he pays no NIC for 2016/17.

C Class 4 NIC is paid on a trader's taxable trading profits less any trading losses brought forward.

D Class 2 NIC is a tax allowable expense for a self-employed trader.

Task 6 (6 marks)

Mark the following statements as true or false. **(6 marks)**

	True	*False*
When a partnership makes a trading loss, all the partners must claim the same method of loss relief.		
When a company makes a trading loss, it can choose not to offset the loss in the current year but instead offset it first in the previous 12 months.		
When a sole trader makes a trading loss, he can choose not to offset the loss in the current year but instead offset it first in the previous tax year.		
A company wishing to offset a trading loss in the current year must submit an election within nine months and one day after the end of the year.		
When a company carries back a trading loss, it can only deduct it from previous periods' trade profits.		
When a company carries forward a trading loss it can deduct it from total profits.		
When a sole trader claims to offset a loss against income of the current year, they cannot restrict the claim to preserve their personal allowance.		

Task 7 (10 marks)

Zahera is a client of your firm. You have agreed the following tax liabilities in recent years.

	2015/16	*2016/17*
	£	£
Income tax liability	16,350	17,550
Tax deducted under PAYE	(9,280)	(7,420)
Income tax payable	7,070	10,130
Class 2 NIC	143	146
Class 4 NIC	2,500	2,370
Capital gains tax	1,670	1,965
	11,383	14,611

Zahera does not understand the tax payment system and wants you to explain:

(a) **how her tax liabilities for 2016/17 are paid** **(7 marks)**

(b) **the effect of making a payment late.** **(3 marks)**

Task 8 (6 marks)

A company has the following information for the year ended 31 March 2017.

	£
Turnover	4,720,000
Trade profits	427,345
Rental income	16,525
Chargeable gains for the year	39,342
Interest received from Government stocks	10,000
Interest paid on loan to buy investment property	4,500
Qualifying charitable donations	2,750

The company has the following losses brought forward:

Trading loss	140,000
Capital loss	8,100

Complete the form CT600 below as far as the information given permits. **(6 marks)**

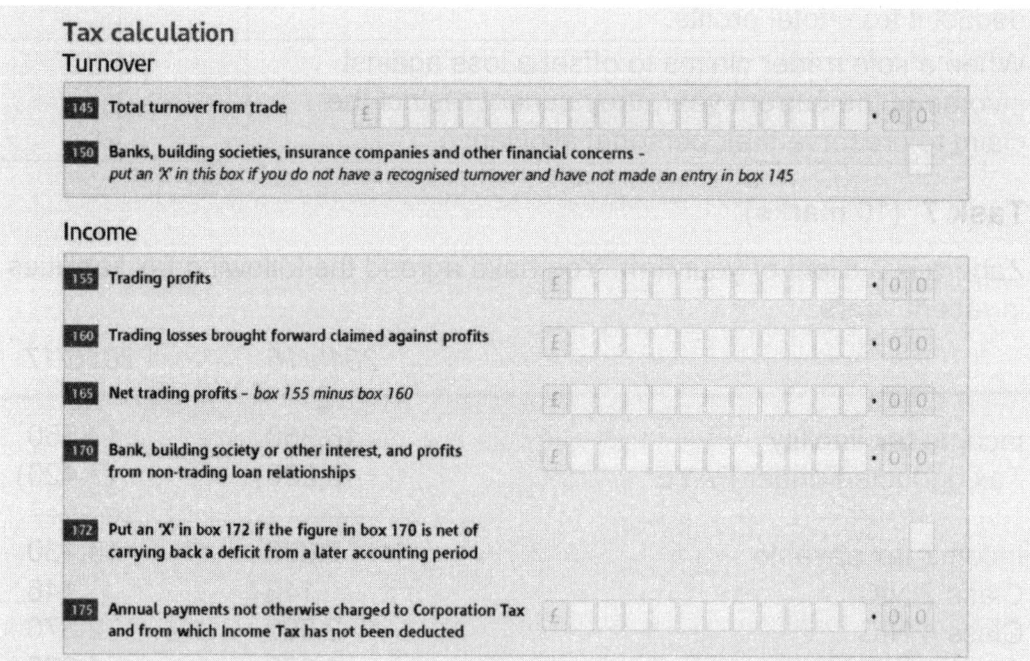

Tax calculation

Turnover

145 Total turnover from trade £ .00

150 Banks, building societies, insurance companies and other financial concerns - *put an 'X' in this box if you do not have a recognised turnover and have not made an entry in box 145*

Income

155 Trading profits £ .00

160 Trading losses brought forward claimed against profits £ .00

165 Net trading profits - *box 155 minus box 160* £ .00

170 Bank, building society or other interest, and profits from non-trading loan relationships £ .00

172 Put an 'X' in box 172 if the figure in box 170 is net of carrying back a deficit from a later accounting period

175 Annual payments not otherwise charged to Corporation Tax and from which Income Tax has not been deducted £ .00

Income *continued*

180	Non-exempt dividends or distributions from non-UK resident companies	£ • 0 0
185	Income from which Income Tax has been deducted	£ • 0 0
190	Income from a property business	£ • 0 0
195	Non-trading gains on intangible fixed assets	£ • 0 0
200	Tonnage Tax profits	£ • 0 0
205	Income not falling under any other heading	£ • 0 0

Chargeable gains

210	Gross chargeable gains	£ • 0 0
215	Allowable losses including losses brought forward	£ • 0 0
220	Net chargeable gains *- box 210 minus box 215*	£ • 0 0

Profits before deductions and reliefs

225	Losses brought forward against certain investment income	£ • 0 0
230	Non-trade deficits on loan relationships (including interest) and derivative contracts (financial instruments) brought forward	£ • 0 0
235	Profits before other deductions and reliefs *- net sum of boxes 165 to 205 and 220 minus sum of boxes 225 and 230*	£ • 0 0

Task 9 (8 marks)

(a) **For each of the following assets, tick the appropriate box to show whether the item is chargeable or exempt for capital gains tax.** **(3 marks)**

	Chargeable	*Exempt*
Half of a racehorse owned jointly with a friend		
£10,000 of 5% Treasury Stock		
Car used by Joe in his business		

(b) Obscure Ltd purchased ten acres of land in December 2008 for £120,000. On 15 March 2017 it sold two acres out of the ten acres for £80,000 incurring £3,420 of legal costs. On 15 March 2017 the remaining eight acres were worth £240,000.

The indexation factor is:

December 2008 – March 2017 0.249

Complete the following computation. Use brackets to indicate numbers to be deducted. **(5 marks)**

	£
Proceeds	
Selling costs	
Cost	
Unindexed gain	
Indexation allowance	
Indexed gain/loss	

Task 10 (10 marks)

Immense plc bought 40,000 shares in Smith plc for £2.20 each in August 2010. There was a bonus issue of 1 for 1 in February 2013 and a rights issue of 1 for 4 at £2.11 each in September 2015. Immense plc took up all its rights. Immense plc sold 75,000 shares in February 2017 for £350,000.

Indexation factors were:

August 2010 – February 2013	0.103
August 2010 – September 2015	0.156
February 2013 – September 2015	0.048
September 2015 – February 2017	0.023

Using the grid below calculate the gain made on this disposal and show the balance of shares carried forward. (10 marks)

Task 11 (6 marks)

(a) **Tick the correct box to show whether the following statements about capital gains are true or false.** **(3 marks)**

	True	*False*
A company can offset a capital loss against its total income of the same accounting period.		
Opera Ltd sells a painting for £12,000. This painting had hung on the wall of the boardroom. This is an exempt disposal.		
An individual taxpayer cannot carry their unused capital gains tax annual exempt amount forward for one year.		

(b) Overs Ltd made a capital gain on the sale of a factory building of £124,300. The building was sold for £500,000 in March 2017. In January 2015, Overs Ltd had bought a new factory building for £481,500.

How much of the gain of £124,300 can be rolled over into the purchase of the new factory? **(1 mark)**

(c) **Which of the following statements about entrepreneurs' relief is correct? Select one answer only.** **(2 marks)**

A The first £10 million of gains on each qualifying disposal is charged at 10%.

B Manuel has owned 10% of the shares in ABC Ltd, a trading company, for 20 years. He does not work for the company. If he sells his shares in ABC Ltd he will be able to claim entrepreneurs' relief.

C Jonah bought a sole trader business, ran it for nine months and then sold it making a gain of £500,000. Jonah will be able to claim entrepreneurs' relief on this disposal.

D Abigail bought a sole trader business which she ran successfully for 10 years. Due to illness she ceased to trade in June 2016. She was unable to sell her business until July 2017. Abigail will be able to claim entrepreneurs' relief on this disposal.

2 Mock Assessment Answers

Task 1

(a) Capital or revenue

	Capital	*Revenue*
Stationery		✓
Legal costs on purchase of a second hand building	✓	
Repairs to the building to make it useable	✓	
Computer software which will be replaced in two years	✓	

(b) Treatment in adjustment of profits computation

	Increase net profit	*Decrease net profit*	*No adjustment needed*
Staff salaries			✓
Profit on the sale of a capital asset		✓	
Decrease in general bad debt provision		✓	
Legal fees for an unsuccessful appeal against a business rating assessment			✓
Costs of installing new machinery	✓		
Food hampers given to staff as Christmas gifts			✓
Boxes of chocolates given to customers who spent over £250	✓		
Leasing costs for car for sales person. The car has CO_2 emissions of 120 g/km			✓

Task 2

Capital allowances computation – year ended 31 March 2017

	AIA/FYA	*Pool*	*Armin's car*		*Total*
			(1)	*(2)*	
	£	£	£	£	£
Tax WDV b/f		74,000	8,200		
Additions – no AIA or FYA				22,000	
Additions with AIA	37,000				
Less: AIA	(37,000)				37,000
	–––––	Nil			
Disposals			(10,000)		
			–––––		
			(1,800)		
BC			1,800	× 60%	(1,080)
			–––––		
		–––––		–––––	
		74,000		22,000	
WDA at 18% × 14/12		(15,540)			15,540
WDA at 8% × 14/12				(2,053)	
				× 60%	1,232
Addition with FYA	12,000				
FYA 100%	(12,000)				12,000
	–––––	Nil			
		–––––		–––––	
Tax WDV c/f		58,460		19,947	
		–––––		–––––	–––––
					64,692
					–––––

Note: In the assessment you do not need to enter lines marking totals and subtotals.

Task 3

(a) Taxable profits

Wasim ceases to trade in 2016/17

Tax year	*Basis period*	*Profit* £
2014/15	Year ended 30 Sept 2014	70,000
2015/16	Year ended 30 Sept 2015	81,000
2016/17	1 Oct 2015 – 31 Jan 2017	61,000

Working:

£56,000 + £13,000 – £8,000 overlap = £61,000

The figure to use for overlap profits brought forward is the original figure with no adjustment for inflation.

(b) Division of profits between partners

	Total	*David*	*George*	*Nick*
	£	£	£	£
Period to 31 Jul 2016				
Salary	0	0	0	0
(4/12 of £180,000)	60,000	20,000	20,000	20,000
Period to 31 Mar 2017				
(8/12 of £180,000)= £120,000				
Salary (8m)	16,000	16,000		
Balance 2:3:1	104,000	34,667	52,000	17,333
	———	———	———	———
	180,000	70,667	72,000	37,333
	———	———	———	———

Task 4

(a) Long period of account

(i) The answer is D.

When a company prepares accounts for a period exceeding 12 months the profits must be split into a 12 month period and a balance period, in this case 3 months.

(ii) Profits before capital allowances are time apportioned.

12/15 £360,000	3/15 £90,000

(iii) Capital allowances are calculated for each period separately. For the second period the WDA must be time apportioned.

£70,000 × 18% = £12,600	(£70,000 – £12,600) × 18% × 3/12 = £2,583

(iv) Corporation tax is due 9 months and 1 day after the end of the accounting period.

First period	1 January 2018
Second period	1 April 2018

(v) The return is filed 7 months late as it was due on 31 December 2017. The penalty will be a fixed penalty of £200 plus 10% of the tax outstanding making a total of £11,400
(£200 + 10% of £112,000)

£11,400

(b) Short period of account – XYZ plc

	£
Augmented profits £420,000 + £12,000 (note 1)	432,000
Limit for determining the date on which the corporation tax liability is due £1,500,000 × 8/12 × 0.5 (note 2)	500,000

Notes:

(1) The dividend from PQR Ltd is not included because it is a 51% group company.

(2) The limit is divided by two because there is a 51% group company, PQR Ltd.

Task 5

(a) Class 4 NICs

£3,441.55

Working:	£
(£43,000 – £8,060) × 9%	3,144.60
(£60,000 – £43,000) × 2%	340.00
	3,484.60

(b) Class 2 NICs

No class 2 NIC is due as the taxpayer is over State Pension age.

(c) NICs

The answer is C.

A is incorrect because class 2 is paid through the self-assessment system on 31 January following the end of the tax year.

B is incorrect because in order to be exempt from class 4 NIC, Joseph must be of State Pension age at the start of the tax year on 6 April 2016.

D is incorrect because the trader's own NIC is never an allowable expense.

Task 6

Losses

	True	*False*
When a partnership makes a trading loss, all the partners must claim the same method of loss relief.		✓
When a company makes a trading loss, it can choose not to offset the loss in the current year but instead offset it first in the previous 12 months.		✓
When a sole trader makes a trading loss, he can choose not to offset the loss in the current year but instead offset it first in the previous tax year.	✓	
A company wishing to offset a trading loss in the current year must submit an election within nine months and one day after the end of the year.		✓
When a company carries back a trading loss, it can only deduct it from previous periods' trade profits.		✓
When a company carries forward a trading loss it can deduct it from total profits.		✓
When a sole trader claims to offset a loss against income of the current year, they cannot restrict the claim to preserve their personal allowance.	✓	

Task 7

(a) Payment of 2016/17 tax liabilities

Payments on account must be made for income tax and class 4 NIC on 31 January 2017 and 31 July 2017. These payments are 50% of the income tax and class 4 NIC payable for 2015/16. Any balance of tax due, together with all the 2016/17 capital gains tax and class 2 NICs, is paid on 31 January 2018. This gives a payment schedule as follows:

Date		*Amount* £
31 January 2017	First payment on account 50% × (£7,070 + £2,500)	4,785
31 July 2017	Second payment on account	4,785
31 January 2018	Balancing payment (£10,130 + £2,370 – £9,570)	2,930
	2016/17 CGT	1,965
	2016/17 Class 2 NICs	146
	Total	5,041

The whole process starts again with the first payment on account of £6,250 (50% × (£10,130 + £2,370) for 2017/18, also due on 31 January 2018.

(b) Effect of late payments

Interest will be charged of any tax paid late from the due date until the date the tax is paid.

In addition, if the tax (excluding Class 2 NIC) of £4,895 due on 31 January 2018 is paid more than 30 days late there will be a penalty equal to 5% of the tax due. Further 5% penalties will be due if the tax is still outstanding after 6 and 12 months after 31 January.

Task 8

CT600 Form

Tax calculation

Turnover

Box	Description	£
145	Total turnover from trade	4720000·00
150	Banks, building societies, insurance companies and other financial concerns – *put an 'X' in this box if you do not have a recognised turnover and have not made an entry in box 145*	

Income

Box	Description	£
155	Trading profits	427345·00
160	Trading losses brought forward claimed against profits	140000·00
165	Net trading profits – *box 155 minus box 160*	287345·00
170	Bank, building society or other interest, and profits from non-trading loan relationships	5500·00 (10,000 - 4,500)
172	Put an 'X' in box 172 if the figure in box 170 is net of carrying back a deficit from a later accounting period	
175	Annual payments not otherwise charged to Corporation Tax and from which Income Tax has not been deducted	·00

Income *continued*

Box	Description	£
180	Non-exempt dividends or distributions from non-UK resident companies	·00
185	Income from which Income Tax has been deducted	·00
190	Income from a property business	16525·00
195	Non-trading gains on intangible fixed assets	·00
200	Tonnage Tax profits	·00
205	Income not falling under any other heading	·00

Chargeable gains

Box	Description	£
210	Gross chargeable gains	39342·00
215	Allowable losses including losses brought forward	8100·00
220	Net chargeable gains – *box 210 minus box 215*	31242·00

Profits before deductions and reliefs

Box	Description	£
225	Losses brought forward against certain investment income	·00
230	Non-trade deficits on loan relationships (including interest) and derivative contracts (financial instruments) brought forward	·00
235	Profits before other deductions and reliefs – *net sum of boxes 165 to 205 and 220 minus sum of boxes 225 and 230*	340612·00

Task 9

(a) Chargeable or exempt assets

	Chargeable	*Exempt*
Half of a racehorse owned jointly with a friend		✓
£10,000 of 5% Treasury Stock		✓
Car used by Joe in his business		✓

Note: A racehorse is exempt as a wasting chattel. It does not matter if two or more people own it.

(b) Chargeable gain – part disposal

	£
Proceeds	80,000
Selling costs	(3,420)
Cost (£120,000 × (£80,000/(£80,000 + £240,000)))	(30,000)
Unindexed gain	46,580
Indexation allowance Cost (£30,000 × 0.249)	(7,470)
Indexed gain/loss	39,110

Task 10

Chargeable gain – Share disposal

Gain calculation		£	
Proceeds		350,000	
Less: Cost (W)		(97,650)	
Less: Indexation (W)			
(£110,429 – £97,650)		(12,779)	
		————	
Chargeable gain		239,571	
		————	
Working: Share pool			
	Number	*Cost*	*Indexed cost*
8.10 Purchase	40,000	88,000	88,000
Feb 2013 Bonus issue 1 for 1	40,000	Nil	Nil
Indexed rise to Sep 2015			
£88,000 × 0.156			13,728
Sep 2015 Rights issue 1 for 4	20,000	42,200	42,200
	————	————	————
	100,000	130,200	143,928
Indexed rise to Feb 2017			
£143,928 × 0.023			3,310
			————
			147,238
Feb 2017 Disposal	(75,000)	[1] (97,650)	[2] (110,429)
	————	————	————
Balance c/f	25,000	32,550	36,809
	————	————	————
[1] 75,000/100,000 × £130,200			
[2] 75,000/100,000 × £147,238			

In the assessment you do not need to enter lines marking totals and subtotals.

Task 11

(a) True or False

	True	*False*
A company can offset a capital loss against its total income of the same accounting period. (Capital losses can only be offset against capital gains)		✓
Opera Ltd sells a painting for £12,000. This painting had hung on the wall of the boardroom. This is an exempt disposal.		✓
An individual taxpayer cannot carry their unused capital gains tax annual exempt amount forward for one year.	✓	

(b) Rollover relief

The answer is Nil.

None of the gain can be rolled over because the purchase of the new factory building is more than 12 months before the disposal of the old factory.

(c) Entrepreneurs' relief

The answer is D.

Abigail's disposal qualifies as it is within 3 years of the cessation of her business and she operated the business for more than 12 months prior to the date of cessation.

A is incorrect because the £10 million is a cumulative lifetime limit covering all disposals, not each disposal.

B is incorrect because entrepreneurs' relief would only be available if Manuel worked for the company.

C is incorrect because qualifying assets must be owned for at least 12 months before disposal.

APPENDIX

Advice on answering extended writing tasks

Advice on extended writing tasks

The chief assessor has offered some tips to help you understand the best way to answer the written task, which will always be marked by an AAT assessor.

These tips were specifically written for the personal tax assessment (PTAX), however they are also extremely helpful when answering the written task in the business tax assessment (BTAX).

Layout of answer

Before we look at the technical aspects of this task, we should begin by considering the practical issues.

Firstly, it's important you understand that the software in which you are answering the task is **not** Microsoft Word. So there's no:

- spell checker
- grammar checker
- automatic correcting of typos.

You won't see any different coloured lines highlighting any of these issues. It's quite clear from assessments we've marked so far that too many students are not proofreading their answers, and are failing to correct obvious mistakes.

So, when you type:

"i DON'T LIKE ANWSERING WRITEN QUETSIONS."

... this is exactly how it will look to the assessor. While the sentence can be read and understood, it's poor practice and would certainly not be allowed in the workplace.

You **must** proofread what you've written and correct any obvious spelling and grammatical errors.

There's often a mark for presentation of the answer, and the assessor is looking for whether the way you've presented your work would be acceptable in the workplace. This mark is independent of the technical answer, and what we look for is whether a client would find the answer acceptable from a visual perspective.

Length of answer

It may not be obvious when you first look at the answer box on the screen, but this is a never-ending answer box. When you get to the last visible line, you can scroll down for extra writing space. So don't start your answer assuming that it needs to be condensed or short.

You should also remember that in many cases, the model answer the assessor is working from is in much more depth than the answer you'd need to give to gain full marks. It's acknowledged that it can be very difficult to write every aspect of all the areas applicable in a written question, and usually it's not necessary to do so.

Before you start to type

You **must** read the question in detail. We've noticed that students often scan read a question, decide what it's about in an instant and then write the answer without giving any thought or consideration to the details. You should:

- read through once to get the general feel of the question
- read through again, slower this time, concentrating on key words or phrases
- plan your answer, ensuring all key areas are covered
- decide the structure of your answer, considering where you'll use things like an email, a memo or bullet points
- type up your answer
- proofread your answer, correcting any errors

Too many times it would seem that students only follow the fifth of these points. If you do this it **will** affect your marks.

Consider exactly who you're writing to. Most likely it will be a client, so this needs to influence your approach.

Remember, if the client is writing to you for advice, they don't know the answer. We often see students give half answers which the assessor will understand, but which a client would not. As a result, they lose marks.

Similarly, be sure to avoid:

- abbreviations
- technical jargon
- SMS/text message speak.

Technical content

What exactly are you going to write?

Let's take the written task from an AQ2010 sample assessment, updated.

Shania has written to you with the following query:

"I am writing to you for some clarification on my father's tax affairs. He is no longer capable of handling his own money, and I have a letter of authorization allowing me to deal with his tax matters.

I have received notification from HMRC of how much tax he has to pay on 31 January 2017. It says he owes £1,400 from 2015/16, and needs to pay £3,500 for 2016/17. I thought he had paid all the tax due for 2015/16, so I don't understand what the £1,400 is for. Also, I know that he has hardly any income this tax year, so where does the £3,500 come from?

If you could explain this to me, it would be much appreciated."

You need to respond appropriately to her query.

Let's break this task down to see exactly what you need to do.

The first line is an introduction only, and gives you the name of the person you are addressing.

The first paragraph of her query is also background, but lets you know two things.

1. It's fine to discuss the father's affairs with Shania.
2. As this tax bill is not hers, Shania will have no understanding of how it has arisen or why, and so you need to explain this in simple but detailed terms.

The second paragraph is the crux of the query, and you must spend time working out the figures and dates from the information given. Let's take a look at the details.

There's a total tax bill of £4,900 to be paid on 31 January 2017. Shania can't understand this, as she knows her father has little income for 2016/17.

Now, ask yourself this question: before you started studying tax, did you know how payments on account worked?

For the majority of people, the answer is 'No'; so you need to put yourself in Shania's position and consider how you're going to clearly and simply explain the £4,900 her father needs to pay.

The question already tells you that £1,400 is from 2015/16, so that must be the balancing figure from that year. But why would there be a balancing figure?

You need to explain the payments on account system, but in very simple terms.

Before you read any further, write your answer to this question and then compare it to the examples below.

Your answer

Now consider the following three typical student answers.

Read them carefully and decide how well they answer the question, before reading the feedback from the chief assessor.

Answer 1

Half of the tax liability for any year is paid by 31 January in that tax year, and the other half is paid by 31 July following the tax year. This is based on an estimate, using the preceding tax year's liability. Therefore, when your father paid his tax liability on 31 January 2016 and 31 July 2016 for 2015/16, this was based on his liability for 2014/15. When the final figures were sent to HMRC, they have worked out that these two instalments are not enough to cover the full liability; hence the £1,400 is the balance of tax due.

Feedback from the chief assessor

Answer 1 is from the model answer and will obviously get full marks.

Answer 2

This is to do with the payments on account system. You need to pay half of your tax bill on 31 January in the year and the other half on 31 July in the year. Anything still to pay needs paying on 31 January after that. So the £1,400 is what is left from 2015/16.

Feedback from the chief assessor

Answer 2 has some good points. Firstly, it uses short sentences, which always makes it easier to read and understand. There are no jargon words. It would therefore get the mark for communication.

However, the crux of the answer, explaining the payments on account, is a problem. The assessor will know which year the answer is referring to, but there's no way a client would. When the answer says '31 January in the year', which year is the student referring to? The tax year, the financial year or the calendar year?

A client wouldn't understand this, so dates written in this manner will lose the student marks. This answer would attract a few marks, but certainly not full marks.

Answer 3

This is to do with POA. You need to pay half of your tax bill in January in the year, and other half in July following that. Then anything left over to pay gets paid in January after that. So the £1,400 is what is left from 2015/16.

Feedback from the chief assessor

> Answer 3 will simply attract no marks at all.
>
> How will a client know what POA means? A day in January in some year also means nothing, and the last sentence is lifted from the question.

How did you do?

Now be honest, and compare the three examples above to your answer and see which one you're the closest to. Ask yourself these questions.

- Have I used abbreviations?
- Have I given the day, month and year accurately?
- Have I proofread my answer?

To finish off, let's consider the rest of the model answer to the question and see if you can understand how to judge the quality of your answer. Again, be honest with yourself on this.

Do you, for instance, realise that as Shania knows her father has 'hardly any income' she needs to understand the implications of this? This leads to the last paragraph of the answer where you can explain to her that he may be entitled to a refund; but that if he makes an incorrect claim to reduce his payments, this may have negative implications.

And finally, when you start the written question, remember this sequence:

- read
- read again
- plan
- structure
- type
- read once again.

Note: below is the full answer to the question to help you.

> Half of the tax liability for any year is paid by 31 January in that tax year, and the other half is paid by 31 July following the tax year. This is based on an estimate, using the preceding tax year's liability. Therefore, when your father paid his tax liability on 31 January 2016 and 31 July 2016 for 2015/16, this was based on his liability for 2014/15.
>
> When the final figures were sent to HMRC, they have worked out that these two instalments are not enough to cover the full liability; hence the £1,400 is the balance of tax due.
>
> As explained, the instalment on 31 January 2017 for this current tax year is based on the accurate liability for 2015/16. If he overpays for 2016/17, he will receive a refund from HMRC.

However, he can claim to reduce these instalments if he knows that his income will not be as high as it was last year. Whilst this is fine, your father needs to be careful. If he makes an incorrect claim to reduce these instalments, then HMRC will charge him interest on the difference between what should have been paid and what was actually paid.

INDEX

Q

R

S

T

W